Oxford American Children's Encyclopedia

9 OXFORD American Children's Encyclopedia

Index, Gazetteer and Timeline of World History

SECOND EDITION

Oxford University Press
New York

Oxford University Press

Oxford New York
Athens Auckland Bangkok Bogotá Buenos Aires Cape Town
Chennoi Dar es Salaam Delhi Florence Hong Kong Istanbul Karachi
Kolkata Kuala Lumpur Madrid Melbourne Mexico City Mumbai Nairobi
Paris Sāu Paulo Shanghai Singapore Taipei Tokyo Toronto Warsaw
and associated companies in
Berlin Ibadan

Copyright © 1998, 2002 by Oxford University Press, Inc.
Second Edition

Published by Oxford University Press, Inc.,
198 Madison Avenue, New York, New York 10016

Oxford is a registered trademark of Oxford University Press.

Library of Congress Cataloguing-in-Publication Data available

ISBN 0-19-515568-8 (complete set)
Volume 9: ISBN 0-19-515791-5 (not for sale separately)

Editor:
Ann T. Keene

Designers:
Cheryl Rodemeyer
Gecko Ltd.
Oxprint Ltd.
Jo Bowers
Jack Donner

A complete list of contributors and consultants
is printed at the end of this volume.

Printed in Hong Kong on acid-free paper.

10 9 8 7 6 5 4 3 2 1

Contents

GAZETTEER

Countries and flags of the world   6–11

TIMELINE OF WORLD HISTORY

Earliest times to 1001 B.C.   12–13

1000 B.C. to 999 A.D.   14–15

1000 A.D. to the present   16–17

INDEX

How to use the index   18

Index   19–104

ACKNOWLEDGMENTS

U.S. contributors and consultants   105

U.K. contributors and consultants   106

Credits   107–112

Countries and flags of the world

A country is often defined as a *sovereign state*—a territory with its own people, its own government and its own laws. There are at present 192 sovereign states in the world, almost all of which are members of the United Nations. The exact number is always changing. Sometimes countries break up into separate states, while others unite. All these countries, apart from the tiny European countries of Liechtenstein, San Marino and Vatican City, appear on the map on the right. In addition, there are many islands and other territories that are part of other countries, which may control their affairs and make their laws. These are known as *dependencies* or *colonies*. Some of these territories also appear on the map, but their names are printed in small letters, not capitals.

All independent (sovereign) countries are listed, with their flags, on the following pages. There are articles in Volumes 1–7 of the encyclopedia on most of these. Those that do *not* have a separate entry are indicated by an asterisk (*). You can find out more about some of the smaller Caribbean countries in the article on the **West Indies**, while several of the smaller Pacific Island states are covered under **Oceania**. Some dependencies, such as **Greenland** and **Bermuda**, have their own entries (with their flags) in the encyclopedia.

The article on each country in Volumes 1–7 includes a locater map to show you the part of the world where it is situated. Many also contain a detailed map of the country. The article on each continent also includes a map. More information on maps in the encyclopedia is given in the **Maps** article.

The articles on **Greenland** and other dependencies include their flags. The article on **Flags** gives more information on certain national flags and includes a selection of other flags.

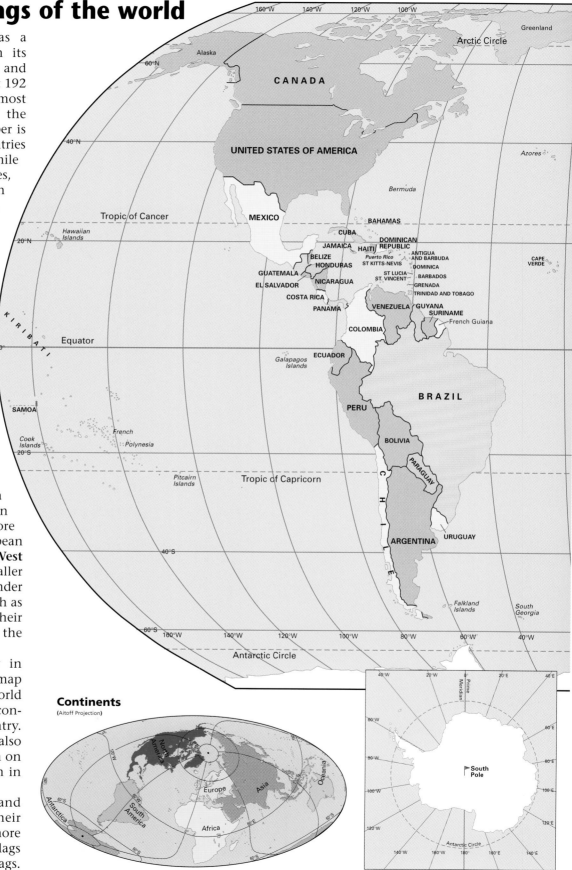

Continents
(Aitoff Projection)

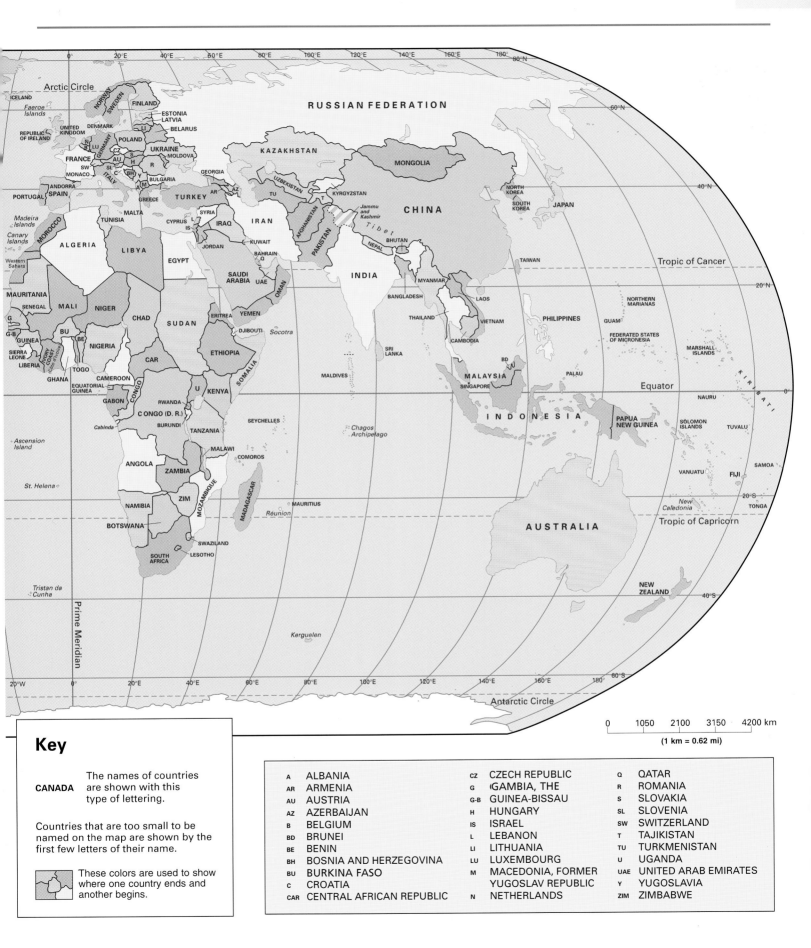

0   1050   2100   3150   4200 km

(1 km = 0.62 mi)

Key

CANADA The names of countries are shown with this type of lettering.

Countries that are too small to be named on the map are shown by the first few letters of their name.

These colors are used to show where one country ends and another begins.

A	ALBANIA	CZ	CZECH REPUBLIC	Q	QATAR
AR	ARMENIA	G	GAMBIA, THE	R	ROMANIA
AU	AUSTRIA	G-B	GUINEA-BISSAU	S	SLOVAKIA
AZ	AZERBAIJAN	H	HUNGARY	SL	SLOVENIA
B	BELGIUM	IS	ISRAEL	SW	SWITZERLAND
BD	BRUNEI	L	LEBANON	T	TAJIKISTAN
BE	BENIN	LI	LITHUANIA	TU	TURKMENISTAN
BH	BOSNIA AND HERZEGOVINA	LU	LUXEMBOURG	U	UGANDA
BU	BURKINA FASO	M	MACEDONIA, FORMER YUGOSLAV REPUBLIC	UAE	UNITED ARAB EMIRATES
C	CROATIA			Y	YUGOSLAVIA
CAR	CENTRAL AFRICAN REPUBLIC	N	NETHERLANDS	ZIM	ZIMBABWE

Afghanistan
Capital Kabul
Population 22,720,000
Area 652,090 sq km (251,772 sq mi)

Albania
Capital Tirana
Population 3,113,000
Area 28,750 sq km (11,100 sq mi)

Algeria
Capital Algiers
Population 31,471,000
Area 2,381,700 sq km (919,590 sq mi)

Andorra
Capital Andorra la Vella
Population 78,000
Area 453 sq km (175 sq mi)

Angola
Capital Luanda
Population 12,878,000
Area 1,246,700 sq km (481,351 sq mi)

*Antigua and Barbuda
Capital St. John's
Population 68,000
Area 440 sq km (170 sq mi)

Argentina
Capital Buenos Aires
Population 37,032,000
Area 2,766,890 sq km
      (1,068,296 sq mi)

Armenia
Capital Yerevan
Population 3,520,000
Area 29,800 sq km (11,506 sq mi)

Australia
Capital Canberra
Population 18,886,000
Area 7,686,850 sq km
      (2,967,893 sq mi)

Austria
Capital Vienna
Population 8,211,000
Area 83,850 sq km (32,374 sq mi)

Azerbaijan
Capital Baku
Population 7,734,000
Area 86,600 sq km (33,436 sq mi)

Bahamas
Capital Nassau
Population 307,000
Area 13,880 sq km (5,359 sq mi)

Bahrain
Capital Manama
Population 617,000
Area 678 sq km (262 sq mi)

Bangladesh
Capital Dhaka
Population 129,155,000
Area 144,000 sq km (55,598 sq mi)

Barbados
Capital Bridgetown
Population 270,000
Area 430 sq km (166 sq mi)

Belarus
Capital Minsk
Population 10,236,000
Area 207,600 sq km (80,154 sq mi)

Belgium
Capital Brussels
Population 10,161,000
Area 30,510 sq km (11,780 sq mi)

Belize
Capital Belmopan
Population 241,000
Area 22,960 sq km (8,865 sq mi)

Benin
Capital Porto-Novo
Population 6,097,000
Area 112,620 sq km (43,483 sq mi)

Bhutan
Capital Thimphu
Population 2,124,000
Area 47,000 sq km (18,147 sq mi)

Bolivia
Capital La Paz
Population 8,329,000
Area 1,098,580 sq km (424,162 sq mi)

Bosnia and Herzegovina
Capital Sarajevo
Population 3,972,000
Area 51,129 sq km (19,745 sq mi)

Botswana
Capital Gaborone
Population 1,622,000
Area 581,730 sq km (224,606 sq mi)

Brazil
Capital Brasília
Population 170,115,000
Area 8,511,970 sq km
      (3,286,472 sq mi)

Brunei
Capital Bandar Seri Begawan
Population 328,000
Area 5,770 sq km (2,228 sq mi)

Bulgaria
Capital Sofia
Population 8,225,000
Area 110,910 sq km (42,822 sq mi)

Burkina Faso
Capital Ouagadougou
Population 11,937,000
Area 274,200 sq km (105,869 sq mi)

Burundi
Capital Bujumbura
Population 6,695,000
Area 27,830 sq km (10,745 sq mi)

Cambodia
Capital Phnom Penh
Population 11,168,000
Area 181,040 sq km (69,900 sq mi)

Cameroon
Capital Yaoundé
Population 15,085,000
Area 475,440 sq km (183,567 sq mi)

Canada
Capital Ottawa
Population 31,147,000
Area 9,976,140 sq km
      (3,851,788 sq mi)

Cape Verde
Capital Praia, on São Tiago
Population 428,000
Area 4,030 sq km (1,556 sq mi)

Central African Republic
Capital Bangui
Population 3,615,000
Area 622,980 sq km (240,533 sq mi)

Chad
Capital N'Djamena
Population 7,651,000
Area 1,284,000 sq km (495,752 sq mi)

Chile
Capital Santiago
Population 15,211,000
Area 756,950 sq km (292,258 sq mi)

China
Capital Beijing
Population 1,277,558,000
Area 9,596,960 sq km
      (3,705,386 sq mi)

Colombia
Capital Bogotá
Population 42,321,000
Area 1,138,910 sq km (439,733 sq mi)

*Comoros
Capital Moroni, on Njazidja
Population 694,000
Area 2,230 sq km (861 sq mi)

Congo, Democratic Republic of (Zaïre)
Capital Kinshasa
Population 51,654,000
Area 2,344,885 sq km
      (905,365 sq mi)

Congo, Republic of
Capital Brazzaville
Population 2,943,000
Area 342,000 sq km (132,046 sq mi)

Costa Rica
Capital San José
Population 4,023,000
Area 51,100 sq km (19,730 sq mi)

Croatia
Capital Zagreb
Population 4,473,000
Area 56,538 sq km (21,824 sq mi)

Cuba
Capital La Habana (Havana)
Population 11,201,000
Area 110,860 sq km (42,803 sq mi)

Cyprus
Capital Nicosia
Population 786,000
Area 9,250 sq km (3,571 sq mi)

Czech Republic
Capital Prague
Population 10,244,000
Area 78,864 sq km (30,449 sq mi)

Denmark
Capital Copenhagen
Population 5,293,000
Area 43,070 sq km (16,629 sq mi)

*Djibouti
Capital Djibouti
Population 638,000
Area 23,200 sq km (8,958 sq mi)

*Dominica
Capital Roseau
Population 71,000
Area 751 sq km (290 sq mi)

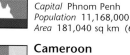

Dominican Republic
Capital Santo Domingo
Population 8,495,000
Area 48,730 sq km (18,815 sq mi)

 Ecuador
Capital Quito
Population 12,646,000
Area 283,560 sq km (109,483 sq mi)

 Egypt
Capital Cairo
Population 68,470,000
Area 1,001,450 sq km (386,660 sq mi)

 El Salvador
Capital San Salvador
Population 6,276,000
Area 21,040 sq km (8,124 sq mi)

 ***Equatorial Guinea**
Capital Malabo
Population 453,000
Area 28,050 sq km (10,830 sq mi)

 Eritrea
Capital Asmara
Population 3,850,000
Area 94,000 sq km (36,293 sq mi)

 Estonia
Capital Tallinn
Population 1,396,000
Area 44,700 sq km (17,300 sq mi)

 Ethiopia
Capital Addis Ababa
Population 62,565,000
Area 1,128,000 sq km (435,521 sq mi)

 Fiji
Capital Suva
Population 817,000
Area 18,270 sq km (7,054 sq mi)

 Finland
Capital Helsinki
Population 5,176,000
Area 338,130 sq km (130,552 sq mi)

 France
Capital Paris
Population 59,080,000
Area 551,500 sq km (212,934 sq mi)

 **Gabon**
Capital Libreville
Population 1,226,000
Area 267,670 sq km (103,347 sq mi)

 **Gambia, The**
Capital Banjul
Population 1,305,000
Area 11,300 sq km (4,363 sq mi)

 **Georgia**
Capital Tbilisi (Tiflis)
Population 4,968,000
Area 69,700 sq km (26,910 sq mi)

Germany
Capital Berlin (formal)
Population 82,220,000
Area 356,910 sq km (137,803 sq mi)

 Ghana
Capital Accra
Population 20,212,000
Area 238,540 sq km (92,100 sq mi)

 **Greece**
Capital Athens
Population 10,645,000
Area 131,990 sq km (50,96 sq mi)

 ***Grenada**
Capital St. George's
Population 94,000
Area 344 sq km (133 sq mi)

 Guatemala
Capital Guatemala City
Population 11,385,000
Area 108,890 sq km (42,042 sq mi)

 Guinea
Capital Conakry
Population 7,430,000
Area 245,860 sq km (94,927 sq mi)

 ***Guinea-Bissau**
Capital Bissau
Population 1,213,000
Area 36,120 sq km (13,946 sq mi)

 Guyana
Capital Georgetown
Population 861,000
Area 214,970 sq km (83,000 sq mi)

 Haiti
Capital Port-au-Prince
Population 8,222,000
Area 27,750 sq km (10,714 sq mi)

 Honduras
Capital Tegucigalpa
Population 6,485,000
Area 112,090 sq km (43,278 sq mi)

 **Hungary**
Capital Budapest
Population 10,036,000
Area 93,030 sq km (35,919 sq mi)

 Iceland
Capital Reykjavík
Population 281,000
Area 103,000 sq km (39,768 sq mi)

 India
Capital New Delhi
Population 1,013,662,000
Area 3,287,590 sq km
 (1,269,338 sq mi)

 Indonesia
Capital Jakarta
Population 212,107,000
Area 1,904,570 sq km (735,354 sq mi)

 Iran
Capital Tehran
Population 67,702,000
Area 1,648,000 sq km (636,293 sq mi)

 **Iraq**
Capital Baghdad
Population 23,115,000
Area 438,320 sq km (169,235 sq mi)

 Ireland
Capital Dublin
Population 3,730,000
Area 70,280 sq km (27,135 sq mi)

 Israel
Capital Jerusalem
Population 6,217,000
Area 26,650 sq km (10,290 sq mi)

 Italy
Capital Rome
Population 57,298,000
Area 301,270 sq km (116,320 sq mi)

 Ivory Coast (Côte d'Ivoire)
Capital Yamoussoukro
Population 14,786,000
Area 322,460 sq km (124,502 sq mi)

 Jamaica
Capital Kingston
Population 2,583,000
Area 10,990 sq km (4,243 sq mi)

 Japan
Capital Tokyo
Population 126,714,000
Area 377,800 sq km (145,869 sq mi)

 Jordan
Capital Amman
Population 6,669,000
Area 89,210 sq km (34,444 sq mi)

 Kazakhstan
Capital Alma-Ata
Population 16,223,000
Area 2,717,300 sq km
 (1,049,150 sq mi)

 Kenya
Capital Nairobi
Population 30,080,000
Area 580,370 sq km (224,081 sq mi)

 ***Kiribati**
Capital Tarawa
Population 83,000
Area 728 sq km (281 sq mi)

 Kuwait
Capital Kuwait City
Population 1,972,000
Area 17,820 sq km (6,880 sq mi)

 Kyrgyzstan
Capital Bishkek
Population 4,699,000
Area 198,500 sq km (76,640 sq mi)

 **Laos**
Capital Vientiane
Population 5,433,000
Area 236,800 sq km (91,428 sq mi)

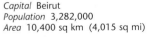 **Latvia**
Capital Riga
Population 2,357,000
Area 64,589 sq km (24,938 sq mi)

 Lebanon
Capital Beirut
Population 3,282,000
Area 10,400 sq km (4,015 sq mi)

 Lesotho
Capital Maseru
Population 2,153,000
Area 30,350 sq km (11,718 sq mi)

 Liberia
Capital Monrovia
Population 3,154,000
Area 111,370 sq km (43,000 sq mi)

 Libya
Capital Tripoli
Population 5,605,000
Area 1,759,540 sq km
 (679,358 sq mi)

Liechtenstein
Capital Vaduz
Population 33,000
Area 157 sq km (61 sq mi)

Lithuania
Capital Vilnius
Population 3,670,000
Area 65,200 sq km (25,200 sq mi)

Luxembourg
Capital Luxembourg
Population 431,000
Area 2,590 sq km (1,000 sq mi)

Macedonia
Capital Skopje
Population 2,024,000
Area 24,900 sq km (9,600 sq mi)

Madagascar
Capital Antananarivo
Population 15,942,000
Area 587,040 sq km (226,656 sq mi)

Malawi
Capital Lilongwe
Population 10,925,000
Area 118,480 sq km (45,745 sq mi)

Malaysia
Capital Kuala Lumpur
Population 22,244,000
Area 329,750 sq km (127,316 sq mi)

*Maldives
Capital Malé
Population 286,000
Area 298 sq km (115 sq mi)

Mali
Capital Bamako
Population 11,234,000
Area 1,240,190 sq km (478,837 sq mi)

Malta
Capital Valletta
Population 389,000
Area 316 sq km (122 sq mi)

Marshall Islands
Capital Dalap-Uliga-Darrit
Population 64,000
Area 181 sq km (70 sq mi)

Mauritania
Capital Nouakchott
Population 2,670,000
Area 1,025,220 sq km (395,593 sq mi)

Mauritius
Capital Port Louis
Population 1,158,000
Area 1,860 sq km (718 sq mi)

Mexico
Capital Mexico City
Population 98,881,000
Area 1,958,200 sq km
(756,061 sq mi)

Micronesia, Federated States of
Capital Palikir
Population 119,000
Area 705 sq km (272 sq mi)

Moldova
Capital Kishinev
Population 4,380,000

Area 33,700 sq km (13,010 sq km)

Monaco
Capital Monaco
Population 34,000
Area 1.5 sq km (0.6 sq mi)

Mongolia
Capital Ulan Bator
Population 2,662,000
Area 1,566,500 sq km
(604,826 sq mi)

Morocco
Capital Rabat
Population 28,351,000
Area 446,550 sq km (172,413 sq mi)

Mozambique
Capital Maputo
Population 19,680,000
Area 801,590 sq km (309,494 sq mi)

Myanmar (Burma)
Capital Yangon (Rangoon)
Population 45,611,000
Area 676,577 sq km (261,228 sq mi)

Namibia
Capital Windhoek
Population 1,726,000
Area 825,414 sq km (318,434 sq mi)

*Nauru
Capital Yaren
Population 12,000
Area 21 sq km (8 sq mi)

Nepal
Capital Kathmandu
Population 23,930,000
Area 140,800 sq km (54,363 sq mi)

Netherlands
Capital Amsterdam
Population 15,786,000
Area 41,526 sq km (16,033 sq mi)

New Zealand
Capital Wellington
Population 3,862,000
Area 270,990 sq km (104,629 sq mi)

Nicaragua
Capital Managua
Population 5,074,000
Area 130,000 sq km (50,193 sq mi)

Niger
Capital Niamey
Population 10,730,000
Area 1,267,000 sq km (489,189 sq mi)

Nigeria
Capital Abuja
Population 111,506,000
Area 923,770 sq km (356,668 sq mi)

North Korea
Capital Pyongyang
Population 24,039,000
Area 120,540 sq km (56,540 sq mi)

Norway
Capital Oslo
Population 4,465,000
Area 323,900 sq km (125,050 sq mi)

Oman
Capital Muscat
Population 2,542,000
Area 212,460 sq km (82,031 sq mi)

Pakistan
Capital Islamabad
Population 156,483,000
Area 796,100 sq km (307,374 sq mi)

Palau (Belau)
Capital Koror
Population 17,000
Area 458 sq km (177 sq mi)

Panama
Capital Panama City
Population 2,856,000
Area 77,080 sq km (29,761 sq mi)

Papua New Guinea
Capital Port Moresby
Population 4,807,00
Area 462,840 sq km (178,703 sq mi)

Paraguay
Capital Asunción
Population 5,496,000
Area 406,750 sq km (157,046 sq mi)

Peru
Capital Lima
Population 25,662,000
Area 1,285,220 sq km (496,223 sq mi)

Philippines
Capital Manila
Population 75,967,000
Area 300,000 sq km (115,300 sq mi)

Poland
Capital Warsaw
Population 38,765,000
Area 312,680 sq km (120,726 sq mi)

Portugal
Capital Lisbon
Population 9,875,000
Area 92,390 sq km (35,670 sq mi)

Qatar
Capital Doha
Population 599,000
Area 11,000 sq km (4,247 sq mi)

Romania
Capital Bucharest
Population 22,327,000
Area 237,500 sq km (91,699 sq mi)

Russian Federation
Capital Moscow
Population 146,934,000
Area 17,075,000 sq km
(6,592,800 sq mi)

Rwanda
Capital Kigali
Population 7,733,000
Area 26,340 sq km (10,170 sq mi)

*St. Kitts and Nevis
Capital Basseterre
Population 38,000
Area 360 sq km (139 sq mi)

St. Lucia
Capital Castries
Population 154,000
Area 610 sq km (236 sq mi)

*St. Vincent & Grenadines
Capital Kingstown
Population 114,000
Area 388 sq km (150 sq mi)

*Samoa
Capital Apia
Population 180,000
Area 2,840 sq km (1,097 sq mi)

San Marino
Capital San Marino
Population 27,000
Area 61 sq km (24 sq mi)

*São Tomé and Principe
Capital São Tomé
Population 147,000
Area 964 sq km (372 sq mi)

Saudi Arabia
Capital Riyadh
Population 21,607,000
Area 2,149,690 sq km
     (829,995 sq mi)

Senegal
Capital Dakar
Population 9,481,000
Area 196,720 sq km (75,954 sq mi)

*Seychelles
Capital Victoria, on Mahé
Population 77,000
Area 455 sq km (176 sq mi)

Sierra Leone
Capital Freetown
Population 4,854,000
Area 71,740 sq km (27,699 sq mi)

Singapore
Capital Singapore
Population 3,567,000
Area 618 sq km (239 sq mi)

Slovak Republic
Capital Bratislava
Population 5,387,000
Area 49,035 sq km (18,932 sq mi)

Slovenia
Capital Ljubljana
Population 1,986,000
Area 20,251 sq km (7,817 sq mi)

*Solomon Islands
Capital Honiara
Population 444,000
Area 28,900 sq km (11,158 sq mi)

Somalia
Capital Mogadishu
Population 10,097,000
Area 637,660 sq km (246,201 sq mi)

South Africa
Capital Pretoria (administrative)
Population 40,377,000
Area 1,219,916 sq km
     (470,566 sq mi)

South Korea
Capital Seoul
Population 46,844,000
Area 99,020 sq km (38,232 sq mi)

Spain
Capital Madrid
Population 39,630,000
Area 504,780 sq km (194,896 sq mi)

Sri Lanka
Capital Colombo
Population 18,827,000
Area 65,610 sq km (25,332 sq mi)

Sudan
Capital Khartoum
Population 29,490,000
Area 2,505,810 sq km
     (967,493 sq mi)

Suriname
Capital Paramaribo
Population 417,000
Area 163,270 sq km (63,039 sq mi)

Swaziland
Capital Mbabane
Population 1,008,000
Area 17,360 sq km (6,703 sq mi)

Sweden
Capital Stockholm
Population 8,910,000
Area 449,960 sq km (173,730 sq mi)

Switzerland
Capital Bern
Population 7,386,000
Area 41,290 sq km (15,942 sq mi)

Syria
Capital Damascus
Population 16,125,000
Area 185,180 sq km (71,498 sq mi)

Taiwan
Capital Taipei
Population 22,191,000
Area 36,000 sq km (13,900 sq mi)

Tajikistan
Capital Dushanbe
Population 6,188,000
Area 143,100 sq km (55,250 sq mi)

Tanzania
Capital Dodoma
Population 33,517,000
Area 945,090 sq km (364,899 sq mi)

Thailand
Capital Bangkok
Population 61,399,000
Area 513,120 sq km (198,116 sq mi)

Togo
Capital Lomé
Population 4,629,000
Area 56,790 sq km (21,927 sq mi)

*Tonga
Capital Nuku'alofa
Population 99,000
Area 750 sq km (290 sq mi)

Trinidad and Tobago
Capital Port of Spain
Population 1,295,000
Area 5,130 sq km (1,981 sq mi)

Tunisia
Capital Tunis
Population 9,586,000
Area 163,610 sq km (63,170 sq mi)

Turkey
Capital Ankara
Population 66,591,000
Area 779,450 sq km (300,946 sq mi)

Turkmenistan
Capital Ashkhabad
Population 4,459,000
Area 488,100 sq km (188,450 sq mi)

*Tuvalu
Capital Fongafale
Population 12,000
Area 24 sq km (9 sq mi)

Uganda
Capital Kampala
Population 21,778,000
Area 235,880 sq km (91,073 sq mi)

Ukraine
Capital Kiev
Population 50,456,000
Area 603,700 sq km (233,100 sq mi)

United Arab Emirates
Capital Abu Dhabi
Population 2,441,000
Area 83,600 sq km (32,278 sq mi)

United Kingdom
Capital London
Population 58,830,000
Area 243,368 sq km (94,202 sq mi)

United States of America
Capital Washington, D.C.
Population 281,422,000
Area 9,372,610 sq km
     (3,618,765 sq mi)

Uruguay
Capital Montevideo
Population 3,337,000
Area 177,410 sq km (68,498 sq mi)

Uzbekistan
Capital Tashkent
Population 24,318,000
Area 447,400 sq km (172,740 sq mi)

*Vanuatu
Capital Port-Vila
Population 190,000
Area 12,190 sq km (4,707 sq mi)

Vatican City
Population 1,000
Area 0.44 sq km (0.17 sq mi)

Venezuela
Capital Caracas
Population 24,170,000
Area 912,050 sq km (352,143 sq mi)

Vietnam
Capital Hanoi
Population 79,832,000
Area 331,689 sq km (128,065 sq mi)

Yemen
Capital Sana
Population 18,112,000
Area 527,970 sq km (203,849 sq mi)

Yugoslavia
Capital Belgrade
Population 10,640,000
Area 102,173 sq km (39,449 sq mi)

Zambia
Capital Lusaka
Population 9,169,000
Area 752,614 sq km (290,586 sq mi)

Zimbabwe
Capital Harare
Population 11,669,000
Area 390,579 sq km (150,873 sq mi)

World history

	before 10,000 B.C.	10,000	9000	8000	7000
Asia	• Hunter-gatherers • From about 50,000 B.C. people were spreading through all continents with a variety of tools—knives, axes, scrapers, harpoons, needles	• Hunter-gatherers • Earliest pottery in Japan, flourishing coastal culture based on fishing	• Hunter-gatherers	• Rice farming in Thailand	• Rice and millet farming spreads
Australia and Oceania	• Hunter-gatherers • Cave drawings in Australia from about 20,000 B.C.	• Hunter-gatherers • Sledges and canoes used	• Hunter-gatherers	• Hunter-gatherers	• Hunter-gatherers • Farming settlements in New Guinea
Africa and the Middle East	• Hunter-gatherers • Engravings in southwest Africa from about 27,000 B.C.	• Hunter-gatherers • Wild wheat gathered in Palestine • Domestication of dogs (wolves)	• Rock paintings in Sahara • Farming of grains • Domestication of sheep and goats • Site of Jericho occupied • Pottery made in Syria	• Farming skills spread through Middle East	• Wheel invented • Pottery and textiles used in Anatolia (Turkey) • Cattle domesticated • Jericho and Çatal Hüyük walled towns
Europe	• Hunter-gatherers • **Cave paintings** from 30,000 B.C. • Female figurines of Great Goddess made across continent • Bow invented	• Hunter-gatherers • Cave paintings • Sledges and canoes used	• Hunter-gatherers	• Hunter-gatherers	*Mainland Groups:* • Farming in Balkans and Greece • Domesticated sheep and goats • Cattle and pigs domesticated *Great Britain:* • Hunter-gatherers
North and South America	• Hunter-gatherers	• Hunter-gatherers • Sledges and canoes used	• Hunter-gatherers	• Hunter-gatherers	• Hunter-gatherers

Archaeologists are working all the time and digging up new evidence. They often disagree on the period when new technology first developed, so the dates given here are only approximate.

A word or phrase in the table printed in **bold** indicates that there is an article in Volumes 1–8 under that heading.

The lists in the far right-hand column of this page indicate other articles in Volumes 1–7 that deal with the region and historical period concerned.

THIS REPRESENTS 1,000 YEARS: A MILLENNIUM

6000	5000	4000	3000	2000	See also
• Farming in China and India • Pottery made in China	• Farming spreads in Huang He (Yellow River) valley, China • Wheat, barley, rice cultivated • Horses domesticated on steppes	• Ploughs used in China • Bronze worked in China and Thailand • Decorated pottery made in Japan • Jade worked in China	• Silk weaving in China • Cities of Harappa and Mohenjo-daro in Indus valley (now Pakistan) • Cotton grown in Indus valley	• Xia dynasty • Shang dynasty • Cities in China • Aryans invade northern India • Hindu religion develops • Rice cultivated in Korea	Ancient world China Evolution India Japan Prehistoric people
• Hunter-gatherers	• Hunter-gatherers	• Hunter-gatherers	• Hunter-gatherers • Melanesian islands settled	• Hunter-gatherers	Aborigines Ancient world Evolution Prehistoric people
• Farming settlements in **Mesopotamia** • Copper used	• Sails used on Nile • Plough invented • Bronze worked and cast • Vines and olives cultivated	• **Hieroglyphics** in Egypt • Farming in central Africa • Cuneiform writing by **Sumerians** • Wheeled vehicles • Pottery in Sudan and East Africa	• Egyptian Old Kingdom ruled by pharaohs • **Pyramids** built • Sumerian civilization • Cities in Iran • Troy founded	• Middle and New Kingdoms in Egypt • **Hittites** establish empire • Hammurabi king of Babylon • Jewish religion develops • Exodus of Jews from Egypt	Africa Ancient world Egypt Evolution Mummies Phoenicians Prehistoric people Seven Wonders of the World Trojan War
Mainland France: • Copper and gold worked *Great Britain:* • Farming and fishing	• Megalithic tombs and standing stones • Flint mines • Horse domesticated in Ukraine	• Farming along Danube • Copper working spreads • Plows drawn by animals • Wheeled vehicles • Vines and olives cultivated around Mediterranean • **Stonehenge**	• Sails used on Aegean Sea • Bronze worked in Britain and Crete • Megalithic tombs spread • Ox-drawn wagons and ploughs	• **Minoan** civilization on Crete • Mycenaean civilization in Greece • Bronze begins to give way to iron	Evolution of people Greece Ireland, Republic of Prehistoric people Scotland Stonehenge Trojan War
• Hunter-gatherers	• Hunter-gatherers • Maize cultivated in Mexico	• Hunter-gatherers • Pottery made in Guyana and Ecuador • Llamas domesticated in Andes	• Hunter-gatherers • Ceremonial centers built in Peru	• Hunter-gatherers • Metalworking and cotton weaving in Peru • Olmec culture in Central America • **Burial mounds** in Mississippi valley	Central America North America South America

	1000	800	600	400	200 B.C.
Asia	• Zhou dynasty in China	• Taoism founded in China • Zhou dynasty establishes legal system	• Ironworking in China • **Confucius** (Kongzi) lived • **Buddha** lived	• Zhou dynasty ends • Qin dynasty • **Great Wall of China** built • **Alexander the Great** of Macedon invades India • **Asoka** emperor of India	• Han dynasty • Roman envoys to China • Buddhism spreads to Southeast Asia and China
Australia and Oceania	• Hunter-gatherers • Settlements in Polynesia	• Hunter-gatherers	• Hunter-gatherers	• Hunter-gatherers	• Hunter-gatherers
Africa and the Middle East	• Kingdom of Kush in Africa • Assyrian empire • Phoenician alphabet • Kingdom of Israel • Carthage founded	• First coins in Lydia (Turkey) • Babylonian empire of Nebuchadnezzar • Assyrians conquer Israel • Zoroastrian religion in Persia (Iran)	• **Persians** establish empire under Cyrus, Darius and **Xerxes** • Persians conquer Egypt • Old Testament of Bible completed • Jews exiled to Babylon	• Nok culture in Africa • Carthage powerful • Persian empire conquered by **Alexander the Great** • Egypt ruled by Ptolemy dynasty	• Carthage destroyed and Syria, Palestine and Egypt conquered by Roman armies • **Jesus** born
Europe	• Celtic tribes migrate to Germany and France • **Etruscans** settle in northern Italy	• Greek alphabet develops • **Homer's** poems composed • Rome founded • Celtic tribes invade and settle Great Britain	• Greek city-states • Athens defeats **Persians** • **Pericles** lived • **Socrates** lived • Parthenon and other temples built • Roman republic founded	• Philip of Macedon conquers Greece • **Alexander the Great** rules Greece and conquers Persians • **Plato** lived • Romans conquer Etruscans, rule all Italy and conquer Spain	• Greece ruled by Romans • Romans conquer Gaul • Civil war between Roman rivals • **Augustus** first Roman emperor • Romans invade Great Britain
North and South America	• Chavín village culture in Peru • Pottery and cotton made	• Olmec civilization in Mexico	• Hieroglyphic system of writing develops in Mexico	• Early **Maya** culture in Guatemala • Olmec civilization ends	• Foundation of Teotihuacán in Mexico

A word or phrase in the table printed in **bold** indicates that there is an article in Volumes 1–8 under that heading.

The lists in the far right-hand column of this page indicate other articles in Volumes 1–7 that deal with the region and historical period concerned.

THIS REPRESENTS 200 YEARS: TWO CENTURIES

1 A.D.	200	400	600	800	See also
• Han dynasty in China • Paper invented in China • Magnetic compass used • Emperors in Japan	• Gupta Empire, India • Great Wall of China extended	• Sui dynasty, China • Horse-collar harness used • Mathematics develops in India	• Tang dynasty, China • Block printing invented in China • Kyoto capital of Japan	• Song dynasty, China • Gunpowder invented in China • Khmer emperor in Southeast Asia • Fujiwara family dominates Japan • Burma unified	China Indian Japan
• **Hunter-gatherers**	• **Hunter-gatherers**	• **Hunter-gatherers**	• **Hunter-gatherers**	• **Hunter-gatherers**	Aborigines Australia Oceania Polynesia
• Ironworking in Zambia • Jesus crucified • **St. Paul's** missions • New Testament written • Jews expelled from Jerusalem	• Ethiopians become Christians • Start of **Byzantine Empire**	• Sassanid Empire in Persia • **Byzantine Empire** powerful	• **Muhammad** founds Islam • Text of Koran established • Muslims conquer northern Africa • Umayyad caliphs rule from Damascus • Arabs develop algebra	• Bantu tribes move into southern Africa • Muslim religion spreads • Abbasid caliphs rule from Baghdad	Africa Egypt Phoenicians Seven Wonders of the World
• Roman Empire most powerful • Emperors Trajan and Hadrian • Christianity spreads	• Franks, Huns, Goths and Vandal tribes attack Roman Empire • Saxons raid Great Britain • Christian missionaries in Great Britain	• Roman Empire in West collapses • **Dark Ages** begin • **Anglo-Saxons** settle England	• Spain conquered by Muslims • Charles Martel defeats Muslims near Poitiers, France • **Vikings** raid and trade in France, Russia and Mediterranean	• Vikings settle Normandy, France; raid and settle Great Britain • **Charlemagne** emperor • Magyars settle Hungary • Bulgars and Russians become Christian • Kingdom of Poland established	Celts; England; Europe; France; Germany; Greece; Ireland, Republic of; Italy; Rome and the Roman Empire; Russia; Scotland; Spain; Wales
• Pyramids, palaces, temples built in Peru	• Maya civilization in Central America	• Teotihuacán temples in Mexico • Complex cities and temples built in Mexico	• Maya astronomical congress	• **Vikings** sail to North America • Toltec civilization in northern Mexico	Central America North America South America

	1000	1100	1200	1300	1400
Asia	• Song dynasty • Movable-type printing • Muslim conquests in northern India	• Song dynasty • Khmer Empire powerful in Southeast Asia • Many kingdoms in India	• **Genghis Khan** extends Mongol Empire • **Kublai Khan** conquers China, Burma, Korea, founds Yuan dynasty • **Marco Polo** in China	• Ming dynasty in China • **Tamerlane** extends Mongol Empire in Central Asia • Muslim sultans rule northern India • **Black Death**	• Ming dynasty • Mongols defeated by Ivan III of Russia • Vasco da **Gama** travels to India
Australia and Oceania	• Hunter-gatherers • Polynesian **Maori** settle in New Zealand	• Hunter-gatherers	• Hunter-gatherers	• Hunter-gatherers	• Hunter-gatherers
Africa and the Middle East	• Zimbabwe • Kingdom of Ghana, West Africa • Turks invade Byzantine Empire and occupy Palestine	• Turks conquer Egypt • Turks attacked by Christian crusaders	• Empire of Mali, West Africa • Mongols attack Baghdad • Turks defeat crusaders and rule Palestine	• Empires of Benin and Mali in West Africa powerful • Ottoman Turks conquer Anatolia and the Balkans • **Black Death**	• Songhai Empire in West Africa • Portuguese explore coast of Africa • Ottoman Turks capture Constantinople 1453
Europe	• **Normans** rule Sicily and southern Italy • **Normans** conquer England 1066 • Roman Catholic and Greek Orthodox Churches split 1054 • First universities • **Crusades** begin	• Romanesque architecture • Cistercian **monasteries** • Crusades establish Christian state in Palestine	• Gothic architecture • Franciscan and Dominican friars founded • Golden Horde of Mongols conquers Russia • French kingdom expands • Christians defeat Muslim states in Spain	• **Black Death** • Hundred Years War • Venice, Florence and Genoa powerful city-states	• First printed books • **Renaissance** in Italy • Muslims driven from southern Spain • Russians drive out Mongols • Wars of the Roses in England
North and South America	• Chimú civilization in Peru	• **Incas** begin to establish empire (Peru) • Aztecs move into Mexico	• Aztec Empire develops in Mexico	• Aztec Empire powerful	• Inca Empire powerful • **Cabot** in Newfoundland • **Columbus** in Caribbean

A word or phrase in the table printed in **bold** indicates that there is an article in Volumes 1–8 under that heading.

The lists in the far right-hand column of this page indicate other articles in Volumes 1–7 that deal with the region and historical period concerned.

THIS REPRESENTS 100 YEARS: A CENTURY

1500	1600	1700	1800	1900	See also
• Ming dynasty ends • Babur founds Mughal Empire, northern India • Sikh religion founded	• Qing (Manchu) dynasty in China • Dutch found empire in East Indies • Taj Mahal built	• Qing (Manchu) dynasty • Chinese export porcelain, silk and tea to Europe • Dutch trade increases • British fight French for control of India	• Opium war • U.S. forces trade with Japan • Britain founds Singapore and takes Hong Kong • India part of British Empire • Independence movement starts in India	• China becomes republic 1911, Communist 1949 • Japan defeats Russia 1905 • Rise and fall of Japanese Empire • **Korean War** 1950–1953 • **Vietnam War** 1957–1975	China Hiroshima India Japan Russia and the Russian Federation World War I World War II
• **Hunter-gatherers**	• **Hunter-gatherers**	• Captain James **Cook** explores coasts of Australia and New Zealand • Australia settled by convicts	• Australia and New Zealand settled	• Continued emigration to Australia	Aborigines Australia New Zealand World War II
• Slave trade from West Africa to Caribbean • **Suleiman I** (the Magnificent) rules **Ottoman Empire**	• Slave trade expands • Dutch settlers (Boers) in South Africa	• Asante kingdom in West Africa • Slave trade continues	• Europeans explore and colonize Africa • Slave trade abolished • Ottoman Empire declines	• African states gain independence • South African policy of apartheid • Ottoman Empire ends • Turkey and Arab states independent • Israel founded	Africa Boer War Crusades Slavery
• **Reformation** • Protestants break from Catholic Church • Wars of Religion • **Ivan the Terrible** rules Russia • **Church of England** founded • Spanish Armada 1588	• Dutch fight Spaniards and gain independence • French power grows under **Louis XIV** • Spanish power declines	• Russian power grows under **Peter the Great** and **Catherine the Great** • Poland partitioned • French Revolution 1789 • Union of Scotland and England 1707 • **Agricultural revolutions** begin • **Industrial Revolution** begins	• **Napoleonic wars** • Russian Empire expands • **Crimean War** • Italian unification • German unification • Industrialization and growth of railways • Emigration to U.S. • British Empire most powerful in world	• **World War I** 1914–1918 • **Russian Revolution** 1917 • **Soviet Union** 1922–1991 • **World War II** 1939–1945 • Communist domination of Eastern Europe 1945–1989 • **European Union**	England; Europe; Feudal system; France; Germany; Holocaust; Italy; Middle Ages; Russia and the Russian Federation; Spain; United Kingdom
• Aztec and Inca empires conquered by Spaniards • Spanish capture Caribbean islands and establish colonies • Magellan's fleet sails around the world • European exploration of North America • St. Augustine (**Florida**) founded 1565	• European colonies founded in North America • **Jamestown** founded 1607 • African slaves imported to North America • **Pilgrims** land at Plymouth Rock 1620	• French and Indian War 1754–1763 • **American Revolution** 1775–1783 • **Declaration of Independence** 1776 • **U.S. Constitution** adopted 1789 • **Bill of Rights** adopted 1791	• **Industrial Revolution** in North America • Louisiana Purchase 1803 • **War of 1812** 1812–1815 • Spanish and French colonies in the Americas gain independence • Slavery abolished in British Empire 1833 • **Civil War**, 1861–1865, ends slavery in U.S.	• **United States of America** becomes world power • **Caribbean** countries gain independence • Technological revolution in industry, transportation and communications • U.S. enters **World War I** 1917 • Great Depression 1929–1939 • U.S. enters **World War II** 1941 • **Civil Rights Movement** in U.S. 1955–1970	Central America* Explorers North America* Slavery South America* United Nations *Country listings and other references can be found under **See also** in these articles.

How to Use the Index

Words in **bold type** indicate that there is an article with this heading.

Words in light type indicate that there is information about this topic on the page or pages listed, but there is not an article with this heading.

Indented index entries indicate pages or articles where you can find information related to the main topic—in this case, advertising.

Words in *italic* may be the names of books, films or musical works, the Latin names of animals, or words from other languages.

Adams, Abigail, 3:82

Adams, John, 8:7, *7*; 1:45; 2:138; 3:82; 4:189; 7:101, 139

Adams, John Quincy, 8:7–8, *8*; 3:82; 4:189; 7:101

Adams, Samuel, 8:8; 1:43, 44; 2:138

Addams, Jane, 8:8–9, *9*; 4:65

addiction, 1:11
    alcoholism, 1:33; 2:172
    to **drugs,** 1:11; 2:50–51, 172
    gambling, 3:144
    glue-sniffing, 3:168
    to **tobacco,** 2:172; 6:151; 7:62

Addis Ababa, Ethiopia, 2:64

additives, food, **3:**112

adhesives, 3:168

Adirondack Mountains, 5:100

adolescence, 1:11; 6:33

Adolfo, 4:33

adoption, 1:11; 5:154

Advent, 2:57

advertising, 1:12–13, *12–13*; 5:13, *90*, 99
    and **design,** 2:146–147, *146, 147*
    logos, 2:146, *146, 147*
    in **magazines,** 4:172; 6:*153*
    posters, 6:12, *12, 50*
    radio, 6:47
    regulation of, 1:12–13
    television, 7:41

Aelian, 3:88

Aenead, 1:13; 3:183

aerial roots, 6:91, *91*

aerobic exercise, 3:92, 192

aerobic respiration, 6:67, *67*

aerosol containers, 1:14, *14*; 3:105; 5:139

Aeschylus, 2:169; 3:183

Aesop's Fables, 2:44; 3:55

aesthetics, 3:77

affirmative action, 2:66

Afghanistan, 1:14, *14*; 6:59, 97

The volume number is given in bold type, the page number or numbers in plain type: in this case, volume **3**, page 82.

The first numbers in this list, **8**:8–9, are the volume and page numbers for the article on **Jane Addams.** The *italic* page number *9* indicates that there is a picture of her on that page. The other page number indicates another place in the encyclopedia where she is mentioned.

Page numbers in *italic* indicate that there is a picture relating to the topic on that page. When the same page number appears twice, once in plain type and once in *italic*, there is information *and* a picture on that page.

Aa

aardvarks, **1**:9
Aaron, Hank, **1**:120
abacuses, **1**:80, 180, *180*
abbeys, **5**:45–46, *45, 46*
abdication, of King Edward VIII, **7**:93
Abdul-Jabbar, Kareem (Lew Alcindor), **1**:19, *120*, 121
Aberdeen, Scotland, **6**:10
abolitionists, **1**:19, 40; **2**:67, 70; **4**:175, 189; **7**:173
Aborigines, **1**:9, *9*
  in **Australia**, **1**:98, 99; **2**:145, 171; **4**:53; **5**:104
  dreamtime of, **2**:171
  as **hunter-gatherers**, **4**:53
  in **Tasmania**, **7**:33
Abraham, **8**:7; **4**:100, 101, 117; **5**:148
Abruzzo, Richard, **1**:113
absolute zero, **2**:88; **7**:19, 43
Abu Dhabi, **7**:90
Abu Simbel, **2**:188
Academy Awards, **5**:62
accelerators, atomic, **1**:96
Accra, Ghana, **3**:162
Achebe, Chinua, **1**:18
Achilles, **4**:26, 64
Achilles tendon, **6**:94
acid rain, **1**:10, *10*; **3**:*30*
acids, **1**:11
acorns, **5**:119
acoustics, **6**:161
Acquired Immune Deficiency Syndrome (AIDS), **1**:23; **2**:158

acrobats, circus, **2**:61, *61*; **8**:*192*
acrylic paints, **5**:141, *146*
acrylics, **1**:171; **7**:29
activities:
  baking bread, **1**:157
  bird-watching, **1**:140
  collecting and creating proverbs and sayings, **6**:32
  doing things with decimals, **2**:137
  embroidery stitches, **3**:38, *38*
  experimenting with levers, **4**:151
  feeding wild birds, **1**:140
  finding the height of a streetlight, **7**:81, *81*
  following a star trail, **6**:144
  growing your own crystals, **2**:128
  hand-made pottery, **6**:13
  investigating magnets, **4**:174
  knitting, **4**:128
  lighting the world, **2**:136
  looking for fossils, **3**:124
  macramé, **4**:129, *129*
  making bubbles, **1**:164
  making a diamond kite, **4**:127
  making garam masala, **6**:176
  making a glove puppet, **6**:38, *38*
  making a pinhole viewer, **1**:184
  making a pulley, **6**:34, *34*
  making a solar system model, **6**:160
  making yogurt cheese, **2**:39
  origami bird, **5**:*138*
  painting techniques, **5**:146
  photography, **5**:167
  sewing, **6**:127, *127*
  sprouting a seed, **6**:122, *122*
  stargazing, **6**:188
  temperature tricks, **7**:43
  testing for symmetry, **7**:27
  testing insulators, **4**:89
  tie-dye, **2**:174
Act of Union (1707), **7**:91–92
actors, dramatic, **2**:169, *169*
acupuncture, **1**:38–39; **5**:13
adages, **6**:32
Adam and Eve, **1**:132
Adams, Abigail, **3**:82
Adams, John, **8**:7, *7*; **1**:45; **2**:138; **3**:82; **4**:189; **7**:101, 139

Adams, John Quincy, **8**:7–8, *8*; **3**:82; **4**:189; **7**:101
Adams, Samuel, **8**:8; **1**:43, 44; **2**:138
Addams, Jane, **8**:8–9, *9*; **4**:65
addiction, **1**:11
  alcoholism, **1**:33; **2**:172
  to **drugs**, **1**:11; **2**:50–51, 172
  gambling, **3**:144
  glue-sniffing, **3**:168
  to **tobacco**, **2**:172; **6**:151; **7**:62
Addis Ababa, Ethiopia, **2**:64
additives, food, **3**:112
adhesives, **3**:168
Adirondack Mountains, **5**:100
adolescence, **1**:11; **6**:33
Adolfo, **4**:33
adoption, **1**:11; **5**:154
Advent, **2**:57
advertising, **1**:12–13, *12–13*; **5**:13, *90*, 99
  and **design**, **2**:146–147, *146, 147*
  logos, **2**:146, *146, 147*
  in **magazines**, **4**:172; **6**:*153*
  posters, **6**:12, *12, 50*
  radio, **6**:47
  regulation of, **1**:12–13
  television, **7**:41
Aelian, **3**:88
Aenead, **1**:13; **3**:*183*
aerial roots, **6**:91, *91*
aerobic exercise, **3**:92, *192*
aerobic respiration, **6**:67, *67*
aerosol containers, **1**:14, *14*; **3**:105; **5**:139
Aeschylus, **2**:169; **3**:183
Aesop's Fables, **2**:44; **3**:55
aesthetics, **3**:77
affirmative action, **2**:66
Afghanistan, **1**:14, *14*; **6**:59, 97
Africa, **1**:15–18; **2**:113
  cave paintings in, **2**:28–29
  cities in, **2**:64
  climate, **1**:16
  coffee in, **2**:87
  dance in, **2**:132, *132*; **4**:84, *84*
  developing countries in, **2**:148–149
  ethnic conflicts in, **1**:174
  European colonies in, **1**:18, *18*, 55, 130, 148, 151, 174, 186; **2**:34, 90,

105, 189; **3**:40, 132, 162, 190; **4**:106, 123, 151, 153, 176, 177; **5**:8, 64, 78, 101, 102; **6**:99, 122, 137, 160; **7**:22, 32, 63, 89, 189
grasslands in, **3**:177, *178*
history, **1**:17–18
immigration from, **4**:67
independence, **1**:18
initiation ceremonies in, **4**:84, *84*
landscapes, **1**:15–16
languages, **1**:16; **2**:34
literature, **1**:18
maps, **1**:*15, 16, 18*
masks of, **4**:188, *188*
and **Middle East**, **5**:30
monarchies in, **4**:126
music, **1**:21, 22; **2**:173, *173*
myths and legends, **1**:21–22
people, **1**:16, 18
prehistoric people, **6**:20–21, 23
proverbs and sayings from, **6**:32
pygmies in, **6**:39, *39*
and **racism**, **6**:43, 162
religion, **1**:16, 17, *17*, 18, 34
Sahara, **6**:99, *99*
slavery in, **1**:17–18, 55, 130; **2**:14; **4**:152, 176; **6**:146–148, *147*
South Africa, **6**:162, *162*
wildlife in, **7**:166, *167, 190*
and **World War I**, **7**:177–178
and **World War II**, **7**:179–181
Zulus, **8**:*215*
see also specific nations
African Americans, **1**:19–20, *20*; **5**:109
and **affirmative action**, **2**:66
and **Black Muslims**, **5**:76; **8**:*153*
and **Civil Rights Movement**, **2**:65–66; **1**:20
and **Ku Klux Klan**, **4**:131, *131*
and music, **1**:147
in public office, **4**:167
and **racism**, **6**:43
separate but equal facilities for, **2**:66
and **spirituals**, **6**:178, *178*
and sports, **1**:120
African music, **1**:21; **1**:22; **2**:173, *173*; **6**:*140*, 141, *141*
African myths and legends, **1**:21–22

afterburning, **4**:114
Agamemnon (Aeschylus), **2**:169, *169*
Age of Reason, The, **8**:185
aggregate (stone), **6**:41
Agincourt, Battle of, **7**:136
Agnon, Samuel, **5**:30
agnostics, **3**:169; **8**:124
Agon (Stravinsky), **2**:*134*
Agra, India, Red Fort in, **2**:*20*
agricultural revolutions, **1**:22–23
in **India**, **4**:72
irrigation in, **4**:99, *99*
and **peasants**, **5**:160
agriculture, *see* **farming**; **farm machinery**
Agrippa (Roman general), **1**:68
AIDS (Acquired Immune Deficiency Syndrome), **1**:23; **2**:158; **6**:128; **7**:*131*
Aiken, Howard, **2**:100
aikido, **4**:186
ailerons, **3**:97
air, **1**:24, *24*; **3**:148; **7**:168, *168*
atmosphere, **1**:94, *94*
balloons and airships, **1**:112–113
and **barometers**, **1**:117
breathing, **1**:158
and **climate**, **2**:72–73
compressed, **2**:191
and **divers**, **2**:159, *159*
pollution of, **5**:186
vacuums, **7**:111
Airbus, **1**:*26*
air-conditioning, **1**:24, *24*
aircraft, **1**:25–27, *25, 26, 27*; **6**:44, *44, 63*; **7**:76, *164*; **8**:*252*
balloons and airships, **1**:112–113, *112, 113*
breaking the sound barrier, **6**:161, *161*
and **electronics**, **3**:12, *12*
flight of, **3**:96–97, *96*
fly-by-wire, **4**:82–83, *82*
gliders, **3**:167, *167*
hang gliders, **4**:13, *13*
helicopters, **4**:23, *23*
jet engines of, **4**:114, *114*
and **solar power**, **3**:22, *22*
in stratosphere, **1**:94
types of, **1**:27

as weapon delivery systems, **7**:150, *151*
wing shapes, **1**:26, *26*
in **World War I**, **7**:178
in **World War II**, **3**:167; **7**:180
air forces, **1**:27
U.S., **1**:27; **2**:93; **7**:106, *106*
in **World War II**, **7**:180, *181*
airports, **1**:28–29, *28, 29*
O'Hare, Chicago, **1**:*28*; **4**:65
terrorists in, **7**:48
X-ray machines in, **7**:185, *185*
air pressure, **7**:153
air supremacy, **7**:180
air traffic controllers, **1**:*28*
Aitchison, Janet, **1**:150
Ajman, **7**:90
Akan language, **1**:16
Akbar, **4**:73
castle of, **2**:*20*
Akers, Michelle, **6**:*155*
Akihito, emperor of Japan, **4**:*111*
Alabama, **1**:29–30; **2**:66, 67; **7**:100
Alamo, **7**:49, *49*
Alaska, **1**:30–31, *31*; **3**:92; **7**:96, 100, 103
glaciers in, **3**:165
Inuit in, **4**:91, *91*
Alaska Oil Pipeline, **1**:31
Alaska Range, **5**:109
Albania, **1**:32; **4**:105
Albany, New York, **5**:99, 100
albatrosses, **1**:138, *138*, 139
albinos, **1**:32; **3**:*157*
Albright, Madeleine, **7**:*105*
albumen, **2**:186
Alcatraz, **6**:29, *29*
alchemy, **8**:29
Alcock, John William, **1**:25; **3**:96
alcohol, **1**:32–33
addiction to, **1**:11, 33; **2**:172
beer, **1**:125; **1**:32; **4**:40; **7**:187
fermentation of, **1**:32, 137
as fuel, **3**:138
and **health**, **4**:18
Prohibition, **6**:30
and temperance movement, **6**:30
wine, **7**:170
Alcoholics Anonymous (AA), **1**:33
alcoholism, **1**:11, 33; **2**:172

Alcott, Louisa May, 8:9, *9*; 2:45;
  4:189
Alderney, 2:37
Aldrin, Edwin "Buzz," 1:93; 5:53;
  6:170
Aleut people, 1:30, 31
Alexander the Great, 8:9; 2:27; 3:50,
  181, 183; 4:94, 169; 5:19, 147
Alexander II, czar of Russia, 6:97, 98
Alexandria, Egypt:
  catacombs of, 6:125
  library of, 4:152
  Pharos of, 4:158; 6:125, *125*
Alfonsín, Raul, 1:79
Alfonso I, king of Spain, 2:21
Alfred, Saxon king, 1:54
Alfred the Great, 2:74–75; 3:26; 5:86
algae, 1:33; 2:30, 70, 115; 3:43;
  5:188; 6:179
  lichens, 4:154
  plankton, 5:123, *123*, 175
  seaweeds, 6:121
algal blooms, 1:33
algebra, 1:34; 3:32; 5:7
Alger, Horatio, 2:45; 4:189
Algeria, 1:34–35; 1:18; 3:132
  cave paintings in, 2:28–29, *28, 29*
alginates, 6:121
Ali, Muhammad, 1:19, 152
Alicante, Spain, 6:*173*
Alice's Adventures in Wonderland,
  illustration, 8:*42*
alimentary canal, 2:152
alkalis, 1:11; 6:153
Allah, 4:100–102; 5:76
allegories, 1:35; 5:152
  fables, 3:55, *55*
Allen, Ethan, 8:10; 1:44; 2:108;
  3:122; 7:119
Allende, Isabel, 4:142
allergies, 1:35; 5:185
  asthma, 1:91
  and **eczema,** 2:185
  hay fever, 4:17
alligators, 1:36, *36*; 1:42; 6:66
alliteration, 5:181–182
alloys, 1:36; 1:39; 2:114; 4:98, 191,
  192; 5:18, 20
All Saints' Day, 3:73; 4:11
allusions, 1:132

Almagro, Diego de, 2:109
almanacs, 1:36
Alomar, Sandy, 1:*119*
alpacas, 4:161
alphabets, 1:37, *37*; 7:183
  Anglo-Saxon runes, 1:54
  braille, 1:154
alpha particles, 6:45, 46
Alps, 1:38, *38*; 1:100, *100*, 103; 5:60,
  60
  French, 3:128
  Swiss, 7:25
alternating current (AC), 3:8
alternative medicine, 1:38–39; 5:15
alternators, 3:8
altiplano, 1:148
altitude, 2:72
aluminum, 1:39; 1:10; 2:40
  mining of, 5:35
  recycling of, 6:55, *55*
a.m. (ante meridiem), 7:60
Amado, Jorge, 4:142
Amahl and the Night Visitors, 8:*165*
amalgams, 5:18
Amazonia, rain forest, 3:119
Amazon River, 1:156; 6:74, 164
amber, 3:124, *124*, 150
America, *see* **Central America; Latin**
  America; North America; South
  America; United States of
  America
American Friends Service Committee
  (AFSC), 6:41
American literature, 1:40–41
  biography and autobiography,
   1:136
  children's books, 2:44–45
American myths and legends,
  1:41–42
  El Dorado, 5:77
  Maya, 5:9
  Paul Bunyan, 5:36, 77
American Revolution, 1:43–45;
  2:107; 3:122; 4:65, 74, 186; 6:165;
  7:119, 136
  African Americans in, 1:19
  and Canada, 1:43, 190
  and Committees of
   Correspondence, 1:43, 44

Declaration of Independence,
  2:138–139, *139*; 1:44, 45
  events leading to, 4:189, *189*
  first naval battle of, 4:174
  and France, 1:45
  Thirteen Colonies and, 7:56
  timeline of, 1:44
American Samoa, 1:46; 5:121, 187;
  7:100
American Sign Language (ASL), 6:137
Americans with Disabilities Act
  (1990), 2:157
America's Cup Race, 6:70; 7:186, *186*
amethyst, 3:150
Amin, Idi, 7:89
amino acids, 3:151
Amish, 1:46, *46*
Amman, Jordan, 4:116
Ammann, Jakob, 1:46
amnesia, 5:17
amniotic fluid, 6:18, *18*
amoebas, 1:47, *47*; 2:30; 6:65
amperes (amps), 3:7
amphibians, 1:47–48, *47, 48*;
  3:44–45; 7:120, *120*
  frogs, 3:134–135, *134–135*
  larvae of, 4:140
  metamorphosis of, 5:21
  salamanders, 6:104, *104*
  toads, 7:62
amplification, 3:12
amplitude, 6:47
amplitude modulation (AM) radio,
  6:47, 48
Amritsar, **pilgrimages** to, 5:169
Amsterdam, Netherlands, 5:92, *92*
Amun (Egyptian god), 2:190
Amundsen, Roald, 8:10, *10*; 1:61
Amur River, 6:74, 96
amusement parks, 1:49, *49*; 3:57, *57*
anaerobic respiration, 6:67
analog transmission, 6:47
anatomy, 5:13, *13*; 7:21
ancient world, 1:50; 2:90; 4:34; 5:27
  aqueducts, 1:68
  art of, 1:*50*
  canals, 1:191
  map, 1:*50*
  medals in, 5:12
  Mesopotamia, 5:19, *19*

Phoenicians, 5:166
prehistoric animals, 6:18–19, *18, 19*
prehistoric people, 6:20–23, *20–21, 22, 23*
Sumerians, 7:17, *17*
tents used in, 1:187
Andersen, Hans Christian, 8:10–11; 2:45; 3:41, 58; 5:19
Anderson, Marian, 8:11 *11*; 1:19; 5:162; 6:178
Andes, 1:51, *51*; 1:50, 79, *148*; 2:46, 90, *185*; 5:60, *60*, 164; 6:164; 7:112, 117
Ando, Tadao, architecture of, 1:*77*
Andorra, 1:51
Andrew, St., 6:102
Andrews, Julie, 5:76
anemia, 1:51, *51*
anemometers, 7:*153*
anemones, 6:65, *65*, 116, *116*
anesthetics, 1:52; 2:172; 7:21, *21*
Angara River, Russia, 6:74
Angel Falls, Venezuela, 7:117, 145
Angelou, Maya, 1:20, 41
angels, 1:52, *52*; 2:57, 149
angiosperms, 7:78
Angkor Wat, 1:183
angles, 3:154, *154, 155*
Anglican Church, 2:60, *61*
angling, 3:88–89, *88*
Anglo-Saxons, 1:53–54; 2:135; 3:26, 27, 28
  Arthurian legends, 1:86–87, *86*
  in Battle of Hastings, 7:136
  burial mounds of, 1:174
  clothes, 1:54, *54*
  houses, 1:*53*
  map, 1:*53*
  names of, 5:78
  writings, 1:54
Angola, 1:55; 1:18
animal behavior, 1:55–56, *55, 56*
  building dams, 1:125
  camouflage, 1:186, *186*
  communication, 2:96, *96*; 1:56, *56*, 140
  eating, 1:59, 64, 124, 139; 2:25; 3:16–17
  flight, 1:139–140, *139, 140*

hibernation, 4:27, *27*
hunting, 2:24, *24*
innate, 1:64
instinct, 1:55–56; 4:88
learning, 1:55–56, 155
mating, 5:7
migration, 1:140; 5:31; 7:84
  triggers of, 1:55
Animal Farm (Orwell), 1:35, *35*
animal parks (zoos), 7:192, *192*
animal rights, 1:57; 2:117
animals, 1:57
  Arctic, 1:78
  brains of, 1:154–155
  cells of, 2:30, *31*
  circus acts, 2:61
  classification of, 2:70; 1:*58–59*
  cloning of, 2:76
  cold-blooded, 1:48
  in **deserts,** 2:*144–145,* 145
  domestication of, 2:165–166
  ears of, 2:175, *175*
  in **ecosystems,** 2:184–185, *184*
  evolution of, 3:44–49, *46, 47, 48–49*
  extinct, *see* **extinct animals and plants**
  eyes of, 3:54, *54*
  farming, 3:60–64, *61, 62, 64*
  feet and hands of, 3:71, *71*
  feral, 2:25, 166
  food chains and webs, 3:114, *114*
  food from, 5:12
  in **forests,** 3:120, 121
  fossils, 3:123–124, *123, 124*
  fur of, 3:140, *140*
  in **grasslands,** 3:177, *177, 178*
  growth of, 3:188, *188*
  habitats of, 4:8
  hormones of, 4:40, *40*
  horns and antlers, 4:41, *41*
  invertebrates, 3:44; 4:92, *92*
  nocturnal, 1:9, 122; 6:149
  in the ocean, 5:122–123, *123, 124*
  and **parasites,** 5:153
  parenthood, 5:154
  as pets, *see* **pets**
  populations of, 5:190–191, *190*
  prehensile tails of, 1:62

  prehistoric, 2:153–156; 6:18–19, *18, 19, 22*
  in and on **rivers,** 6:71–72, *72*
  species, 6:175
  in stream habitats, 7:12–13, *12*
  territories of, 4:8
  venomous, 6:116, *116,* 152, *152,* 177, *177*; 7:118, *118*
  vertebrates, 3:44; 7:120, *120*
  warm- and cold-blooded, 7:134
  wild, 7:165–167, *167*
animal tracks and signs, 1:59, *59*
animation (movies), 2:17–19
Ankara, Turkey, 7:86
Annam, 7:124
Annan, Kofi, 7:95
Annapolis, Maryland, 4:186; 7:107
Anne, queen of England, 7:91
Anne of Green Gables (Montgomery), 2:45
anniversaries, wedding, 4:184
Anno Domini (A.D.), 2:56
annuals (plants), 3:102
anorexia nervosa, 2:180
Anschluss, 7:179
Antarctica, 1:60–61; 2:71, 113; 3:165, 168; 4:59–60, *60*; 5:31, 161
  climate of, 2:73, 144
  exploration, 1:60–61
  map, 1:*60*
  research in, 1:61
Antarctic Ocean, 5:122, 125, *125*
Antarctic Treaty (1959), 1:61
anteaters, 1:62, *62*; 1:9; 2:186
antelopes, 1:62, *62*; 2:26
anthems, 1:63
  national, 5:80
  see also **"Star-Spangled Banner, The"**
Anthony, Susan B., 8:12, *12*; 4:189; 7:173
anthracite, 2:81
anthropologists, 1:63
antibiotics, 1:63; 1:107; 2:172; 3:139
antibodies, 4:68
Antietam, Battle of, 2:68, *69*
antigens, 4:68
Antigua, 7:157
antlers, 4:41, *41*
ants, 1:64, *64*; 1:62

termites, 7:48, *48*
Antwerp, Belgium, 1:128, *128*
Anyaoku, Chief Emeka, 2:95
apartheid, 6:162
apes, 1:65–66, *65, 66;* 6:25
    baboons, 4:178, *178*
    chimpanzees, 2:46, *46*
    evolution of, 3:47, 48, *48*
    gorillas, 3:171, *171*
    knuckle walking of, 1:65
aphids, 1:64, *64,* 168
Aphrodite (Greek goddess), 3:185
Apollo (Greek god), 3:185
Apollonia, St., 2:142
Apollonius of Rhodes, 3:183
Apollo spacecraft, 5:80; 6:169, 170
apostles, 1:66; 2:54
Appalachian Mountains, 1:30; 5:110
appeasement, 7:179
appendix, 1:66
apples, 3:136, 137
Appleseed, Johnny, 8:12, *12;* 1:42;
    5:128
apprentices, 2:44
aquariums, 1:67, *67*
aqueducts, 1:68, *68*
Aquino, Corazon, 5:165
Arabia, 1:69
Arabian Nights, 1:68; 3:58; 5:30
Arabic language, 1:16, 37, *37*
Arabs, 1:69, *69;* 1:130; 2:36, 187;
    5:30
    explorers, 3:50
    in **Iraq,** 4:95
    and **Israelis,** 4:103
    in **Jordan,** 4:116
    in **Morocco,** 5:54
    paper made by, 5:151
    in **Saudi Arabia,** 6:107
    in **Syria,** 7:29
Arafat, Yasser, 8:13; 4:103; 5:148
Ararat, Mount, 7:86
arcades, 1:73
Arc de Triomphe, 3:129
archaeologists, 1:70–71, *70, 71;* 6:13;
    7:8
    carbon dating by, 2:10
    in **China,** 2:49, 51, *51*
    in cities, 2:65
    and **dinosaurs,** 2:154

in **Mexico,** 1:104, *104–105*
and **prehistoric animals,** 6:18–19
and **prehistoric people,** 6:20–23
archangels, 1:52
Archbishop of Canterbury, 2:60, *60*
archbishops, 2:23
arch bridges, 1:160, *160,* 161, *161*
archery, 1:72, *72;* 7:150, *150*
arches, 1:72–73, *73;* 1:76
Archimedean screw, 4:99
Archimedes, 8:13; 3:17
archipelago, 4:103
architecture, 1:74–77, *75, 76, 77*
    arches, 1:72–73, *73*
    bridges, 1:160, *160*
    cathedrals, 2:22–23, *22, 23*
    churches, 2:58, 59, *59;* 1:76–77,
        76–77
    conservation of, 2:110, *110*
    design of, 1:74–75, *75, 76;*
        2:146–147
    drawings of, 2:171
    Gothic style, 1:73, 76–77, *76–77;*
        2:59
    "green," 1:74
    history of, 1:75–77
    Renaissance, 6:64, *64*
    rules for, 1:74
    skyscrapers, 6:145, *145*
    symmetry in, 7:27, *27*
    of **Thailand,** 7:52
the Arctic, 1:78, *78;* 4:59–60, *59;*
    5:31, *31,* 114
    Greenland in, 3:187, *187*
    Inuit in, 4:91, *91*
    tundra in, 7:84, *84*
Arctic Circle, map, 1:*78*
Arctic Ocean, 1:78; 5:122, 125, *125*
Arctic Slope, 1:31
area codes, 1:79
Ares (Greek god), 3:185
Argentina, 1:79; 3:62; 6:164; 7:109
    Andes in, 5:60, *60*
    and **Falkland Islands,** 3:58
    pampas of, 3:177, *178*
Ariosto, Ludovico, 3:41
Aristophanes, 3:183
Aristotle, 8:13; 1:95; 3:77, 181; 5:165
arithmetic, 1:80; 3:32; 5:7
    algebra, 1:34

averages, 1:104
calculators, 1:179–180
decimals, 2:137
fractions, 3:127
infinity, 4:81
mental, 1:80
numbers, 5:116–117, *117*
percentages, 5:164
sets, 6:124, *124*
Arizona, 1:81–82; 5:98; 7:100, 103
    Grand Canyon in, *see* Grand
      Canyon
    meteor craters in, 5:21, *21;* 6:125
Arkansas, 1:82–83; 2:68; 7:100
Arkwright, Richard, 4:78
Arlington National Cemetery, 2:33;
    7:141
armadillos, 1:83, *83*
Armenia, 1:84; 1:88, 104; 2:*178;*
    6:98, 168
armies, 1:84; 2:27, 78
    and **forts,** 3:122, *122*
    medals of, 5:12, *12*
    of **Napoleon,** 5:*80*
    and **police,** 5:184
    Roman Empire, 6:88
    Spanish, 6:*174*
    U.S., 7:101, 107, *107*
armistice, 7:178
armor, 1:85, *85;* 4:128; 5:*28;* 8:191
    helmets, 7:*17*
Armstrong, Edwin, 6:48
Armstrong, Louis, 8:14, *14;* 1:19;
    4:112, 113, 167
Armstrong, Neil, 8:14, *14;* 1:93;
    5:53, 127, 128; 6:170
Armstrong, William, 2:45
Arnaz, Desi, 4:33
Arnold, Benedict, 8:14–15
Arnold, Matthew, 3:29
aromatherapy, 1:39
art:
    abstract, 6:116
    Bible and, 1:132
    by children, 2:*43*
    Chinese, 2:170
    collages, 2:89, *89*
    and **design,** 2:146–147, *146, 147*
    drawing, 2:170–171, *170, 171*
    fine arts, 3:77

folk, 3:77, 107
frescoes, 3:133, *133*; 5:*23*, 140
icons, 4:62, *62*
illuminated manuscripts, 3:*130*,
   172; 4:66
meanings of the word, 3:77
mosaics, 1:*177*; 2:*54*; 4:105; 5:54,
   54; 6:*89*
and mythology, 5:142
origami, 5:138, *138*
painting, 5:140–146
portraits, 6:8, *8*; 3:77; 5:144, *167*;
   6:8, *8*, 115
posters, 6:12, *12*; 6:*50, 98*; 8:*198,
   216, 220–221*
of **prehistoric people,** 6:*114*
printmaking, 6:28, *28*
propaganda, 6:*98*
religious, 5:142, *142*
Renaissance, 4:104, 105;
   5:142–143; 6:63–64, *63, 64*
sculpture, 5:9, *19*; 6:112–116, *112,
   113, 114, 115, 116*
of Sumer, 1:50
see also **fine arts;** *specific genres*
Artemis (Greek god), 3:185
   temple of, 6:124–125, *125*
arteries, 4:19, *19*
artesian wells, 7:156, *157*
art historians, 3:77
arthritis, 1:85; 6:68
Arthur, Chester A., 8:15, *15*; 7:101,
   118, 119
Arthurian legends, 1:86–87, *86*;
   1:136; 2:32, 52, 135; 3:29; 5:14, 77
articulated trucks, 7:82, *82*
artificial lakes, 4:135, *135*
artificial limbs, 1:87
artillery, 1:84; 2:27; 7:150–151
artists, 2:122; 3:77
Aruba, 7:157
Asante people, legends, 1:22
asbestos, 1:87
ASCII code, 2:86
asexual organisms, 6:127
Ashe, Arthur, 1:19; 7:*46*
Asia, 1:88–89; 2:113
   beans from, 1:123
   Buddhism in, 1:165–167
   climate, 1:88

colonies in, **4:**39, 77, 176
developing countries in,
   2:148–149
European colonies in, 3:40, 76,
   132; 5:76; 6:139, 183; 7:124
grasslands in, 3:177, *178*
immigration from, 4:67–68
India, 4:70–73, *70, 71, 72*
Japan, 4:109–111, *110, 111*
landscapes, 1:88
maps, 1:*88, 89*
and **Middle East,** 5:30
monarchies in, 4:126
monsoons in, 5:50, *50*
people, 1:88
U.S. territories in, 3:189
wildlife in, 7:166, 167, *167*
Asian literature, 1:90; 2:104
   Indian myths and legends, 4:76,
      76; 4:30–31, *30*
Asimov, Isaac, 6:110
Asoka, 8:15; 4:73
Assad, Hafez al-, 7:29
assemblages, 2:89
Assisi, Italy, 4:105
Assyrians, 5:19, *19*
Astaire, Fred, 2:*133*; 5:76
asteroids, 1:91; 5:172; 6:159
asthma, 1:91
Astley, Philip, 2:61
astrology, 1:92; 2:111
astronauts, 1:93, *93*; 5:53; 6:80,
   169–172
astronomers, 1:93; 1:112; 5:120, *120*;
   6:159, 188
   Big Bang theory of, 1:134
   and **black holes,** 1:145
   and **constellations,** 2:111, *111*
   Maya, 5:9
   and **planets,** 5:171–174
   and **telescopes,** 7:40, *40*
   and the **Universe,** 7:108, *108*
Asturias, Miguel Angel, 4:142
Asunción, Paraguay, 5:153, *153*
Aswan dam, 2:*188*
Atacama Desert, 2:46, 144
Atahualpa, 8:16; 2:109; 4:69
Atatürk, Mustafa Kemal, 7:86
atheists, 3:169
Athene (Greek goddess), 3:185

Athens, Greece, 2:64; 3:180, 181, *182*,
   183
Atlanta, Georgia, 2:70; 3:156, *157*
Atlantic Ocean, 5:122, *125*
   Bermuda Triangle in, 1:130
   and Northwest Passage, 1:78
   transatlantic cable under, 1:178
Atlas (Greek god), 3:184
Atlas Mountains, 1:15; 6:99
atmosphere, 1:94, *94*; 2:177; 3:30
   air, 1:24
   and **barometers,** 1:117
   and **climate,** 2:72–73
   and **clouds,** 2:80, *80*
   cosmic rays in, 2:117
   and **greenhouse effect,** 3:186, *186*;
      3:22, 121, 168
   northern lights, 5:113, *113*
   oxygen in, 3:43
   and **ozone,** 1:14, 94
   radiation in, 1:94, 134
   and **vacuums,** 7:111, *111*
atolls, 6:116
atomic bomb (A-bomb), 1:96, *96*;
   1:149
atomic clocks, 7:61
atomic numbers, 3:14
atoms, 1:95–96, *95*; 1:134; 3:7, 14,
   20; 5:8
   in **crystals,** 2:128
   and **heat,** 4:20
   and **lasers,** 4:141
   and **nuclear power,** 5:115
   particles, 5:157, *157*
   radioactive, 2:10
Attila, 8:16
Attucks, Crispus, 1:19, 44; 4:189
Auden, W. H., 3:29
audiocassettes, 2:19
Audubon, John James, 8:16; 1:142
   painting by, 8:*16*
augmented systems, 7:130
Augusta, Maine, 4:174
Augustine of Canterbury, St., 1:53;
   2:135
Augustine of Hippo, St., 8:17; 1:136
Augustus, 8:17; 1:13; 3:183
Aung San Suu Kyi, 8:18, *18*
aurochs, 2:26, 165

auroras (**northern lights**), 5:113, *113*; 7:19

Auschwitz, 2:103

Austen, Jane, 8:18; 3:29

Austin, Stephen F., 7:49

Austin, Texas, 7:49, 50

Australia, 1:97–99, *98*, *99*; 2:90; 5:121, 161

  Aborigines, 1:9, *9*, 98, 99; 2:145, 171

  Ayers Rock, 1:*98*; 6:125

  cave paintings in, 2:28–29

  caves in, 2:29

  climate in, 2:72

  in the Commonwealth, 2:95

  gold in, 3:170

  government, 1:98

  Great Barrier Reef, 2:115; 5:81; 6:125

  history, 1:99

  kangaroos in, 4:119, *119*

  koalas in, 4:130, *130*

  map, 1:*97*

  marsupials in, 4:185

  outback, 1:97

  parliament of, 5:156

  platypuses in, 5:180, *180*

  rain forest in, 3:*120*

  and **Tasmania,** 7:33

  underwater canyon in, 7:112

  wildlife in, 7:167, *167*

  and world wars, 7:177–178, 179–181

Australopithecus, 3:48, *48*

Austria, 1:100, *100*; 3:41, 160; 4:52; 6:150; 7:177–178, 179

autobiography, 1:136, 140; 3:29

autogiros, 4:23

automobiles, 1:101–102, *101*, *102*; 5:24–25; 7:76

  brakes of, 1:102, 155, *155*

  catalytic converters of, 1:10, 102

  drunk driving in, 1:32

  electric, 1:102

  gasoline and diesel engines, 3:149, *149*

  insulation of, 4:88, *88–89*, 89

  manufacture of, 3:*128*; 6:78, *78*

  mass production of, 4:190

  pollution from, 1:10, 102; 2:64

  racing, 3:129

  roads and highways, 6:76–77, *76*, *77*

  and safety, 1:101–102

  suspensions of, 2:191

  tires of, 7:62

  traffic jams, 2:64, *64*

auto racing, 1:103, *103*; 4:75

Autry, Gene, 2:119

avalanches, 1:103

averages, 1:104

awards, **medals,** 5:12, *12*

axial-flow turbines, 7:86

axles, 4:170, *170*

axolotls, 1:48

aye-aye, 3:*19*

Ayers Rock (Uluru), Australia, 1:*98*; 6:125

Azerbaijan, 1:88; 1:104; 6:98, 168

Aztecs, 1:104–105; 2:85, 109; 4:28; 5:22, 82; 6:21, 151

  ancient civilization of, 1:50

  Montezuma II, 1:105

  myths of, 1:41

Babbage, Charles, 8:18; 1:180; 2:102

babies, 1:106, *106*; 4:51; 6:18, *18*

  birth of, 1:144, *144*

  bones of, 1:149

  cells of, 2:30

  with Down's syndrome, 2:166

  growth of, 3:188

  swaddling bands for, 2:78

baboons, 4:178, *178*

Babylon, 1:50; 5:19, 120

  Hanging Gardens of, 6:124, *125*

  laws of, 4:144

Baca, Judy, 4:33

Bach, Johann Sebastian, 8:18–19; 2:103; 5:67

backpacking, 1:187

backstitch, 3:18, *18*

Bacon, Francis, 8:19, *19*

bacteria, 1:107; 2:70, 76, 88, *88*; 3:115, 161; 4:56; 6:179

  and **antibiotics,** 1:63

  and **Black Death,** 1:144

  cells of, 2:30, *31*

  and **disease,** 2:158; 1:107

  and fermentation, 1:137

  and insulin, 2:150

  intestinal flora, 2:152

  and protective clothing, 2:*78*

  in **yogurt,** 7:188

Baden-Powell, Robert, 8:19, *19*; 1:153; 3:164

badgers, 1:107, *107*

badminton, 1:108, *108*

Baez, Joan, 3:108

bagels, 1:157

Baghdad, Iraq, 4:95; 5:19

bagpipes, 1:*115*

Bahaism, 1:108

Bahamas, 1:108; 2:95; 7:157

Baha'u'llah, 1:108

Bahrain, 1:109; 4:126; 5:30

Baird, John Logie, 7:42

Baisakhi (holiday), 3:74

balance, 1:109; 2:175

balance of nature, 5:190

Balanchine, George, 2:134

Balboa, Vasco Núñez de, 8:20; 2:109

Baldwin, James, 1:20, 41

baleen whales, 7:163

Bali, gamelans of, 5:*135*

ballads, 1:109; 2:119

ballet, 1:110–111, *110*, *111*; 2:134, *134*

balloons and airships, 1:112–113, *112*, *113*; 1:27; 3:97, 148, *148*

  flight of, 3:96–97, *96*

  and **weather,** 1:94, 112; 7:*153*

balls, bouncing, 2:*191*

Baltimore, Maryland, **4**:186, 187; **7**:10
Baluchitherium, **3**:46
Balzac, Honoré de, **3**:41
bamboo, **3**:175, 176
bananas, **3**:136, *136*
Band Aid charity benefit, **2**:38
Bandaranaike, Sirimavo, **6**:25
bandicoots, **4**:*185*
bands (musical), **1**:114–115, *114–115*;
    2:15, *15*
Bangkok, Thailand, **5**:*147*; **7**:52, *52*
Bangladesh, **1**:116; **1**:88; **2**:85, 95;
    5:147
    famine in, **3**:60
    floods in, **3**:*99*
    poverty in, **6**:15
banks, **1**:116
    and **money,** **5**:46–47, *46, 47*
Banneker, Benjamin, 8:20; **1**:19, 20;
    4:186
Bantu languages, **1**:16
Bantus, **6**:162
baptism, **1**:116; **2**:55–56, *55*
Barbados, **1**:116; **2**:95; **7**:157
Barbarossa, **5**:170
Barbary pirates, **5**:170
Barber, Samuel, 8:20; **5**:67
Barbie dolls, **1**:*164*
Barbuda, **7**:157
Barcelona, Spain, **6**:173
bar codes, **2**:86; **4**:83, *83*, 141
Bardeen, John, **3**:13
bark, of trees, **7**:*78, 79*, 80
barley, **3**:173, *173*, 176
barnacles, **1**:117, *117*; **2**:*127*; **6**:118
Barnard, Christiaan, **7**:75
Barnum, P. T., 2:61; **8**:20–21; **2**:108
Barnum and Bailey's Circus, **2**:61
Barocci, Federico, painting by, **1**:*13*
barographs, **7**:*153*
barometers, **1**:117, *117*; **1**:24
barques, **6**:*101*
Barrie, J. M., 8:21
Barron, Robert, **4**:164
barrows (burial mounds), **1**:174
barter, **5**:46; **7**:73
Bartok, Béla, **5**:67
Barton, Clara, 8:22, *22*; **4**:189
Baryshnikov, Mikhail, **1**:111
basal metabolic rate (BMR), **3**:110

baseball, **1**:118–120, *118, 119*; **6**:156;
    8:59
Basho, 8:22
Basie, Count, **4**:112
basilicas, **2**:58
basketball, **1**:120–121, *120, 121*;
    7:187
basket making, **1**:121, *121*; **5**:*84*
Basques, **6**:173
bassoons, **5**:*70*
batik, **7**:*51*
Baton Rouge, Louisiana, **4**:167
bats, **1**:122, *122*; **2**:*175*, 181; **6**:123
    claws of, **5**:*77*
    vampires, **7**:115
batteries, **1**:123
    of electric cars, **1**:102
    and **electricity,** **3**:7, 8, 21
    flashlight, **3**:94, *94*
    mercury in, **5**:18
Batuta, Ibn, **3**:50
Bauhaus, **1**:77
Baum, L. Frank, **2**:45; **4**:121
bauxite, **1**:39
Baykal, Lake (Russia), **4**:134; **6**:96
Bay of Bengal, **4**:70
Bay Psalm Book, **1**:40
Beach Boys, **3**:11; **6**:81
beaches, **4**:*17*
beam bridges, **1**:160, *161*
beans, **1**:123, *123*; **6**:122
Beard, Daniel Carter, **1**:153
Bearden, Romare, **1**:19
bears, **1**:124, *124*
Beatles, **2**:99; **6**:81, *81*
Beatrix, queen of Netherlands, **4**:125,
    126
Beaufort scale, **7**:168, *168*
Beauregard, P. T., **2**:68
Beauvoir, Simone de, **7**:173
beavers, **1**:125, *125*; **6**:86
Beckett, Samuel, **3**:29
Becquerel, Henri, **6**:46
Bede, Venerable, **1**:131
Bedouin, **2**:145, *145*; **5**:104
beer, **1**:125; **1**:32; **4**:40; **7**:187
bees, **1**:126, *126*; **4**:87; **7**:118
    communication by, **1**:56, *56*
    and **honey,** **4**:38, *38*
    nests of, **5**:92

    pupae of, **6**:37, *37*
    worker, **1**:*126*
beeswax, **7**:149
Beethoven, Ludwig van, 8:22–23,
    23; **2**:36, 99, 103; **5**:67
beetles, **1**:127, *127*; **3**:80, *80*; **4**:87
Beijing, China, **2**:47–48, *49*, 50, 52,
    62; **5**:148
Beirut, Lebanon, **4**:148, *148*
Belarus (Belorussia), **1**:128; **6**:168
Belfast, Northern Ireland, **5**:112
Belgium, **1**:128; **3**:41; **4**:126, 169
    African colonies of, **2**:105; **6**:99
    and world wars, **7**:177–178,
    179–181
Belgrade, Yugoslavia, **7**:188
Belize, **1**:129; **2**:34–35, 95
Bell, Alexander Graham, 8:23, *23*;
    4:92, 189; **7**:38, 39
Bellini, Giovanni, 8:24;
    painting by, **8**:*24*
Bellini, Vincenzo, **5**:132
Bellow, Saul, **1**:40; **6**:34
bells, **1**:129, *129*
    Liberty Bell, **4**:152; **5**:163
beltways, **2**:65
Benedictine monks, **5**:45
Benelux, **4**:169
Benesh dance notation, **2**:134
Ben-Gurion, David, 8:24
Benin, **1**:130; **1**:17
Bennett, Michael, **5**:75
Beowulf, **3**:28, 29
Berbers, **1**:130
Berg, Alban, **5**:67
Bergen-Belsen, **2**:103
Bergh, Henry, **1**:57
Bergman, Ingmar, **5**:63
Bering, Vitus, **3**:51
Bering Strait, **1**:30; **3**:51
Berlin, Germany, **3**:158, 160
Berlin, Irving, **5**:75
Berlin Wall, **3**:160
Berlioz, Hector, **1**:13; **5**:67
Bermuda, **1**:130; **2**:95
Bermuda Triangle, **1**:130
Bern, Switzerland, **7**:25
Bernadette, St., **6**:102
Bernard, St., **6**:102

Bernini, Gian Lorenzo, portrait by, 6:*8*

Bernstein, Leonard, 8:24–25, *25;* 4:189; 5:67, 75

berries, 3:136–137, *136*

Bes (Egyptian god), 2:190

Bessemer, Henry, 4:98

beta particles, 6:45, 46

Bethlehem, 2:56, 57; 5:169

Bethune, Mary McLeod, 1:19

Bharata Natya, 2:*132,* 133

Bhutan, 1:130; 4:126

Bhutto, Benazir, 5:147; 6:25

Bible, 1:131–132, *131;* 2:44, 55, 56, 57, 59; 3:29; 4:22, 117; 6:31; 7:28

drama in, 2:169

illuminated manuscripts and, 4:66

King James, 3:29

and **Kwanza,** 4:*132*

miracles described in, 5:37

parables in, 5:152

prophets of, 6:30

proverbs and sayings in, 6:32

and religious painting, 5:142, *142*

bicycles, 1:133, *134;* 3:*134;* 4:*192;* 7:75, *75*

and camping, 1:187

pumps, 6:36, *36*

racing, 2:129, *129*

tires, 7:62

tire valves of, 7:115, *115*

wheels of, 4:169, *169*

biennials (plants), 3:102

Big Bang theory, 1:134; 2:177; 7:108; 8:122

Bigfoot, 1:42; 5:51

bilateral symmetry, 7:27, *27*

billiards and pool, 1:135

Billings, William, 1:63

Bill of Rights, 1:135–136; 2:112

Billy the Kid, 8:25, *25;* 3:146; 5:97

bimetal thermostats, 7:55, *55*

binary system, 1:179; 2:97; 5:117

Bingham, Hiram, 4:69

binoculars, 1:136, *136;* 4:150; 5:133

biochemists, 2:41

biodegradable materials, 4:192

biodiversity, 7:165

biofeedback, 1:39

biogas, 1:137

biogenesis, 8:124

biogeographical zones, **wildlife** in, 7:165–167, *167*

biography and autobiography, 1:136, 140; 3:29

biological control, 5:153; 7:142, 168

biologists, 1:137; 2:182; 4:133

biosphere, 3:30

biotechnology, 1:137

genetic engineering, 3:150

Bird, Larry, 1:121; 4:74

birds, 1:138–143, *138, 141, 142, 143;* 7:120, *120,* 165–167, *167*

bills of, 1:*139;* 3:*42*

bittern, 6:*56*

classifications of, 1:141–143

claws of, 5:77

on **cliffs,** 2:71, *71*

crow, 8:*16*

diets of, 1:139

eggs of, 2:186, *186*

evolution of, 1:139; 3:*42,* 46, *46*

extinction of, 3:52–53, *52–53;* 3:19

feathers of, 3:70, *70*

feeding, 1:140

flightless, 5:161–162, *161*

flight of, 1:139–140, *139, 140;* 3:96

habitats of, 4:8, *8*

hawks, 6:*123*

imprinting of, 4:88

mating, 5:7

migration of, 1:138, 140; 4:27, 88; 5:31; 7:159

nests of, 4:8

owls, 1:141, *143;* 3:*54*

parenthood of, 5:154, *154*

parrots, 5:156

pellets of, 1:59

as pets, 1:141

and **ponds,** 5:188, *188*

populations of, 5:190–191, *191*

poultry, 2:42, *42*

preen glands of, 7:149

ritual displays of, 1:*55*

robin, 1:*141*

and **seashore,** 6:119

songs of, 1:56, 140

sparrows, 1:139, 141

starlings, 1:139, *139*

and **streams,** 7:12, *12*

terns, 1:138, *138,* 140

turkeys, 7:87, *87*

in **wetlands,** 7:159–161, *160–161*

see also **chickens**

bird-watching, 1:140, 142

Birmingham, Alabama, 1:30

birth, 1:144, *144;* 6:18, *18,* 71

pregnancy and, 6:18, *18*

reproduction, 6:65, *65*

birth control, 6:128

Bishop, Elizabeth, 1:41

bishops (priests), 2:23, *56*

Bismarck, North Dakota, 5:111

Bismarck, Otto von, 8:26; 3:160

bison, 1:144, *144;* 2:*26;* 3:177; 5:82

bits (computer), 2:97, 101

bitterns, 6:*56*

bitumen, 7:81, *81*

bituminous coal, 2:81

bivalves, 5:44

Bizet, Georges, 8:26; 5:132

Blackbeard the Pirate (Teach), 5:170

blackbirds, 1:*143*

Black Death, 1:144; 3:31; 5:27; 6:53

Black Forest mountains, 5:61, *61*

Black Hawk War (1832), 7:171

Black Hills, 6:167

black holes, 1:145

Black Muslims, 2:66; 5:76

Black Panther Party, 1:20; 2:66

blacks, *see* **African Americans**

Blackstone, Harry, 4:173

Blair, Tony, 7:94

Blake, Peter, collage by, 2:*89*

Blake, William, 8:26; 3:29

illustration by, 8:*26*

Blakey, Art, 4:112

blazon, 4:25

bleeding, first aid for, 3:81

Blériot, Louis, 1:25; 3:96

blimps (dirigibles), 1:112–113, *113*

blindness, 1:145, 154

blind worms, 1:47–48, *47*

Blitzkrieg, 7:179

Block, Adriaen, 6:69

blockboard, 7:174, *174*

blood, 1:146, *146*

anemia, 1:51, *51*
bleeding, 3:81, *81*
circulation of, 4:19, *19*, 50, *50*
and digestion, 2:152
and HIV, 1:23
in **human body,** 4:48, 49, 50, *50*,
124
and **pulse,** 6:35, *35*
Bloodaxe, Eric, 7:125
blowholes, 7:162
bluebirds, 1:*142*
blue jays, 1:*142*
blues, 1:147; 5:39, 68
Blume, Judy, 2:45
boars, 5:168
boats, 1:147–148, *147*; 2:*108*; 4:*71*,
177; 7:76, 147
and **canals,** 1:191–192, *191*, *192*;
4:163, *163*
canoes and kayaks, 2:9, *9*; 5:*121*
catamarans, 7:186
Chinese junks, 2:48; 5:170
and **coast guards,** 2:83, *83*
and **docks,** 2:161, *161*
dugout canoe, 6:*71*
ice, 7:170
junks, 6:100, *101*
lifeboats, 5:155, *155*
and **lighthouses,** 4:158, *158*
at Mystic Seaport, 2:*108*
on the Nile, 5:102, *102*
ports and harbors, 6:9–10, *10*
rowing, 6:92
sailing, 6:100, *100*; 5:*121*; 6:69, 70
ships, 6:132–133, *132–133*
and sonar, 2:181
steamboats, 5:*40*, 41
U-boats, 7:178, 180
yachts, 7:186, *186*
bobsleds, 7:170
Boccaccio, Giovanni, 3:41
bocce, 1:152
bodhisattvas, 6:103, *103*
Boeing 747, 1:*25*, 28
Boeing 777, 1:*27*
Boer War (1899–1902), 1:148; 1:18;
2:103; 6:162; 7:93
Bogart, Humphrey, 5:*63*
bog mosses, 7:160
Bogotá, Colombia, 2:90
Bohr, Niels, 8:27; 1:95

Boise, Idaho, 4:63
Bolívar, Simón, 8:27, *27*; 1:148; 2:90;
7:117
Bolivia, 1:148; 6:164
Böll, Heinrich, 3:41
boll weevils, 1:127
Bombay, India, 2:64; 4:71
bombers, 1:27, 113
bombs, 1:149; 1:96; 4:32, 111; 7:151,
181
nuclear, 5:115
and **peace movement,** 5:159
bone china, 6:13
bones, 1:149, *149*; 4:48, *48*; 7:120,
120
first aid for, 3:81
fossilized, 3:47, *47*
fractures of, 3:127, *127*
skeletons, 6:142, *142*
Bonn, Germany, 3:158
Bonnie and Clyde, 1:42
bonobos, 2:46
Book of the Dead, The, 2:*189*
books, 1:150–151, *150*
censorship of, 2:33
for **children,** 2:44–45
copyrights of, 2:115
encyclopedias, 3:18
in **libraries,** 4:152
novels, 5:114
printing, 6:26–27, *26*, *27*
boomerangs, 1:9
Boone, Daniel, 8:27–28, *27*; 1:42;
4:122
Booth, William and Catherine,
8:28; 6:105
Borden, Lizzie, 1:42
bores, tidal, 7:58
Borg, Bjorn, 7:*46*
Borges, Jorge Luis, 4:142
Borneo, 1:151; 4:176
Borromini, Francesco, 1:74
Boru, Brian, 4:97
Bosley, Keith, 5:181
Bosnia and Herzegovina, 1:100,
151; 2:125; 3:34; 6:124, 148; 7:188
bosons, 5:157
Boston, Massachusetts:
Boston Massacre, 1:43, 44, *44*;
4:189
Boston Tea Party, 1:44; 4:189

marathon, 4:184
Boswell, James, 1:136; 3:29
Botswana, 1:151; 1:175; 2:95; 7:*69*,
160
Botticelli, Sandro, 8:28–29
painting by, 8:*28*
Botticini, Francesco, painting by,
5:*142*
Boublil, Alain, 5:75
Boudicca, 4:26
Boulez, Pierre, 3:11
Bourges cathedral, France, 1:*76–77*
boutiques, 7:9
Boutros-Ghalli, Boutros, 7:95
Bowie, Jim, 7:49
bowling, 1:152
Boxer Rebellion (1900), 2:51
box-girder bridges, 1:160
boxing, 1:152–153
Boyle, Robert, 8:29
Boy Scouts, 1:153, *153*
Brachiosaurus, 2:152
Bradbury, Ray, 6:110
Bradford, William, 8:29; 1:40; 4:190
Bradley, Troy, 1:113
Bradstreet, Anne, 8:29–30; 1:40
Brady, Mathew, 2:70
photography by, 3:*82*
Bragi (Norse god), 5:107
Brahe, Tycho, 8:30
Brahmaputra River, 3:146
Brahms, Johannes, 8:30, *30*; 2:36,
103; 5:67
braille, 1:154; 1:145
Braille, Louis, 8:31; 1:154
brains, 1:154–155, *155*
human, 4:17, 51, *51*
and **memory,** 5:17
and **nervous systems,** 5:91, *91*
and **senses,** 6:123
as **thermostats,** 7:55
brakes, 1:155, *155*; 1:24
anti-lock, 1:102
bicycle, 1:133, *134*
friction of, 3:134
hydraulic, 4:54
locomotive, 4:165
Bramah, Joseph, 4:164
Bramaputra River, 4:70
Brandeis, Louis, 4:145
brand names, 7:74, *74*

brandy, 1:33
Branson, Richard, 1:113
Brasília, Brazil, 1:156; 2:23
brass, 1:36; 7:191
brass instruments, 5:71, *71*, 134
Bratislava, Slovakia, 6:149
Brattain, Walter, 3:13
Braun, Wernher von, 8:31; 6:80
Brazil, 1:156, *156*; 2:63, 72; 6:164;
    7:109
    folk dance in, 3:*106*
    Native Americans in, 5:*82*
    poverty in, 6:15
    rain forest in, 3:*121*
Brazil nuts, 5:119
bread, 1:157, *157*; 3:173, *173*
breathing, 1:158, *158*; 1:24
    asthma, 1:91
    and **disease,** 2:158
    human, 4:49, *49*, 168
    lungs and, 4:168
    respiration, 6:67, *67*
    in singing, 6:140
    underwater, 2:159, *159*
Brecht, Bertolt, 3:41
brewer's yeast, 7:187
Breyer, Stephen, 4:*145*
bricks, 1:159, *159*; 2:188–189
bridge (card game), 2:11, *11*
Bridger, Jim, 2:92
bridges, 1:160, *160*, *161*
    aqueducts, 1:68, *68*
    concrete in, 2:104, *104*
    Oakland, California, 7:*96*
    suspension, 1:160, *160*, 161, *161*;
    2:50
    Tacoma Narrows, 7:*121*
Briggs, Robert, 2:76
Britain, Battle of, 7:180
British Antarctic Survey team, 1:*61*
British Isles, 1:162–163; 7:90–94,
    90–94
    Anglo-Saxons in, 1:53–54
    archaeology in, 1:54, *54*
    burial mounds in, 1:174
    climate of, 1:163
    countries and people of, 1:163
    England, 3:24–27
    Irish Republic, 4:96–97
    landscapes, 1:163, *163*
    map, 1:*162*

    monasteries in, 5:45–46, *46*
    national anthem of, 5:80
    Normans in, 5:105–106, *105*, *106*
    Northern Ireland, 3:25; 4:97;
      5:112, *112*; 7:90–94
    observatories in, 5:*120*
    power station in, 5:*115*
    prehistory in, 6:20, 23
    Scotland, 6:111, *111*
    Wales, 7:134
    see also **United Kingdom**
Britten, Benjamin, 8:31–32, 155,
    163; 1:132; 5:67, 132
brittle materials, 2:191
broadcasting, 6:47–48, *47*, *48*
brocade, 7:51
Brodsky, Joseph, 5:182
bronchodilators, 1:91
Brontë family, 8:32, *32*; 3:29; 7:122
bronze, 1:36; 5:20, *20*; 6:23, *23*
    sculpture of, 6:112–115, *113*
Bronze Age, 5:20
Brook Farm, Massachusetts, 7:110
Brooklyn-Battery Tunnel, New York,
    7:85
Brooks, Garth, 2:*119*
Brooks, Gwendolyn, 1:20, 41; 4:65;
    5:182
Brooks Range, 1:31; 2:113
Broom, Rev. Andrew, 1:57
Brown, Arthur, 3:96
Brown, Arthur Whitten, 1:25
Brown, James (singer), 6:81
Brown, John, 8:32–33, *33*; 2:67;
    7:158
**Browning, Elizabeth Barrett and
    Robert,** 8:33; 3:29; 7:122
Brown v. *Board of Education,* 1:20;
    2:65, 66; 8:156–157
Brubeck, Dave, 4:113
Bruegel, Pieter, 8:34
    painting by, 8:*34*
bruises, 1:164
Brule, Étienne, 5:24
Brunei, 1:164
Brunel, Isambard Kingdom, 3:23;
    4:78
Brunelleschi, Filippo, 8:34; 6:64
Brussels, Belgium, 1:128
Bryant, William Cullen, 1:40

Bryan, William Jennings, 8:34–35,
    35; 4:65; 5:88; 7:45
bubbles, 1:164, *164*
Bubka, Sergey, 7:*72*
buccaneers (pirates), 5:170
Buchanan, James, 8:35–36, *35*; 3:82;
    5:162; 7:101
Bucharest, Romania, 6:87
Buchenwald, 2:103, *103*
Buck, Pearl S., 8:36; 1:41; 6:34;
    7:158
Buckland, Dean, 2:153
Budapest, Hungary, 4:52, *52*
Buddha, 8:36; 1:165, *165*; 3:74;
    5:169; 6:61
Buddhism, 1:165–167; 2:50; 5:155;
    6:61–62, 102, *103*; 7:117
    burial mounds of, 1:*166*
    festivals, 3:73–74
    funerals in, 3:139
    literature of, 1:90
    map, 1:*167*
    meditation in, 5:15
    monasteries, 5:45, *45*
    pilgrimages of, 5:169
    reincarnation, 6:60
    rites and rituals, 4:84–85, *85*, 139
    teachings of, 1:165
    temples of, 1:*130*, *167*; 7:43–44, *52*
    way of life, 1:166–167, *166*
    Zen, 1:167
    see also **Buddha**
buds, 7:79
Buenos Aires, Argentina, 1:79
buffalo, 1:168, *168*; 1:144, *144*; 2:24,
    39, 166; 5:82
"Buffalo Bill," *see* **Cody, William F.**
bugs, 1:168, *168*; 4:86–87, *86–87*
    centipedes, 2:33, *33*
    millipedes, 3:*120*
    see also **insects**
Bugs Bunny, 2:19
building, 1:169–171, *170*
    aircraft construction, 1:26
    in cities, 2:64–65
    concrete in, 2:104
    conservation of, 2:110, *110*
    cranes, 2:123, *123*
    dams, 2:131
    earthquakes and, 2:179; 1:169
    houses, 4:45–46, *45*

materials, 4:191–192
mud bricks for, 2:188–189
skyscrapers, 6:145, *145*
stone quarries for, 2:188
see also **architecture; housing**
building codes, 1:169
bulbs and corms, 1:172, *172*
Bulgaria, 1:172; 2:87; 6:148;
 7:177–178, 179
bulimia, 2:180
bulldozers, 1:173, *173*; 4:54
bullet-proof vests, 1:85
bullfighting, 1:173, *173*
Bull Run (Manassas), Battles of, 2:68
bumblebees, 1:126, *126*
Bunche, Ralph, 8:37; 1:19
Bunker Hill, Battle of, 1:44, 45
Bunyan, John, 8:37; 1:35; 2:44; 3:29;
 5:169
Bunyan, Paul, 1:42
buoys, 4:*158*
bupivacaine, 1:52
Burger, Warren, 5:36
burial mounds, 1:174; 3:139; 5:127
 Buddhist, 1:*166*
 cemeteries, 2:33
Burke, Robert, 3:51
Burkina Faso, 1:174
Burma (Myanmar), 5:76, *76*; 1:88;
 2:95
burners, stove, 7:11
burns, first aid for, 3:81, *81*
Burns, Robert, 8:38, *38*; 3:29
Burnside, Ambrose, 2:68
Burton, Richard, 1:68
Burundi, 1:174
Bush, George, 8:38–39, *38*; 7:49, 101
Bush, George W., 8:39
Bushmen, 1:175, *175*; 1:151; 2:29,
 145; 4:53; 5:104; 6:162
Bushnell, David, 7:15
businesses, 1:175
 advertising by, 1:12–13
 and **biotechnology,** 1:137
 and **calculators,** 1:179–180
 chemical, 2:40, *40*
 codes and ciphers in, 2:86, *86*
 and **economics,** 2:183, *183*
 employment, 3:18
 factories, 3:56, *56, 115*; 4:190
 factors of production in, 3:56

fax machines, 3:68, *68*
industry, 4:79–80
international trade, 2:51, 52
labor unions, 4:133
logos of, 2:146, *146, 147*
trademarks of, 7:74, *74*
trade of, 7:73
see also **industry**
butterflies, 1:176, *176*; 1:186; 2:22;
 4:87
 endangered species, 3:19
 larvae of, 4:140
 metamorphosis of, 5:21, *21*
 migration of, 1:176
 symmetry of, 7:27, *27*
Byron, Lord, 8:39; 3:29
bytes (computer), 2:101
Byzantine Empire, 1:177; 3:38, 182;
 5:139; 6:91
 churches, 2:*54*, 55, 56, 58–59, *58*
 laws in, 4:144

Cable, George Washington, 1:40
cablegrams, 7:37
cables, 1:178
 bridges, 1:160, *161*
 electric, 3:9–10, 21
 elevators (hoisting ropes), 3:17
 fiber optics, 3:75, *75*
 rope, 6:92
 wire, 7:170
cable-stayed bridges, 1:160, 161, *161*
cable television, 7:42
cabochon, 3:150

Cabot, John and Sebastian, 8:39;
 1:190; 4:174; 7:103
Cabral, Pedro, 6:11
Cabrini, St. Frances Xavier, 8:40;
 4:65
cacti, 1:178, *178*; 1:82; 2:145, *145*;
 3:*102*
CAD (computer-aided design), 4:82
Caesar, Julius, 8:40; 1:181; 2:31, 150;
 3:27, 183; 6:23, 89
caffeine, 2:87
Cahill, Thaddeus, 3:11
caimans, 1:36
Cairo, Egypt, 2:187, *187*
Cajuns, 4:167
Calamity Jane, 6:167
calculators, 1:179–180, *179, 180*;
 1:80; 4:82
Calcutta, India, 4:71
Caldecott, Randolph, 2:45
Calder, Alexander, 8:40–41
 sculpture by, 8:*40*
calendars, 1:181, *181*; 7:60
 Anno Domini on, 2:56
 astrology, 1:92
 Aztec, 1:105
 festivals and holidays, 3:73–74,
 73, 74
 stone circles, 7:7–8, 8
Calhoun, John C., 8:41; 6:165
California, 1:182–183; 2:67; 7:100,
 102, 103
 Death Valley in, 7:113
 earthquakes in, 2:179; 7:98
 gold in, 3:170
 Hollywood, 4:36, *36*
 San Diego Animal Park in, 7:*192*
 Yosemite National Park in, 1:183;
 5:81, *81*
Callimachus, 3:183
calories, 3:110
Calvin, John, 8:41; 3:130; 4:47; 6:31,
 57
Cambodia, 1:183; 1:88, 89; 6:59
camcorders, 7:123
camels, 1:184, *184*; 2:26, 39,
 144–145, 145, 166
camera obscura, 1:185
cameras, 1:184–185, *184, 185*; 4:*81*,
 150; 5:133, 167
 television, 7:41–42

video, 7:41, 123, *123*
Cameroon, 1:186; 2:36
camouflage, 1:186, *186*; 3:70, 176
    of **butterflies,** 1:176
    of **caterpillars,** 2:22
    of **chameleons,** 2:37, *37*
    cosmetics, 2:117
    stick insects, 6:192, *192*
camping, 1:187, *187*
Camus, Albert, 3:41
Can (musical group), 3:11
Canaanite people, alphabet, 1:37
Canada, 1:188–190; 2:90; 3:92;
    5:108, 109, 136–137; 7:137
    acid rain in, 1:10
    agriculture in, 1:23
    and Alaska, 1:30
    and **American Revolution,** 1:43,
    190
    British victory in, 7:91
    cities of, 1:189, *189*
    climate, 1:188; 2:72
    in the Commonwealth, 2:95
    farming, 3:*178*
    flag, 3:93
    French and Indian War, 3:132
    gold in, 3:170, *170*
    Grand Banks, 3:91
    history of, 1:190
    ice ages in, 4:58, *58*
    Inuit in, 4:91, *91*
    languages of, 1:189
    and **Maine,** 4:175
    map, 1:*188*
    and NAFTA, 5:22; 7:73, 101
    Native Americans in, 5:85, 85
    Niagara Falls in, 7:145
    northern lights in, 5:113, *113*
    parliament of, 5:156
    people and culture of, 1:189
    provinces and territories of, 1:190
    Quebec bridge in, 1:161
    resources of, 1:189
    St. Lawrence Seaway, 1:192
    sawmill in, 7:*174*
    War of 1812 in, 7:135
    West Edmonton Mall in, 7:10
    and world wars, 7:177–178,
    179–181

canals, 1:191–192, *191, 192*; 2:50;
    4:78
    Erie, 5:99–100
    locks of, 4:163, *163*
    in Netherlands, 5:92, *92*
    and the Nile, 5:102
    Panama, 5:149, *149*; 6:175
    Suez, 5:16
canard arrangement, 1:26
Canary Islands, 2:7; 7:133
Canberra, Australia, 1:97, 99
cancer, 2:7; 5:115
candles, 2:7; 2:74–75; 3:78; 4:*156,*
    157; 7:149
canine teeth, 7:36, *36*
cannibalism, 2:8, *8*
Cannon, Annie Jump, 6:186
cannons, 2:8, *8*; 3:190; 7:150, *150,*
    151
canoeing, 2:9, *9*; 1:147; 7:147
canonization, 6:102
Canseco, José, 4:33
Canterbury Tales (Chaucer), 5:169
    illustration,
    8:*52*
cantilever bridges, 1:160, 161, *161*
canyons, 7:112, 113, *114*
capacitors, 3:12
Cape Canaveral, Florida, 3:100
Cape Cod, Massachusetts, 4:190
Capek, Karel, 6:78
Cape Town, South Africa, 6:162, *162*
Cape Verde, 2:9
capillaries, 4:19
capital cities, 2:65
capitalism, 2:183
Capitol Building, U.S., 7:139, 140,
    140, 141
Capone, Al, 1:42; 3:146; 6:30
Caracas, Venezuela, 7:117
carats, 3:170
carbohydrates, 2:10; 3:110
carbon, 2:10, *10*; 1:95; 2:40, 150;
    3:14, 150, 186
carbon dating, 1:71; 2:10
carbon dioxide, 1:24, 102, 146; 2:10;
    6:67
Carboniferous period, 2:81
carbon monoxide, 1:102
cardinals (birds), 1:*141*

cardinals (priests), 2:23
cardiopulmonary resuscitation (CPR),
    3:81
cardiovascular surgeons, 7:21
Cardozo, Benjamin N., 4:145; 5:100
cards and card games, 2:11–12, *11,*
    12; 3:146
Caribbean, 2:13–14; 4:103
    African influence in, 2:14, 90
    Cuba, 2:128
    developing countries in,
    2:148–149
    European colonies in, 6:33, *33*, 102
    European influence in, 2:14, 90
    Hispanics from, 4:32–34, *33*
    history, 2:14
    hurricanes in, 4:54, *54*
    Jamaica, 4:107
    in Latin America, 6:163
    literature of, 4:141–142
    map, 2:*13*
    Native Americans of, 5:82
    and Panama Canal, 5:149, *149*
    pirates in, 5:170
    Puerto Rico, 6:33, *33*
    Rastafarians in, 6:52, *52*
    reggae in, 6:60, *60*; 6:52
    St. Lucia, 6:102, *102*
    slavery in, 6:146–147, *147*
    Spanish colonies in, 4:107
    steel bands in, 1:114–115, *115*
    West Indies in, 7:157, *157*
caribou (**reindeer**), 6:60, *60*
caricatures, 2:17
carillons, 1:129
Carl Gustav, king of Sweden, 4:125
Carlsbad Caverns, 1:122; 5:98
Carlyle, Thomas, 3:29
Carmichael, Hoagy, 4:74
carnauba wax, 7:149
Carnegie, Andrew, 8:42; 4:152;
    5:163
Carnegie Hall, 1:24
carnivals, 2:15, *15*; 3:73–74; *see also*
    festivals and holidays
carnivores, *see* **flesh-eaters**
carols, 2:16, *16*; 2:57; 4:56; 8:244
Carothers, Wallace, 7:29
carpentry, 2:16–17, *16, 17*; 7:174
carpets, 6:93, *93*

Carpue, Joseph, 5:178
carrageen, 6:121
carrier frequency, 6:47
carrier waves, 6:47
Carroll, Charles, 2:139
Carroll, Lewis, 8:42–43; 2:45; 5:18
cars, *see* **automobiles**
Carson, Kit, 2:92; 5:93, 97
Carson, Rachel, 8:43; 5:162
Carson City, Nevada, 5:93
Carter, James Earl, 8:43–44, *43;* 3:156; 7:101
Carthage, 1:68; 5:166; 7:85
Cartier, Jacques, 8:44; 1:190; 3:130
cartilage, 1:85, 149
cartographers, 4:180–183
cartoons and comics, 2:17–19, *18;* 2:170; 4:172
Cartwright, Alexander, 1:118
Cartwright, Edmund, 4:78
Caruso, Enrico, 5:*132*
Carver, George Washington, 8:44–45, *45;* 1:20, 29; 5:41
Casablanca (movie), 5:*63*
Cascade Range, 5:109, 137
case law, 4:143
Cash, Johnny, 2:119
cash registers, 1:180
Caspian Sea, 1:89; 3:37; 4:134
Cassatt, Mary, 8:45
    painting by, 8:*45*
cassette players, 2:19, *19;* 6:54; 7:123, *123*
cassiterite, 7:62
castles, 2:20–21, *20–21;* 2:126; 5:27, 105–106, *105*
castrato, 6:140
Castro, Fidel, 8:46; 2:128
Castro, Raul H., 4:33
CAT (Computerized Axial Tomography) scanners, 6:108
catacombs of Alexandria, 6:125
catamarans, 7:186
catapults, 6:88; 7:150, *150*
cataracts, 1:145
caterpillars, 2:22, *22;* 4:140
    butterflies, 1:176
    camouflage, 1:186
    metamorphosis of, 5:21, *21*
    and **moths,** 5:57

and **parasites,** 5:*153*
cathedrals, 2:22–23, *22, 23;* 1:*76–77;* 2:58; 3:129, 130; 6:95; 7:89
    in **Middle Ages,** 5:27
    Norman, 5:*106*
    Renaissance, 6:64, *64*
    stained glass in, 6:183, *183*
Cather, Willa, 8:46, *46;* 1:40, 41; 5:88, 89
Catherine of Alexandria, St., 6:102
Catherine of Aragon, 2:60
Catherine the Great, 8:46–47, *47;* 6:97
Catherine wheel, 6:102
catholic, use of word, 2:23
Catholicism, Roman, 2:23; 2:54–56; 7:116, *155*
    churches of, 2:58–59, *58*
    monasteries, 5:45–46, *45, 46*
    popes, *see* **popes**
    priests of, 6:24
    and **Reformation,** 6:57, *57*
    rites and rituals of, 4:84, *84*
    saints, 6:102, *102, 103*
    and **Vatican City,** 7:116, *116*
catkins, 7:79, *80*
Catlin, George, painting by, 5:*84*
cats, 2:24–25, *24, 25;* 2:166
    cheetahs, 2:40, *40*
    claws of, 5:*77*
    feral, 2:25, 166
    jaguars, 4:107, *107*
    leopards, 4:150, *150*
    lions, 4:159, *159*
    pumas, 6:36, *36*
    saber-toothed, 6:*19*
    as **symbols,** 7:26, *26*
    tigers, 7:59, *59*
Cats (Lloyd Weber), 5:76
Catskill Mountains, 5:100
Catt, Carrie Chapman, 8:47; 7:171
cattle, 2:26, *26;* 2:120, 121, *121,* 152; 5:32, *104;* 7:25
    farming, 3:62, *62,* 178, *178*
    horns of, 4:41
    prehistoric, 6:*22*
    ranches, 6:52, *52*
cavalry, 2:27, *27;* 1:84; 6:88
Cavazos, Laura, 4:33

cave paintings, 2:28–29, *28–29;* 3:77; 5:140; 6:18, *18,* 19
caves, 2:29, *29;* 1:151; 4:123
    Carlsbad Caverns, 5:98, *98*
    stalactites and stalagmites in, 6:184, *184*
Cavour, Camillo, 4:105
Caxton, William, 8:47; 1:151; 2:44
Cayley, George, 1:25; 3:96
CCDs (charge-coupled devices), 7:41
CD-ROM, 5:65
CDs (**compact discs**), 2:97; 4:141; 6:54
Ceausescu, Nicolae, 6:87
celestial sphere, 6:144, *144*
cellos, 5:73, *73*
cells, 2:30, *30, 31;* 7:131
    cancer, 2:7
    cloning from, 2:76
    and **DNA,** 2:160
    evolution of, 3:43, 47
    genetic engineering, 3:150
    genetics, 3:151, *151*
    growth of, 3:188
    and **heredity,** 4:26
    in **human body,** 4:48, *48*
    nerve, 5:91, *91*
    and **proteins,** 6:31
    solar, 3:22
cells and cell phones, 7:39
cellulose, 7:29
Celsius, Anders, 7:23
Celsius scale, 7:43, *43*
Celts, 2:31–32, *32;* 3:163; 4:11; 6:23
    Arthurian legends, 1:86–87, *86*
    of **England,** 3:26, 27
    of **France,** 3:130
    of **Ireland,** 4:96–97
    of **Wales,** 7:134
cement, 2:33; 2:104; 3:168
cemeteries, 2:33; 2:58, 59
    sculpture in, 6:114
    tombs in, 7:63
censorship, 2:33
Census, U.S., 2:106; 5:191
centigrade (Celsius) scale, 7:43, *43*
centipedes, 2:33, *33*
Central African Republic, 2:34
Central America, 2:34–35; 5:109
    in **ancient world,** 1:50

bullfighting in, 1:173
colonies in, 3:16, 40, 189; 4:38, 69
conquistadores in, 2:109; 1:105;
  6:174
in Latin America, 6:163
literature of, 4:141–142
map, 2:13
Maya in, 5:9, 9
Native Americans in, 5:82
see also Latin America; specific
  countries
central banks, 1:116
centurions, 6:88
ceramics, 4:192; 6:13–14, 13, 14
cereals, 3:173, 173, 176, 178
  corn, 2:116, 116
  rice, 6:70, 70
  wheat, 7:163, 163
cerebellum, 1:154
cerebral cortex, 1:154
cerebral palsy, 2:35
cerebrum, 1:154
Ceres (asteroid), 1:91; 5:172
Cervantes, Miguel de, 8:48; 3:41
cesarean birth (C-section), 1:144
Ceylon (Sri Lanka), 6:183, 183; 1:88;
  2:95
Cézanne, Paul, 8:48–49
  painting by, 8:48
CFCs (chlorofluorocarbons), 1:14; 3:186
Chad, 2:36
Chad, Lake, 1:15–16; 2:36
Chagall, Marc, 8:49
  painting by, 8:49
chain hoists, 4:170, 170
chain reactions, 1:96; 5:115
chains, bicycle, 4:169, 169
Challenger spacecraft, 1:93; 6:169
Chamberlain, Wilt, 1:121
chamber music, 2:36, 36
chameleons, 2:37, 37
Champa, 7:124
Champlain, Samuel de, 5:94; 7:118
Chancellorsville, Battle of, 2:68, 69
change-ringing, 1:129
Changi Airport, Singapore, 1:28
Chang Jiang (Yangtze River), 1:50, 88,
  89
Channel Islands, 2:37, 37; 7:90

Channel Tunnel, 2:38; 6:50, 50–51;
  7:85, 85, 94
chaos theory, 2:38; 3:126
Chaplin, Charlie, 5:63, 63
charcoal drawings, 2:170–171
Chardonnet, Hilaire, 7:29
Charge of the Light Brigade, 2:27,
  124
chariots, 7:150
charities, 2:38
  American Friends Service
    Committee, 6:41
  Live Aid, 6:81
  Red Cross, 6:56
  Salvation Army, 6:105
Charlemagne, 8:49; 2:135; 3:39, 130
Charles I, king of England, 8:50, 50;
  3:27; 4:125; 6:39, 165
Charles II, king of England, 8:50;
  1:190; 3:27; 4:125; 5:162, 170;
  6:165
Charles V, Holy Roman emperor,
  8:50–51; 1:100; 3:159–160
Charles, Prince of Wales, 8:51, 51;
  6:14
Charleston, South Carolina, 6:165,
  165, 166
Charleston, West Virginia, 7:158
Charlotte's Web (White), 2:45; 8:246
Chartres Cathedral, 2:22, 23; 3:130
Chase, Salmon P., 5:94
Chattanooga, Battle of, 2:68, 69
Chatterjee, Bankim Chandra, 1:90
Chaucer, Geoffrey, 8:52; 3:27–28, 29,
  107; 5:169
Chávez, César, 4:33
Chavez, Karla, 4:33
Chechnya, 6:98
checkmate, 2:41
cheese, 2:39, 39; 3:128; 5:32
cheetahs, 2:40, 40; 2:24–25; 5:77;
  6:94
Chekhov, Anton, 3:41; 6:98; 8:231
chemical energy, 3:20
chemical products, from wood, 7:59
chemical reactions, 2:40
chemicals, 2:40
  acids, 1:11
  and coal, 2:82
  dyes, 2:174

fertilizers, 3:72
  poison, 5:182
  in pollution, 2:64
chemists, 2:41; 4:133, 133
Cheops, 2:188
Chernobyl, 5:115; 7:89
cherubs, cherubim, 1:52
chess, 2:41, 41
Chester, England, 2:110
chestnuts, 5:119
Cheyenne, Wyoming, 7:184, 184
Chiang Kai-shek, 8:52; 2:51–52; 7:30
Chicago, Illinois, 4:65, 66
  Columbian Exposition in, 1:49, 49
  Great Fire in, 3:79, 80
  skyscrapers in, 4:65; 6:145
chickens, 2:42, 42; 2:166; 3:62, 62
Chieftains, 3:108
chiffon, 7:51
children, 2:43–44, 43
  adoption of, 1:11
  child labor, 2:44, 82; 4:78
  in the city, 3:30
  clothing of, 2:78
  crusade of, 2:126
  energy of, 3:20, 112
  foster, 3:125
  in Japan, 4:110
  rights of, 2:44
  teaching of, 2:55
  toys of, see toys
children's books, 2:44–45
  fables, 3:55
  nursery rhymes, 5:118, 118
Chile, 2:46; 1:84; 3:92; 6:164
chillis, 6:176, 176
chimpanzees, 2:46, 46; 1:65, 65;
  2:96; 3:47, 48; 6:25, 123
China, 2:47–52, 47, 49; 1:88, 89;
  2:98
  acupuncture in, 1:38–39
  alphabet, 1:37
  in ancient world, 1:50
  archaeological discovery in, 2:49,
    51, 51
  art in, 2:170
  astrology in, 1:92
  Buddhism in, 1:167
  coins of, 2:87, 87
  and Cold War, 7:104–105

Communism in, **2**:97; **2**:51–52
Confucianism in, **2**:104
conscripted army in, **1**:84
dragons in, **2**:*167*, 168
dynasties of, **2**:49–50
earthquake in, **2**:178
emperor of, **2**:49
floods in, **3**:98
Grand Canal, **1**:191, *191*
Great Wall of, **2**:49, 50; **3**:179, *179*; **6**:125
history of, **2**:49–50
ideograms, **7**:183, *183*
Imperial Palace in, **5**:148
and **Japan**, **2**:52; **4**:111
languages in, **2**:47, 50, *50*, 51
literature, **1**:90
Long March in, **2**:52
map, **2**:*48*
martial arts of, **4**:186
medicines of, **2**:172
metals discovered in, **6**:23
monsoons in, **5**:50
Nationalist, **2**:51–52
New Year's Day in, **2**:*167*
painting in, **5**:*141*, 144
paper in, **1**:151; **5**:151
pirates of, **5**:170
Porcelain Tower of Nanking, **6**:125
pottery of, **6**:13, *14*
prehistory in, **6**:20
printing in, **6**:27, *27*
revolution in, **6**:68
rice grown in, **6**:70
silk production in, **2**:49
smugglers in, **6**:151
and **Taiwan**, **7**:30, *30*
Taoism in, **7**:32
and **Tibet**, **7**:57
and **World War II**, **7**:179
Zheng's tomb in, **7**:63
China clay (kaolin), **6**:13
Ching Chihlung, **5**:170
chinooks, **7**:168
Chippendale, Thomas, **3**:141
chiropractic, **1**:39
chivalry, **2**:52, *52*; **4**:128; **5**:28, *28*
in France, **3**:130
heraldry of, **4**:24–25, *24–25*
chlorine gas, **7**:148

chlorofluorocarbons (CFCs), **1**:14; **3**:186
chlorophyll, **2**:30; **4**:147; **5**:168, 175; **6**:121
chloroplasts, **5**:168
chocolate, **2**:53, *53*; **2**:85
choirs, **2**:53, *53*; **6**:141
African, **1**:21
hymns of, **4**:56
choking, first aid for, **3**:81
cholesterol, **3**:111
Chopin, Frederick, **8**:52–53; **5**:67
chopsticks, **2**:48
choreographers, **1**:110–111; **2**:132, 133, 134; **3**:77
choruses (Greek), **2**:169, *169*
choruses (music), **2**:53
Christ Church Cathedral, Missouri, **2**:22
Christianity, **2**:54–56; **3**:38, 169; **5**:30; **6**:61–62, *61*
apostles, **1**:66; **2**:54
baptism in, **1**:116; **2**:55–56, *55*
and **Bible**, **1**:131–132
and **carols**, **2**:16, *16*
and **Christmas**, **2**:57, *57*; **2**:56
and **churches**, **2**:58–59, *58*, *59*
converting people to, **1**:53, 81, 182; **2**:54, 55
crosses of, **2**:*31*, 58–59
and **Dark Ages**, **2**:135
and **days of the week**, **2**:136
and **Easter**, **2**:180, *180*
festivals and holidays, **3**:73–74, *73, 74*
funerals in, **3**:139
and **God**, **3**:169
heretics, **4**:26
hymns in, **4**:56
icons in, **4**:62, *62*
in Ireland, **4**:96–97, *96*
Jesus Christ, *see* **Jesus**
and **Latin**, **1**:54; **2**:56
in **Middle Ages**, **5**:27–29
monasteries, **5**:45–46, *45, 46*
pilgrimages of, **5**:169
prophets of, **6**:30
Protestant, **6**:31, 39
Reformation, **6**:57, *57*
rites and rituals in, **4**:84, *84*

Roman Catholicism, **2**:23
saints, **6**:102, *102, 103*
Christian Science, **2**:57
Christmas, **2**:57, *57*; **2**:56; **3**:73, *73*
carols, **2**:16, *16*
mince pies for, **3**:113
chromosomes, **2**:30; **3**:151, *151*; **4**:26; **6**:127–128
chronometers, **2**:75
churches, **2**:58–59, *58*, *59*, *141*
architecture of, **1**:76–77, *76–77*; **2**:58, 59, *59*
art in, **1**:*177*; **2**:59
choirs of, **2**:53, *53*
Christian Science, **2**:57
and **Christmas**, **2**:57, *57*
in **Middle Ages**, **5**:27
stained glass in, **6**:183, *183*
see also **Christianity**
Churchill, Winston, **8**:53, *53*; **6**:25
Church of England, **2**:60, *60*; **3**:26; **6**:39, 57
cigarettes, **7**:62
cigars, **7**:62
Ciller, Tansu, **6**:25
Cincinnati, Ohio, **5**:128
cinemas, **7**:53
cinnamon, **6**:176, *176*
ciphers, **2**:86, *86*
circles, **6**:129, *129*
circuit breakers, **3**:10, *10*
circuits:
electric, **3**:8
electronic, **3**:12, 13
integrated, **3**:13
circulation, blood, **4**:19, *19*, 50, *50*
circumpolar stars, **6**:144
circuses, **2**:61, *61*
CIS, *see* **Commonwealth of Independent States**
Cisneros, Henry G., **4**:33
Cistercian monks, **5**:46
cities and towns, **2**:62–65, *62, 63, 64*; **7**:99
children in, **3**:30
on the coast, **2**:84–85
in **Europe**, **3**:37
games in, **3**:145, *145*
greenbelts of, **2**:65
land use in, **4**:138

map of, 2:*63*
migration to, 2:63
museums in, 5:66
oldest, 2:65
parks in, 5:154–155, *154*, *155*
poverty in, 6:15, *15*
riots in, 2:66
of **Roman Empire**, 6:87–89, *88*
skyscrapers in, 6:145, *145*
subways in, 7:15–16, *15*, *16*
transportation in, 7:75–76, *75*
Citizen Kane, 8:111
citrine, 3:150
citrus fruits, 3:137, *137*
"Civil Disobedience," 8:229
civil law, 4:143
civil liberties, in **Bill of Rights**,
    1:135–136; 2:112
Civil Rights Act (1964), 2:66
Civil Rights Movement, 2:65–66;
    1:20; 5:40, 110
    in Alabama, 1:30; 2:66
    in Arkansas, 1:83
    and **Ku Klux Klan**, 4:131, *131*
    and NAACP, 1:19
civil servants, 3:172
Civil War, U.S., 2:67–70, *70*; 3:156;
    4:120, 187, 189; 5:39–41, *86*,
    162–163; 6:165; 7:45, 128, 136
    battles of, 2:68–70
    and **cavalry**, 2:27, *27*
    end of, 2:67, 70
    and **Gettysburg Address**, 3:161,
    161
    secession and, 2:67–68
    and slavery, 1:19; 2:67, 70
    spies in, 2:147
clapboards, 5:62
clapper bridges, 1:161, *161*
Clare, John, 5:182
clarinets, 5:70, *70*
Clark, George Rogers, 8:53; 4:65, 74
Clark, William (Lewis and Clark),
    8:146–147, *210*; 3:51; 4:63, 120;
    5:51, 88, 112, 136; 6:166; 7:103,
    128
Clarke, Arthur C., 6:110
classification of living things, 2:70
    animal kingdom, 1:*58–59*
    bacteria, 1:107

birds, 1:141–143
plants, 5:175, *176*
species, 6:175
in taxonomic groups, 2:70
warm- and cold-bloodedness,
    4:27; 6:66; 7:134
Claudius, emperor of Rome, 3:26
claws and nails, 5:77, *77*; 2:25; 3:71
clay, 2:33
    pottery, 6:13, *13*
Clay, Henry, 8:54; 7:128
Cleary, Beverly, 2:45; 5:136
Clemente, Roberto, 4:33
Cleopatra, 8:54
Cleveland, Grover, 8:55, *55*; 7:101
Cleveland, Ohio, 5:127, 128
cliffs, 2:71, *71*; 1:*163*; 2:29, 84
climate, 2:72–73
    deserts, 2:144–145
    drought, 2:172
    global warming, 3:168, *168*
    greenhouse effect, 3:186, *186*
    ice ages, 4:58, *58*
    Mediterranean, 5:16
clinics, 2:74, *74*; 4:44, *44*
clinkers, 2:33
Clinton, Bill, 8:55–56, *55*; 1:82;
    7:101, *105*
clipper ships, 6:100, *101*
clitoris, 6:128
clocks and watches, 2:74–75, *74*, *75*;
    2:50; 6:181, *181*; 7:60–61, *60–61*
    atomic, 5:*10*, *10*, 11
    candles, 2:7
    pendulums on, 5:*10*, 161
clones, 2:76; 3:176; 6:179
closed-circuit television, 7:41
clothing, 2:76–79, *77*, *78*, *79*
    design, 2:76–77
    fashion, 3:66, *66*
    of **first ladies**, 3:82, *82*
    from **fur**, 4:*91*
    hats and headdresses, 4:15, *15*
    national dress, 2:76, 78, *78*, *79*
    protective, 2:78, *78*
    sewing, 6:126–127, *127*
    shoes, 6:134, *134*
    uniforms, 2:78
clouds, 2:80, *80*
    and **climate**, 2:72, 73

formation of, 1:94
and **hailstones**, 4:8
rain, 6:51, *51*
and **thunderstorms**, 7:57, *57*
cloven hooves, 2:26
cloves, 6:176, *176*
Clovis the Frank, 3:130
clowns, 2:18, 61, *61*, 117; 5:33
coal, 2:81–82, *81*, *82*; 3:124, 138;
    4:78; 5:35, *35*
coast guards, 2:83, *83*
    lifeboats of, 4:155, *155*
    and **lighthouses**, 4:158, *158*
Coast Ranges, 5:109
coasts, 2:84–85, *84*
    cliffs, 2:71, *71*, 84
    seashore, 6:118–119, *118*, *119*
Coatlicue, Aztec monster, 5:51
Cobb, Ty, 1:120
cobras, 7:*118*
cocaine, 2:90, *90*
Cochise, 1:81
cockatoos, salmon-crested, 3:19
cockroaches, 2:85; 1:127, *127*; 6:123
cocoa, 2:85, *85*; 2:53, *53*
coconuts, 5:119
codes and ciphers, 2:86, *86*
code talkers, 7:181
Cody, Samuel Franklin, 4:*127*
Cody, William F. "Buffalo Bill,"
    8:56, *56*; 1:42; 4:93; 5:88
Coelophysis, 2:*153*
coffee, 2:87, *87*
cog ships, 6:*101*
Cohan, George M., 5:75
coins, 2:87, *87*; 3:170; 6:23, 89, 115,
    139
coke (fuel), 2:82
cold, 2:88; 7:43, *43*, 55
    hypothermia, 4:56
    ice, 4:57, *57*
    refrigerators, 6:58, *58*
    snow, 6:153, *153*
    and **superconductivity**, 7:19, *19*
colds and coughs, 2:88; 2:158; 7:131
Cold War, 2:88; 1:100; 7:104–105
    and **peace movement**, 5:159
Coleman, Ornette, 4:112, 113
Coleridge, Samuel Taylor, 3:29
collagen, 1:149

collages, 2:89, *89*
collar cells, 6:179
collating, 5:166
colleges and universities, 2:89
 bands, 1:114–115, *114*
 degrees granted by, 2:89
 demonstrations on campuses of,
  1:183
 football played in, 3:116
 Ivy League, 2:89
 sports, 1:118, 120, 147
 teachers in, 2:161
Collins, Michael, 6:170
Collodi, C., 2:45
Colombia, 2:90, *90*; 2:34, 55, 64;
 6:164
Colombo, Sri Lanka, 6:183, *183*
Colonial Williamsburg, Virginia,
 7:*56*, 129
colonies, 2:90
 in **Africa,** 1:18, *18*, 55, 130, 148,
  151, 174, 186; 2:34, 90, 105, 189;
  3:40, 132, 162, 190; 4:106, 123,
  151, 153, 176, 177; 5:8, 64, 78,
  101, 102; 6:99, 122, 137, 160;
  7:22, 32, 63, 89, 189
 in America, 1:29, 82, 116, 129,
  190; 2:14, 34, 46, 128, 166, 185;
  3:99, 190; 4:33, 108, *108*, 167,
  174, 189; 5:22, 110; 6:164; 7:22,
  45, 49, 56, 117, 157
 in Asia, 1:183; 3:40, 76, 132; 4:39,
  77, 176; 5:76; 6:139, 183; 7:124
 in the **Caribbean,** 6:33, *33*, 102
 in **Central America,** 3:16, 40, 189
 in **Commonwealth of Nations,**
  2:95
 and English Parliament, 1:43–44
 in **Europe,** 3:163
 in Indian Ocean, 5:8
 in Middle East, 5:131
 in the Pacific, 5:113, 121, 165
 and **slavery,** 6:146–148, *148*
 U.S., *see* **Thirteen Colonies**
color, 2:91–92, *91, 92*
 camouflage, 1:186
 and **design,** 2:146
 and **light,** 4:156
 rainbows, 6:51
 as **symbol,** 7:26, *155*

Colorado, 2:92–93; 3:*62*; 5:98; 7:100
 Air Force Academy in, 7:106, *106*
 Rocky Mountains, 6:85, *85*
Colorado River, 6:73, 125; 7:97–98
 Aqueduct, 1:68
 Grand Canyon, *see* **Grand Canyon**
 Hoover Dam, 2:*131*
Colorado River (Texas), 7:49
Colosseum (Rome), 6:91, 125
Colossus of Rhodes, 6:125, *125*
Colt, Samuel, 2:107–108
Coltrane, John, 1:19; 4:112, 113
Columba, St., 6:111
Columbia (spacecraft), 6:169
Columbia, South Carolina, 6:165
Columbian Exposition, Chicago
 (1893), 1:49, *49*
Columbia River, 7:138
Columbus, Bartholomew, 2:166
Columbus, Christopher, 8:56–57;
 1:49, 108; 2:14; 3:50; 4:38; 6:174;
 7:17, 129, 157, 163
 map, 8:*57*
Columbus, Ohio, 5:127, *127*
combines, 3:65; 7:*163*
combustion, 5:139
comedies, 2:169
comedy, musical, 5:75–76
comets, 2:94, *94*; 5:173; 6:159
comic books, 2:17–18
comic strips, 2:17–18, *18*, 170; 4:172
commedia dell'arte, 5:33; 6:38
commemorative stamps, 6:185, *185*
commercials, **television,** 7:41
commissions, 6:192
**Commonwealth of Independent
 States (CIS),** 2:94; 6:98, 168
Commonwealth of Nations, 2:95
communication, 2:96, *96*
 of animals, 1:56, *56*, 140; 2:96, *96*
 of birds, 1:140
 e-mail, 4:90; 6:12
 fax machines, 3:68, *68*
 fiber optics, 3:75, *75*
 Internet, 4:90, *90*
 languages and, 4:138–139
 microwaves in, 5:26
 and **postal services,** 6:11–12
 radio, 6:47–48, *47, 48*
 satellites, 6:106

 sign language, 6:137, *137*
 telegraph, 7:37, *37*
 telephones, 7:38–39, *38, 39*
 television, 7:41-42, *41, 42*
 voice, 7:131, *131*
 within the U.S., 7:99–100
 writing systems, 7:183, *183*
 see also **language**
Communism, 2:97; 2:183; 3:40, 69;
 6:98, 156, 168
 in **China,** 2:51–52
 and **Cold War,** 2:88; 1:100
 in **Cuba,** 2:97, 128
 see also **Russia; Soviet Union**
communities, 2:182
community theaters, 7:54
commuters, 7:75–76, 127
compact discs (CDs), 2:97; 4:141;
 6:54
compasses, 2:98, *98*; 2:50; 3:50;
 4:173
 gyroscopes as, 4:7
 and **maps,** 4:182
 navigation, 5:87
 orienteering, 5:138
composers, 2:98–99; 2:103; 3:77;
 5:67
 of **electronic music,** 3:11
 of **operas,** 5:132
composite materials, 4:192, *192*
composite photographs, 5:167
compost, 7:77
compound eyes, 3:54
compounds, chemical, 2:40
compression, 3:117
computer games, 2:99, *99*
computers, 2:100–102, *100, 101,
 102*; 3:69; 4:82–83, *82, 83*; 7:176
 in airliners, 1:27
 arithmetic with, 1:80
 ASCII code, 2:86
 and **calculators,** 1:180
 codes for, 2:86, *86*
 communication with, 2:96
 design via, 2:147
 and **electronic music,** 3:11, *11*
 and **electronics,** 3:12–13, *13*
 and **fax machines,** 3:68
 hardware and software of, 2:100
 history of, 2:102

image enhancement on, 5:26
and the **Internet,** 4:90, *90*
manufacture of, 1:183
microchips for, 7:19
multimedia, 5:65
music composed on, 2:99
parallel processing of, 2:101
peripherals for, 2:102
and **robots,** 6:79, *79*
and **scanners,** 6:108, *108*
and **science fiction,** 6:110
and **virtual reality,** 7:130
words about, 2:100
concentration camps, 2:103, *103*;
    3:160; 4:7, 37, 118; 5:87; 6:43
conception, 6:18
concertmasters, 5:134–135
concertos, 2:103
Concord, Battle of, 1:44; 4:189, *189*
Concord, New Hampshire, 5:94
Concorde SST, 1:*25*, 26, 27
"Concord Hymn" (Emerson), 1:44
concrete, 2:104, *104*; 1:160; 2:33
concussion, 1:155
condensed milk, 5:32
condoms, 6:128
condors, 1:143
conduction, heat, 4:20, *20*
conductors (electric), 3:7, 8
conductors (metals), 7:19
conductors (orchestra), 5:134–135
Conestoga wagon, 5:*88*
Coney Island, New York, 1:49
Confederate States of America,
    2:67–70
Confederation of the United States of
    America, 1:44, 45
Confucianism, 2:104
Confucius, 8:57; 1:90; 2:50, 104;
    6:32, 102
Congo, 2:105, *105*
Congo (Democratic Republic of),
    2:105, *105*
Congress, U.S., 2:106–107; 5:156;
    7:96, 101
    and **American Revolution,** 1:44
    and apportionment, 2:106
    and civil rights, 1:20
    and **Civil War,** 2:67
    and **coast guard,** 2:83

and **Constitution,** 2:107, 112
    election of, 2:192
    and **government,** 3:172
    House of Representatives, 2:107
    poets appointed by, 5:182
    Senate, 2:106–107
    and separation of powers, 2:112
    and **slavery,** 2:70; 6:148
    war declared by, 5:160
Congressional Medal of Honor, 5:12,
    12
Congreve, William, 3:29
conifer trees, 3:101, 119, *119*; 7:78,
    80
Connecticut, 2:107–108; 7:56, 100
conquistadores, 2:109; 1:105, 148;
    4:33, 38, 69, 141; 5:22, 77, 82,
    164; 6:174
Conrad, Joseph, 3:29
conscription, army, 1:84
conservation, 2:109–110; 2:182;
    3:19, 30
    animal rights, 1:57
    fishing and, 3:89, 91
    and **green movement,** 3:187, *187*
    of **habitats,** 4:8
    national parks, 5:81, *81*
    of **wetlands,** 7:161
    of **wildlife,** 7:166, 192
Constable, John, painting by, 5:*143*
Constantine the Great, 8:57–58, *58*;
    1:76, *177*; 2:55, 136; 6:91
Constantinople, 1:177; 2:55, 56; 3:38,
    182; 5:139; 7:86
    and **crusades,** 2:126
    see also Istanbul, Turkey
constellations, 2:111, *111*; 5:32, *32*,
    89, *89*
    pulsars, 6:35, *35*
    sky, 6:144
    stars, 6:186–188
    zodiac, 1:92, *92*, 181
Constitution, U.S., 2:112; 4:143–145;
    5:162
    13th Amendment, 1:19
    14th Amendment, 1:19
    16th Amendment, 2:112
    and African Americans, 1:19, 20
    amendments to, 2:112
    Bill of Rights, 1:135–136; 2:112

and Congress, 2:107, 112
and *Federalist,* 1:40
and **government,** 3:172
implied powers, 8:156
judicial review, 8:156
and **Prohibition** amendments,
    6:30
and voting rights, 7:1 , 173
construction, *see* **building**
consumers, 2:183
Conté, Nicolas-Jacques, 2:171
Continental Congress, 1:44–45;
    2:107, 138
Continental Divide, 2:35, 92, 113;
    5:52; 6:85
continental drift, 2:177
continents, 2:113, *113*; 2:177, *177*;
    4:136
    Africa, 1:15–18
    Antarctica, 1:60–61
    Asia, 1:88–89
    Australia, 1:97–99
    Europe, 3:36–40
    North America, 5:108–109
    Oceania, 5:121, *121*
    and **plate tectonics,** 4:136; 5:*179*
contraception, 6:128
conurbations, 2:62
convection, heat, 4:20, *20*
convenience stores, 7:9
convents, 2:114
Cook, James, 8:58; 1:60, 99; 3:51;
    4:16, 142, 179; 5:121, 136
    map, 8:58
cooking, 2:114; 3:113; 5:26
    and **heat,** 4:20
    herbs for, 4:25, *25*
    spices in, 6:176, *176*
Cook Islands, 5:121
Coolidge, Calvin, 8:59, *59*; 7:101,
    118, 119
Cooper, James Fenimore, 8:59; 1:40;
    5:100
Cooper, Susan, 2:45
Copenhagen, Denmark, 2:142
    Little Mermaid in, 5:*19*
    Tivoli Gardens, 1:49
copepods, 5:*175*
Copernicus, Nicolas, 8:59–60

Copland, Aaron, 8:60; 3:11; 5:67, 100

copper, 2:114; 1:36, 82; 6:23, *23*

copyrights, 2:115; 5:158

coral, 2:115, *115*; 1:116; 6:116
  islands, 4:103
  reefs, 6:116, 125

Coral Sea, Battle of, 7:136

Corbett, Jim, 1:152

Cordero, Angel, 4:33

corduroy, 7:51

Corelli, Arcangelo, 2:103

Corinth Canal, Greece, 1:191, *191*

cork, 2:116

Cormier, Robert, 2:45

cormorants, 1:139, 141

corms, 1:172, *172*

corn (maize), 2:116, *116*; 3:63, 173, *173*, 176; 4:93, *93*

Cornwallis, Charles, 1:45; 7:128

Coronado, Francisco Vásquez de, 5:77, 88, 97, 129; 7:103

coronation, 4:126, *126*

corporate colonies, 7:56

corpus callosum, 1:154

corries, 4:134

corrosive acids, 1:11

Cortázar, Julio, 4:142

Cortés, Hernán, 8:60; 1:105; 2:109; 7:103

corticosteroids, 1:91

Cosa Nostra (Mafia), 4:171, *171*

Cosby, Bill, 1:20

cosmetics, 2:117, *117*

cosmetic surgery, 5:178

cosmic rays, 2:117; 6:45, 46

cosmology, 7:108

cosmonauts, 1:93

cosmos, 7:108, *108*

Costa Rica, 2:118; 2:34–35, *35*

Côte d'Ivoire (Ivory Coast), 4:106

cottage industry, 4:80, *80*

cotton, 2:118–119, *118*, *119*; 1:30; 3:76, 156; 5:39, 40; 7:51
  and boll weevils, 1:127
  spinning, 6:178

cotton gin, 8:*248*

cotyledons, 6:122

Coubertin, Baron Pierre de, 5:131

cougars, 6:36, *36*

coughs and colds, 2:88; 2:158; 7:131

Counter-Reformation, 6:57

counter-urbanization, 2:63

country and western music, 2:119; 5:68; 6:141; 7:44, *44*, 45

county fairs, 3:57

Court, Margaret, 7:47

courts (law), 4:143–145, *143*

Cousteau, Jacques, 8:60

Coverdale, Miles, 1:131

cowboys, 2:120, *120*; 4:120
  gauchos, 7:109
  music of, 2:119
  ranches, 6:52, *52*
  in a rodeo, 7:*184*
  in sculpture, 6:*115*

cows, 2:121, *121*; 2:26, 39, 166; 3:60, *61*, 65; 5:32

"Coyote and the Goat, The," 3:55

CPR (cardiopulmonary resuscitation), 3:81

crabs, 2:122, *122*; 2:*127*; 6:118, 119

crafts, 2:122

Crane, Stephen, 8:60–61; 1:40

cranes (mechanical), 2:123, *123*

crater lakes, 4:134, *135*

craters, asteroid, 1:91

crayfish, 4:162

Crazy Horse, 8:61; 6:166–167

Crécy, Battle of, 7:136

credit cards, 5:47

Creole, 2:124; 4:139

Crete, 1:50; 3:*64*, 133, 180

Crick, Francis, and Watson, James, 8:61

crickets, 3:176

Crimean War, 2:124; 2:27; 7:93

criminal law, 4:143

Crisis, 8:185

Croatia, 2:125; 1:151; 6:124, 148; 7:188

Crockett, Davy, 8:61; 1:42; 6:43; 7:44, 49

crocodiles, 2:125, *125*; 1:36; 3:45; 6:66, *66*, 72

Crompton, Samuel, 4:78

Cromwell, Oliver, 8:62; 1:84; 3:27; 4:97, 107

Crosby, Bing, 5:76; 7:137

crosses:

Celtic, 2:*31*

Christian, 2:58–59
  cruciform churches, 2:58–59

cross-pollination, 3:103

cross stitch, 3:18, *18*

crow, 8:*16*

crowns (teeth), 7:36, *37*

crude oil, 5:129

Crusades, 2:126, *126*; 1:73, 177; 3:26; 5:28, 105
  castles from, 2:20, *20*
  and chivalry, 2:52
  knights of, 4:128

crustaceans, 2:127, *127*; 4:92, *92*; 6:118, 119
  barnacles, 1:117, *117*; 2:*127*
  crabs, 2:122, *122*, 127
  larvae of, 4:140, *140*
  lobsters, 4:*140*, 162, *162*
  metamorphosis of, 5:21
  shrimp, 6:135, *135*

Cruz, Celia, 4:33

Cruz, Juana Inés de la, 4:141

cryosurgery, 7:21

cryptograms, 2:86

Crystal Cathedral, California, 2:*22*, 23

Crystal Palace, 7:92, *92*, 122

crystals, 2:128, *128*; 5:34, *34*
  carbon, 2:10
  diamonds, 2:150, *150*
  gems, 3:150
  ice, 4:57
  lasers, 4:140–141
  rock, 6:82, 84
  salt, 6:104–105, *104*
  silicon, 6:138
  snow, 6:153, *153*

C-section (cesarean birth), 1:144

Ctesibius, 6:36

Cuba, 2:128, *128*; 6:175; 7:104, 157
  Communism in, 2:97, 128
  Hispanics from, 4:32–34
  Independence Day, 4:34

cubes, 6:129, *129*

Cuchulain, 2:32, *32*

cuckoopint, 3:136, *136*

cuckoos, 2:186

cud, chewing, 1:62; 2:26, *26*

Cudworth, Kyle, 7:*40*

Cullen, William, 6:58

cultivation, shifting, 3:61

cultivators, 3:65

Cumberland Gap, Kentucky, 4:122

cumin seeds, 6:176

cuneiform writing, 5:19; 7:183

Cunningham, Merce, 2:133; 2:*132*, 134

cupronickel, 1:36

curds and whey, 2:39

Curie, Marie, 8:62–63, *62*; 6:46

curlews, 1:*139*

currency, 5:47

current, electric, 3:7

curry, 6:176

Curtis, Charles, 5:85

cuscus, 4:*185*

Custer, George Armstrong, 8:63, *63*; 2:27; 5:51

customs duties (taxes), 6:151

cuticles, 6:142

cuttlefish, 4:*92*; 5:44

cyberpunk, 6:110

cycling, 2:129, *129*; 5:*154*

cyclones (hurricanes), 4:54, *54*; 1:116

Cyclopes, 3:*184–185*

cyclosporin, 7:75

cylinder locks, 4:164, *164*

Cyprus, 2:130; 1:50; 2:95

Cyrillic alphabet, 1:*37*

Cyrus, king of Persia, 2:27; 3:50

cytoplasm, 2:30

czars, 6:97

Czechoslovakia, 3:160; 7:179, *179*

Czech Republic, 2:130; 6:148, 149, 168

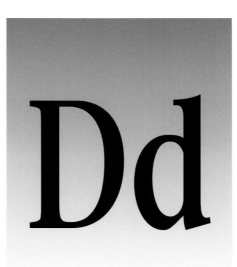

Dachau, 2:103

Daffy Duck, 2:19

Daggett, Samuel, 5:66

Daguerre, Louis, 8:63–64; 5:167

Daimler, Gottlieb, 5:58

dairy farming, 2:121; 3:60, *61*

Dalai Lama, 8:64, *64*; 7:57

Dalton, John, 8:65; 1:95

Damascus, Syria, 5:19; 7:29, *29*

damask, 7:51

dams, 2:131, *131*; 2:*188*; 7:25, 146, 148

   and artificial **lakes,** 4:135, *135*

   Aswan, 5:102

   beaver, 1:125

   Hoover, 5:93, 94

   and **hydroelectric power,** 4:55

   for **irrigation,** 4:99

   and **tidal power,** 7:58

   TVA, 7:45

dance, 2:132–134, *134*; 3:77

   African, 2:132, *132*

   ballet, 1:110–111, *110, 111*

   of the Caribbean, 2:14

   folk, 3:106, *106*

   of India, 2:132–133, *132*; 4:75

   in **initiation ceremonies,** 4:84, *84*

   Maori, 4:*179*

   and **mime,** 5:33, *33*

   modern, 2:*132*, 133, *134*

   in **musicals,** 5:75

   notation system for, 2:134

   social, 2:132, 133, *133*

Dance Theater of Harlem, 2:*134*

D'Annunzio, Gabriele, 3:41

Dante Alighieri, 8:65; 3:41; 4:105

Danube River, 1:38, 100, 172; 3:37; 4:52; 6:87

Darby, Abraham, 4:78

Dare, Virginia, 5:109–110

Dark Ages, 2:135; 3:38; 5:27

   Arthurian legends, 1:86–87, *86*

   in **Italy,** 4:105

Darrow, Clarence, 8:65–66; 4:65; 5:127, 128; 7:45

darts, 2:135, *135*

Darwin, Charles, 8:66–67, *66*; 3:42; 7:45

data (**statistics**), 6:190

David, 8:67, *72, 166*; 1:132; 3:163; 4:126

Davis, Benjamin O., Sr., 1:19

Davis, Jefferson, 8:67

Davis, Miles, 1:19; 4:112, *112*, 113

Davy, Humphry, 8:68

day and night, 2:136, *136*; 3:32; 6:120; 7:60–61, *60–61*

daydreaming, 2:171

Daylight Saving Time (DST), 7:61

days of the week, 2:136; 1:181

D-Day, 7:181, *181*

DDT, 5:182; 8:43

deadlocks, 4:164

Dead Sea, 1:89

deadweight, 5:18

deafness, 2:137; 6:161

   and **sign language,** 6:137, *137*

death, 2:137; 2:158, 189; 6:71

   and **cemeteries,** 2:33

   and **funerals,** 3:139

   and **mummies,** 5:65, *65*

   and **tombs,** 7:63, *63*

Death Valley, California, 1:183; 5:108; 7:113

Debussy, Claude, 8:68; 3:132; 5:67

decathlons, 7:71

decibels, 6:161

deciduous trees, 7:78, 175, *175*

decimals, 2:137

decimal system, 5:117

Declaration of Independence, 2:138–139, *139*; 1:44, 45; 4:152; 5:162, 163

and **human rights,** 4:52
  Thirteen Colonies and, 7:56
deer, 2:140, *140*; 6:60, *60*
  antlers of, 4:41, *41*
  cloven hooves of, 2:26
  and deer ticks, 1:85
  as ruminants, 2:26
Deere, John, 1:23; 4:65
defendants, 4:143
Defoe, Daniel, 8:68; 2:44; 3:29;
  5:114
De Forest, Lee, 3:13
deforestation, 3:19, 30, 121, *121*, 186
Degas, Edgar, 8:68–69;
  painting by, 8:*69*
  sculpture by, 6:*113*
de Gaulle, Charles, 8:69; 3:132
De Havilland Comet (aircraft), 1:25;
  4:114
de Klerk, F. W., 8:69; 6:162
de la Renta, Oscar, 4:33
Delaware, 2:140–141; 2:112; 7:56,
  100
de Lesseps, Ferdinand, 1:192
Delmarva Peninsula, 2:141; 4:187
deltas, 2:84
demesne, 3:75
Demeter (Greek goddess), 3:184, *184*,
  185
demigods, 4:26
de Mille, Agnes, 1:42
De Mille, Cecil B., 5:63
democracy, 2:141; 3:172, 181
  elections in, 2:192, *192*
  law and legal systems, 4:143–145
  popular sovereignty in, 2:67
Democratic Party, 5:185
Dempsey, Jack, 1:152
Deng Jie, 3:73
Deng Xiaoping, 8:70
denim, 7:51
Denmark, 2:142; 4:61, 126; 6:107;
  7:179
  and **Greenland,** 3:187, *187*
  literature of, 3:41
  Vikings of, 7:125
dentine, 7:36
dentists, 2:142; 7:36–37, *37*
Denver, Colorado, 2:87, 92, 93
deoxyribonucleic acid, *see* **DNA**

department stores, 7:9
Depression, Great, 2:143, *143*; 1:182;
  3:18; 6:192; 8:119
dermatology, 5:13
dermis, 6:143, *143*
derricks, 5:128
Desai, Anita, 1:90
desalinization, 6:40, 105; 7:87
Descartes, René, 8:70
deserts, 2:144–145, *144–145*
  in Africa, 1:16
  in Asia, 1:88
  in Australia, 1:97
  cacti in, 1:178, *178*; 2:145, *145*
  camels in, 1:184, *185*; 2:*144–145*,
    145
  climate of, 2:72–73
  mirages in, 5:38, *38*
  oases in, 1:*34*; 2:145; 5:119
  see also specific deserts
design, 2:146–147, *146, 147*
  clothing, 2:76–77
  engineers, 3:23
  gardens, 3:147, *147*
  posters, 6:12, *12, 50, 98*
Des Moines, Iowa, 4:93, 94
de Soto, Hernando, 8:70; 1:29;
  2:109; 5:39; 7:103
detectives, 2:147
detergents, 2:148, *148*; 6:153
detritus feeders, 3:87
Detroit, Michigan, 5:24, 25
de Vaca, Alvar Núñez Cabeza, 2:109
Devambez, André, painting by, 7:*178*
Devanagari alphabet, 1:*37*
developing countries, 2:148–149
  employment in, 3:18
  energy used in, 3:22, *22*
  LDCs, 7:55
  poverty in, 6:15, *15*
  starvation in, 6:189
Devil, 2:149; 1:52; 4:24
Dewar, James, 1:24
Dewey, George, 6:175
Dewey, John, 7:118
Dewey decimal system, 4:152
dhows, 6:100, *101*
diabetes, 2:150; 4:40
dialects, 3:27

diamonds, 2:150, *150*; 1:82; 2:10,
  128; 3:150; 5:35
Diamond Sutra, 6:27
Diana, Princess of Wales, 6:*14*; 8:51
Diana, temple of, 6:124–125, *125*
diaphragm (human body), 4:168
diaphragms (birth control), 6:128
Dias, Bartolomeu, 8:70–71; 6:11
diatoms, 1:*33*; 5:175, *175*, 188
Díaz del Castillo, Bernal, 4:141
Dickens, Charles, 8:71; 3:29; 7:122
Dickinson, Emily, 8:71, *71*; 1:40;
  4:189
"Dick Tracy" (Gould), 2:18
dictators, 2:150
dictionaries, 2:151
diesel engines, 3:149, *149*
diesel fuel, 5:129
dies (molds), 7:170
diets, 2:151; 2:158; 3:111–12, *111*;
  4:18
  and **eating disorders,** 2:180
  and **fats,** 3:67, 110
  and **malnutrition,** 4:177
  and nutrition, 3:110–111; 4:18
  proteins in, 6:31
  vegetarian, 7:117
digestive systems, 2:152, *152*; 3:165;
  4:49, *49*; 7:7, *7*
digital tapes/recordings, 2:19
dikes, 5:92
Dillinger, John, 1:42; 3:69
dinosaurs, 2:153–156, *153–157*;
  3:124; 6:18, 66
  and birds, 1:139
  evolution of, 3:46, *153*
  extinction of, 1:91; 3:53, *153*
diodes, 3:12, 13
Dionysus (Greek god), 3:185
direct current (DC), 3:8
dirigibles, 1:112–113, *113*
disabilities, 2:157, *157*
  blindness, 1:145, 154
  deafness, 2:137; 6:161
Discovery spacecraft, 6:169, *169*
discus throw, 7:71, *71*
diseases, 2:158, *158*; 3:161
  AIDS, 1:23; 6:128
  and **antibiotics,** 1:63
  asthma, 1:91

and **bacteria**, 1:107; 2:158
Black Death, 1:144
and **blindness**, 1:145
and **blood**, 1:146
cancer, 2:7
cerebral palsy, 2:35
and **charities**, 2:38
and **clinics**, 2:74, *74*
colds and coughs, 2:88, 158
death caused by, 2:137, 158
diabetes, 2:150
epidemics, 3:31
fleas and, 3:94
flies and, 3:95
and **hygiene**, 4:56
and **immunity**, 4:68
influenza, 4:81
malaria, 4:176
and **medicine**, 5:13, *13*
mental illness, 5:18
and **mosquitoes**, 5:56
pneumonia, 5:180
polio, 5:184–185, *184*
prevention of, 2:158
quarantine and, 6:41
rats and, 6:53
rheumatism, 6:68
sexually transmitted, 6:128
from **ticks**, 7:58
tuberculosis, 7:83
vaccinations against, 7:111
from **viruses**, 7:131, *131*
Disney, Walt, 1:49; 2:18–19; 5:63
Disneyland, 1:49
Disney World, 1:49, 67; 3:100
Disraeli, Benjamin, 6:25
distaff, 6:178
distilled water, 7:143
distribution, statistical, 6:190, *190*
divers, 2:159, *159*
Divine Comedy, The, illustration, 8:*65*
diving, 7:146–147, *146*
divining rods, 3:*107*
division (arithmetic), 1:80
division of labor, 2:183
divorce, 2:159
Diwali, 3:73
Dix, Dorothea, 8:72
DNA, 2:160, *161*; 2:30, 76, 86
and **evolution**, 3:42, 47

genetic engineering, 3:150
and **genetics**, 3:151, *151*
and **heredity**, 4:26
docks, 2:161, *161*; 3:97
and **locks**, 4:163
doctors, 2:161; 4:44; 5:13, *13*
and **clinics**, 2:74
and **hospitals**, 4:44
surgeons, 7:21, *21*
training of, 7:*130*
see also **medicine**
dodos, 1:143
dogs, 2:162–163, *162–163*
domestication of, 2:162, 165, 166
jackals, 4:106, *106*
Seeing Eye, 1:145, *145*
doldrums, 7:168
doll houses, 7:*69*
dolls, 2:164, *164*; 7:68–69
dolphins, 2:165, *165*; 6:7, 72
Dome of the Rock, Jerusalem, 1:73; 4:*102*; 5:55, 148
domes, 1:73, *73*, 76, *177*
building, 1:171, *171*
onion-shaped, 1:*58*
Domesday Book, 3:27
domestication, 2:165–166
of **camels**, 1:184, *184*
of **cats**, 2:24–25
of **cattle**, 2:26
of **dogs**, 2:162, 165, 166
of **elephants**, 3:15; 4:*70*
of **goats**, 3:169
of **horses**, 2:165–166; 4:42–43
of **llamas**, 4:161, *161*
of **pets**, 5:165
of **reindeer**, 6:60, *60*
of **sheep**, 6:131, *131*
Dominica, 7:157; 2:95
Dominican monks, 5:46
Dominican Republic, 2:166; 7:157
Donald Duck, 2:19
Donatello, 8:72;
sculpture by, 6:*103*; 8:*72*
Donizetti, Gaetano, 5:132; 8:159
Donne, John, 8:72–73; 3:29
"Doonesbury" (Trudeau), 2:18
Doppler effect, 6:161
dormouse, 4:27
Dorris, Michael, 5:85

Dostoevsky, Fyodor, 8:73; 3:41
Doubleday, Abner, 1:118
double helix, 2:160, *161*
double jeopardy, 1:135
Douglas, Stephen A., 8:73; 4:65; 7:118
Douglas, William O., 4:145
Douglass, Frederick, 8:73–74, *74*; 1:19, 40
dove, as symbol, 7:26, *26*
Dove, Rita, 5:182
Down syndrome, 2:166
dowsing, 3:*107*
Doyle, Arthur Conan, 8:74
Dracula (movie), 7:*115*
draft, in army, 1:84
drag (air resistance), 3:97
dragonflies, 2:167, *167*; 4:*86*, 87
dragons, 2:167–168, *167*, *168*
Drake, Edwin, 5:162
Drake, Francis, 8:74–75; 5:170; 7:103
Drakensberg Range, 1:15
drama, 2:169, *169*; 3:29, 77, 183
Bible and, 1:132
copyrights of, 2:115
Japanese, 1:90
masks for, 4:188, *188*
and **mime**, 5:33, *33*
theaters, 7:53–54, *53*, *54*
drawing, 2:170–171, *170*, *171*; 3:77; 6:8
dreams, 2:171
dreamtime, of Aborigines, 1:9; 2:171
Drebbel, Cornelius, 7:15
Dreiser, Theodore, 1:40, 41; 4:74
Drew, Charles R., 8:75; 1:20
dripstone, 6:184, *184*
drop spindle, 6:178
drought, 2:172; 3:34; 4:99, 120
drugs, 2:172; 3:19, 146; 6:151
addiction to, 1:11
anesthetics, 1:52
cocaine, 2:90, *90*
nicotine, 7:62
opium, 2:50–51, 172, *172*
Druids, 2:31–32; 4:11
drums, 2:173, *173*; 5:74, *74*
African, 1:21, *21*; 2:55, 173, *173*
in **Indian music**, 4:75
steel, 2:114–115, *115*; 2:15, *15*

Dryden, John, **3**:29; **5**:182

Dubai, **7**:90, *90*

Dublin, Ireland, **4**:95–97, *96*

Du Bois, W. E. B., 8:75, *75*; **1**:19

Dubos, René, **1**:63

Dubrovnik, Croatia, **2**:*125*

ducks, **1**:139, 141–142; **2**:166

dude ranches, **6**:52

due process, and 14th Amendment, **2**:112

dugongs, **7**:162

Duke, James B., **5**:110

Dumas, Alexandre, Sr., **3**:41

dump trucks, **7**:*82*

Dunant, Jean Henri, **6**:56

Dunbar, Paul Laurence, 8:75–76; **1**:20, 40; **5**:127, 128

dung beetles, **7**:166

Du Pont de Nemours, E. I., **2**:141

duralumin, **1**:36

Dürer, Albrecht, 8:76

Durga Puja, **3**:73

Du Sable, Jean Baptiste Point, 8:76; **1**:19; **4**:65

Dussehra, **3**:73

dust bowls, 2:174, *174*; **2**:172; **4**:120

Dutch, *see* Netherlands

duty-free airports, **1**:28

Duvalier, "Papa Doc," **4**:10

Dvořák, Antonín, 8:76; **2**:36, 103; **3**:108; **5**:67

dyes, 2:174, *174*; **2**:91–92

Dylan, Bob, **3**:108; **5**:36; **6**:81

dynamite, **3**:52

dynasties, royal, **4**:125–126

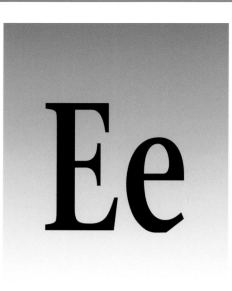

eagles, **1**:*139, 141*; **3**:19; **5**:77, *154*

Eakins, Thomas, 8:76–77; **5**:162
 painting by, **8**:*77*

Eames, Charles and Ray Kaiser, **3**:142

Earhart, Amelia, 8:77,*77*; **4**:120

Early, Jubal, **2**:70

earmuffs, **4**:174

Earp, Wyatt, **1**:81; **4**:120

ears, **2**:175, *175*; **6**:123
 and balance, **1**:109; **2**:175
 and **deafness, 2**:137
 and **sound, 6**:161

Earth, **2**:176–177, *176, 177*; **3**:154; **5**:171, 172, *172*; **7**:108, *108*
 and **astrology, 1**:92
 astronauts in orbit around, **1**:93
 and **atmosphere, 1**:94, *94*
 Big Bang theory, 1:134; **2**:177; **7**:108
 and **calendars, 1**:181
 as center of universe, **1**:93
 climate of, **2**:72–73
 continents, *see* **continents**
 and **cosmic rays, 2**:117
 day and night on, **2**:136, *136*
 environments on, **3**:30
 Equator and, **3**:32
 escape velocity of, **6**:172
 forces and, **3**:117, 179
 and **geological time, 3**:152–153, *152, 153*
 global warming of, **3**:168, *168*
 gravity, 3:117, 179; **5**:157, 168

 ice ages on, **4**:58, *58*
 landforms on, **4**:136–137, *136, 137*
 maps of, **4**:180–183, *180, 181*
 metals in, **5**:20
 meteors and meteorites in, **5**:21, *21*
 minerals in, **5**:34, *34*
 and **Moon, 5**:53, *53*
 and **mountains, 5**:60–61, *60, 61*
 oceans and seas on, **5**:122–125, *122, 125*
 and **plate tectonics, 5**:179, *179*
 and **poles, 5**:183
 population of, **5**:191–192, *192*
 and **rocks, 6**:82–84, *82, 83, 84*
 rotation of, **7**:61
 satellites orbiting, **6**:106, *106*
 and **sky, 6**:144
 soil, 6:157, *157*
 and **solar system, 6**:159–160, *159*
 and **space exploration, 6**:169–172, *169, 170*
 and **Sun, 7**:18–19
 and **tides, 7**:58, *58*

earthenware, **6**:13

earthquakes, 2:178–179, *178*; **1**:31; **3**:16; **4**:109; **5**:179, *179*; **7**:98
 in Armenia, **1**:84; **2**:*178*
 in Asia, **1**:88; **2**:178
 in California, **2**:179; **7**:98
 and construction, **1**:169; **2**:179
 epicenter of, **2**:178
 in **Japan, 2**:179
 map, **2**:*179*
 measuring damage of, **2**:178
 in **Nicaragua, 5**:101
 in **South America, 6**:164
 in U.S., **2**:178, 179

earthworms, 2:179, *179*; **4**:92; **6**:157; **7**:182, *182*

earwigs, **4**:87

Easter, 2:180, *180*; **2**:55, 56; **3**:74, *74*

Easter Island, **5**:187

Eastman, George, **1**:185

eating disorders, 2:180

echoes, **2**:181, *181*

echolocation, **1**:122; **2**:181, *181*

Eckert's projection, **4**:181, *181*

eclipses, 2:181, *181*

ecology, 2:182, 184; 3:30
   and **conservation**, 2:109–110
   wetlands, 7:159–161, *160–161*
economic cycle, 2:*183*
economics, 2:183, *183*; 2:143; 3:18
   of **forests**, 3:120
   Great Depression, 2:143
   and **socialism**, 6:156
   stock market, 6:192, *192*
   trade, 7:73, *73*
ecosystems, 2:184–185, *184*; 3:30,
   114
   conservation of, 2:109–110, 182
   forests, 3:118–121, *119*
   woodlands, 7:175, *175*
Ecuador, 2:185; 6:164
eczema, 2:185
Eddy, Mary Baker, 8:78; 2:57; 5:94
Edinburgh, Scotland, 2:62; 6:111, *111*
Edison, Thomas Alva, 8:78; 4:92;
   5:62, 97, 127, 128; 6:54
education, *see* schools
Edward VII, king of England, 7:92, 93
Edward VIII, king of England,
   abdication of, 7:93
Edward the Confessor, 3:26
Edwards, Jonathan, 8:79; 1:40;
   2:108
eels, 3:*87*
eggs, 2:186, *186*
   boiling, 2:40
   chickens and, 2:42
   fertilization of, 6:65, *65*, 127
   of **fish**, 3:84–85, 89
   of **frogs**, 3:134
   yolks of, 6:65
Egypt, 2:187–189, *187*; 1:69, 84;
   2:*188*; 3:98; 5:30, 148
   in **ancient world**, 1:50
   catacombs of Alexandria, 6:125
   cosmetics in, 2:117
   glass made in, 3:166
   hieroglyphics in, 4:28–29, *28, 29*
   history of, 2:187, 188
   irrigation in, 4:99, *99*
   library in, 4:152
   medicines in, 2:172
   mummies in, 5:65, *65*
   Nile in, 5:102, *102*
   palaces in, 5:148

papyrus in, 1:151; 2:188; 5:151
   pets in, 5:165
   pharaohs of, 2:188
   Pharos of Alexandria, 6:125, *125*
   pyramids in, 6:40, *40*, 124, *125*
   religions in, 2:189
   scarab beetles in, 1:127
   slavery in, 6:146
   Suez Canal, 1:191
   temples in, 7:43
Egyptian multiplication, 1:80
Egyptian mythology, 2:190, *190*;
   2:189
eid, 2:191; 3:74, *74*
Eiffel, Gustave, 3:23, 129
Eiffel Tower, 3:23, *129*
Einstein, Albert, 8:79, *79*; 3:32;
   4:141; 6:61; 7:60
Eisenhower, Dwight D., 8:79–80, *80*;
   4:120, 131; 5:162; 7:49, 101, 107
Eisenstein, Sergei, 5:63
ejaculation, 6:128
elastic, 2:191, *191*
elastomers, 6:181
El Cid, 3:41; 5:14–15
El Dorado, 2:90
elections, 2:192, *192*
electrical energy, 3:19
electricity, 3:7–10, *7, 8, 9–10*;
   3:20–22, *22*, 138; 5:168
   and **batteries**, 1:123; 1:102
   cables, 1:178
   dams for, 7:45
   and **greenhouse effect**, 3:186
   and **heat**, 4:20
   hydroelectric power, 4:55, *55*
   and **insulation**, 4:88–89
   for **light**, 4:157, *157*
   motors, 5:58, *58*
   and **nuclear power**, 5:115
   power stations, 6:16–17, *16, 17*
   solar power for, 6:158, *158*
   and **superconductivity**, 7:19, *19*
   in **thunderstorms**, 7:57
   and **transformers**, 7:74, *74*
   and **turbines**, 7:86, *86*
   water power and, 7:146
electrolysis, 5:20
electromagnetic force, 3:117; 5:157

electromagnetic waves, 6:45, *45*, 46;
   7:121, 149
electromagnets, 3:7, *8*; 4:174; 7:19
electronic mail (e-mail), 4:90; 6:12
electronic music, 3:11, *11*; 2:98–99,
   173
electronics, 3:12–13, *12, 13*; 4:78;
   6:138; 7:123, *123*
   calculators, 1:179–180, *179, 180*
   cassette players, 2:19, *19*
   compact discs, 2:97
   computer games, 2:99, *99*
   computers, 2:100–102, *100, 101,
      102*
   fax machines, 3:68, *68*
   and **information technology**,
      4:82–83, *82, 83*
   recording, 6:54, *54*
electronic total stations, 7:22
electronic toys, 7:69
electron microscopes, 5:26, *26*
electrons, 1:95, 96, 134; 3:7–9; 5:157;
   7:185
elements, 3:14, *14*; 1:95; 2:40
   and compounds, 3:14
   isotopes of, 3:14
   list of, 3:*14*
elephants, 3:15–16, *15, 16*; 4:*70*, 106;
   5:114
elevators, 3:17, *17*; 3:97
Elgar, Edward, 2:103
El Greco, 8:80
   painting by, 8:*80*
Eliot, George, 8:80; 3:29
Eliot, T. S., 8:81; 1:40, 41; 5:41
Elizabeth I, queen of England,
   8:81–82, *81*; 2:60, 169; 3:26–27;
   4:73, 125, 126; 6:39, 57; 7:53, 128
Elizabeth II, queen of England, 8:82,
   82, 51; 1:190; 2:60, 95; 4:125,
   126, *126*; 7:94
Ellington, Duke, 8:82; 1:19; 4:112
Ellison, Ralph, 1:20, 40, 41; 5:130
El Niño, 7:153
El Salvador, 3:16; 2:34–35
elves, 3:56, *56*
e-mail (electronic mail), 4:90; 6:12
Emancipation Proclamation (1863),
   2:67, 68–69, 70; 6:148
embroidery, 3:18, *18*

embryos, 6:18, 65
emeralds, 3:150, *150*
Emerson, Ralph Waldo, 8:83; 1:40, 44; 4:189
Emerson, Roy, 7:47
emigrants, 5:31, 78
Emile, 8:208
employment, 3:18; 2:183; 4:133
enamel, 7:36, *37*
encryption, 2:86
encyclopedias, 3:18
endangered species, 3:19, *19*; 2:109–110
   bats, 1:122
   bears, 1:124
   butterflies, 1:176
   cats, 2:25
   conservation of, 2:109–110
   elephants, 3:*15*, 16, *16*
   gorillas, 3:171
   hyenas, 4:55
   lemurs, 4:149, *149*
   list, 3:*19*
   orangutans, 5:133, *133*
   orchids, 5:136
   otters, 5:138, *138*
   pandas, 5:150, *150*
   rhinoceroses, 6:68
   tigers, 7:59
   tortoises and turtles, 7:*66*, 67
   whales, 3:19, *19*; 7:163
   zoos, 7:192
endorphins, 1:39
endoscopes, 7:21
energy, 3:20–22, *20–21, 22*; 2:185; 5:168; 6:55, 67
   alternative, 3:22
   and **Big Bang theory,** 1:134
   and **biotechnology,** 1:137
   $E = mc^2$, 3:32; 6:61
   and **ecosystems,** 2:185
   electricity, 3:7–10
   from **food,** 1:158; 3:20, *20*, 110
   and **fuel,** 3:20–21, *21*, 138, *138*
   geothermal, 3:22
   and heat, 4:20, 21
   nuclear, 1:96; 5:115
   oil, 5:128–129
   photosynthesis, 5:168
   power stations, 6:16–17, *16, 17*

radiation, 6:45–46, *45*
solar power, 6:158, *158*
stars and, 6:186, *186*
storage of, 2:191
from **Sun,** 7:18, *18*
Engels, Friedrich, 2:97; 6:156; 8:157
engineers, 3:23
   in ancient Egypt, 2:188
   army, 1:84
   in industrial design, 2:147
engines, 3:23
   automobile, 1:101, *101*, 102
   on boats, 1:147–148
   diesel, 1:102
   gasoline and diesel, 3:149, *149*
   internal-combustion, 3:149, *149*
   jet, 1:24, 26, 27; 4:114, *114*
   locomotive, 4:164–165, *164–165*
   motors, 5:58, *58*
   piston, 1:26
   steam, 1:23, *23*; 6:191, *191*
   turbines, 7:86
   turboprop, 1:26
England, 3:24–27, *24–25*; 7:90–94, *91*
   agriculture, 1:22; 3:*61*
   and **American Revolution,** 1:43–45
   Bill of Rights in, 1:135
   bridges in, 1:*160*, *161*
   Buckingham Palace, 5:147, *148*
   Channel Tunnel, 2:38; 6:*50–51*; 7:*85*, *94*
   common law of, 4:143
   Cromwell in, 1:84
   Dover cross-Channel ferry port, 6:10, *10*
   explorers from, 3:26, 51; 7:103
   vs. **France,** 3:26, 39
   history of, 3:*24–25*, 26–27, 39; 7:91–94
   Industrial Revolution in, 7:91, *92*
   kings and queens of, 4:125–126
   Parliament of, 1:43–44; 3:26
   and **smugglers,** 6:151, *151*
   Stonehenge in, 5:120; 6:125; 7:7–8, *8*
   and **Thirteen Colonies,** 7:56
   wars and warfare, 7:136

   see also **British Isles; United Kingdom**
English Channel, 1:163; 2:37, 38
   Channel Tunnel, 6:50, *50–51*
   swimming, 7:24
English language, 3:27–28
English literature, 3:29; 1:86
engraving, 6:28
Enlightenment, 8:240
ENT surgery, 7:21
environments, 3:30, *30*; 2:182
   ecosystems, 2:184–185, *184*
   and **endangered species,** 3:19, *19*
   forest, 3:118, *119*, 120
   and **green movement,** 3:187, *187*
   habitats, 4:8, *8*
   landforms, 4:136–137, *136, 137*
   and **land use,** 4:138
enzymes, 3:31; 2:148, 152; 3:165; 6:31; 7:7
épée, 3:72
Ephesus, temple of Artemis/Diana, 6:124–125, *125*
Epictetus, 3:183
epidemics, 3:31; 6:41
epidermis, 6:143, *143*
epilepsy, 3:31
Epiphany, 2:57
epitaphs, 2:59
epoxy glues, 3:168
equations, 3:32; 1:34
Equator, 3:32; 4:142; 7:82
   and **Africa,** 1:15–16
   and **Asia,** 1:88
   and **climate,** 2:72–73
   and **seasons,** 6:120, *120*
equinoxes, 2:136
Erasmus, Desiderius, 8:83
Ercilla y Zuñiga, Alonso de, 4:141
Erdich, Louise, 5:85
erection (sexual), 6:128
ergonomics, 3:141
Ericsson, Leif: *see* **Leif Ericsson**
Eric the Red, 8:83
Erie, Lake, 4:135; 7:135
Erie Canal, New York, 1:191, 192
Eritrea, 3:32; 3:34
Ernst, Max, 2:89
erosion, 3:33, *33*; 3:30; 4:136–137; 6:73

of **coasts**, 2:84–85, *84*
in **deserts**, 2:144–145
and **dust bowls**, 2:174
of **rocks**, 5:34; 6:*82*
of **valleys**, 7:112–114, *112–114*
waterfalls and, 7:145, *145*
escalators, 3:33, *33*
escape velocity, 6:172
escrima, 4:186
esophagus, 2:152, *152*
espresso coffee, 2:87
Estafan, Gloria, 4:33
Estonia, 3:34; 6:168
estuaries (**rivers**), 6:74, *74*, 119; 7:159
etching, 3:105; 6:28
ethanol, 1:32, 137
ethics, 3:34
Ethiopia, 3:34; 3:32, 98; 4:105
famine in, 3:*60*
flag, 3:93
Rastafarians in, 6:52
"ethnic cleansing," 3:34
ethnic groups, 3:34
immigration of, 4:67–68, *67*
and **racism**, 6:43
ethylene glycol, 1:32
etiquette, 3:35
Etruscans, 3:35
Euclid, 8:84
Euphrates River, 1:50; 2:65; 5:30
Eurasia, 1:88–89, maps, 1:*88* and
1:*89*; 3:36
Euripides, 3:183
EuroDisney, 1:49
Europe, 3:36–40; 2:113
colonies of, *see* **colonies**
colonies within, 3:163
countries and languages of,
3:36–37
Dark Ages in, 2:135
Eurasia, 11.88–89, maps, 1:*88*, *89*
explorers from, 3:50–51
feudal system in, 3:75
history of, 3:38–40, *38–40*
immigration from, 4:67–68, *67*
languages in, 4:138–139
maps, 3:*36*, *37*
in **Middle Ages**, 5:27–29, *28*, *29*
and **Middle East**, 5:30
monarchies in, 4:125–126, *126*

Napoleonic wars in, 5:79–80, *79*,
80
NATO in, 5:86
painting in, 5:140–146, *140*,
142–143
palaces in, 5:147–148, *148*
Reformation in, 6:57
religions in, 3:37, 38, 39
Renaissance in, 6:63–64, *63*, *64*
roads and highways in, 6:77, *77*
and **slavery**, 6:146–148, *146*, *147*
Warsaw Pact in, 5:86
wildlife in, 7:166, *167*
European Community, and
Commonwealth of Nations,
2:95
European literature, 3:41; 3:183
European Union, 3:41; 3:40, 182;
4:105; 5:47; 7:90
in Brussels, 1:128
flag, 3:93
laws and legal systems, 4:145
passports in, 5:158
Evans, Bill, 4:112
Evans, Gil, 4:112, 113
evaporated milk, 5:32
Eve (Bible), 1:132
Everest, Mount, 1:89; 4:29, *29*; 5:59,
61; 6:125
Everglades National Park, 3:99, *100*
evergreen trees, 7:78
Everly Brothers, 6:81
Evers, Medgar, 5:40
Evita (Lloyd Webber), 1:79
evolution, 3:42–49, *42–49*; 3:*153*
of **birds**, 1:139
of **dinosaurs**, 2:153–156
and **islands**, 4:103
of **mammals**, 4:178
of **plants**, 5:175
and Scopes trial, 7:45
excretory system, 4:50, *50*
exercise:
and **breathing**, 1:158
dance, 2:*134*
and **fitness**, 3:92
and **pulse** rate, 6:35
exoskeletons, 4:86–87, 92, 162, *162*
exosphere, 1:94
explorers, 3:50–51

to the Americas, 2:90, 109; 4:174;
7:103
to Antarctica, 1:60–61
to Australia, 1:99
boats of, 5:*121*
from **England**, 1:68; 3:26, 51;
6:174; 7:103
from **Europe**, 3:50–51, 130; 6:11;
7:103
in **India**, 4:73
maps of, 4:180–183, *180*
Vikings, 7:125–126, *125*, *126*
see also **space exploration**
explosives, 3:52, *52*; 7:48
exports, 7:73
extended family, 3:59
extinct animals and plants,
3:52–53, *52–53*; 2:165–166; 3:46,
46
birds, 1:143
dinosaurs, 2:153–156; 1:91
endangered species and, 3:19, *19*
fossils of, 3:123–124, *123*, *124*
prehistoric, 6:18–19, *18*, *19*
Tasmanian wolf, 4:*185*
eyes, 3:54, *54*; 3:167; 6:123, *123*
blindness, 1:145, 154
of **cats**, 2:24
lenses of, 4:150
and **optics**, 5:133
optometrists and opticians,
5:133, *133*
Eyre, Edward, 3:51

Ff

F-15 Eagle fighter jet, 1:*27*
fables, 3:55, *55*; 2:44–45
Fables of Bidpai, 3:58
facets, of **gems,** 3:150
factories, 3:56, *56*; 4:78–80, *80*, 98, *98*
  air-conditioning in, 1:24
  car manufacturing, 3:*128*
  children working in, 2:44
  in **cities,** 2:63, 64, 65
  and **fishing industry,** 3:91
  food processing in, 3:115, *115*
  manufacturing in, 2:76, 77
  mass production in, 4:190
  pollution from, 2:64, *64*; 3:*30*
  textile, 7:51, *51*
  see also **businesses; industry**
Faeroe Islands, 6:107
Fahrenheit scale, 7:43
Fairhall, Neroli, 1:*72*
fairies, 3:56, *56*
fairs, 3:57, *57*; 3:*125*
fairy tales, 3:58, *58*; 3:41, 107, *107*, 109, *109*; 8:*11*
  in ballet, 1:110, 111
  in **children's books,** 2:44–45
falcons, 1:138, *138*, 140, 142, *143*
Falkland Islands (Islas Malvinas), 3:58, *58*; 1:79; 2:95; 7:94
Falla, Manuel de, 8:84
fallout, nuclear, 1:96
Fall River Legend (de Mille), 1:42
families, 3:59, *59*; 3:151, *151*

and **adoption,** 1:11
  foster children, 3:125
  parenthood, 5:154
family trees, 3:59, *59*
famine, 3:60, *60*; 3:139; 4:97, 177; 6:189
FAO Schwarz, New York City, 7:68
Faraday, Michael, 8:84; 3:8
farming, 3:60–64, *60, 61, 62, 63, 64*; 4:40, *74*
  agricultural revolutions, 1:22–23
  in **ancient world,** 1:50
  aquaculture, 3:91
  and **archaeological sites,** 1:70
  in Asia, 1:88–89
  beans, 1:123, *123*
  and **calendars,** 1:181
  in California, 1:182, 183
  corn, 2:116, *116*; 4:93, *93*
  dairy, 2:121
  and **drought,** 2:172
  and **ecology,** 2:182
  in Egypt, 2:188
  fertilizers used in, 3:62, 64, 72
  in **France,** 3:128, *128*
  fur, 3:140
  green movement in, 3:63, 64; 4:73
  harvest, 3:65, *65*; 4:14
  in India, 4:72
  irrigation for, 4:99, *99*
  and **land conservation,** 7:161, *161*
  and **land use,** 4:138, *138*
  in **Mediterranean** area, 5:16
  and **milk,** 5:32
  organic, 3:64
  by **peasants,** 5:160
  pig, 5:168, *168*
  in Poland, 5:*183*
  and **pollution,** 5:186, *186*
  by **prehistoric people,** 6:22, *22*
  and **rain,** 5:50
  rice, 4:*138*; 6:*160*
  sunflowers, 4:*120*, 121
  tea, 7:34
  in U.S., 7:100–101
  wheat, 3:178, *178*; 7:163, *163*
  winnowing grain, 7:*32*
farm machinery, 3:65, *65*; 1:23, *23*; 2:63, 119; 4:65; 7:*163*
Farnsworth, Philo T., 7:42

Farragut, David G., 2:68; 4:167; 7:44
fascism, 3:66; 4:105
fashion, 3:66, *66*; 2:76–79, *77*, 146
fasting, 3:67; 4:101
fats, 3:67, *67*; 3:110
Faulkner, William, 8:84–85, *85*; 1:40, *41*; 5:39; 6:34
Faust, legend of, 5:15, *15*
fax machines, 3:68, *68*; 2:96; 6:12
FBI, 3:69, *69*; 3:77
feathers, 3:70, *70*; 1:138, 139, 140
Federalist, The, 1:40
feet and hands, 3:71, *71*; 5:77, *77*
Felix the Cat, 2:18
Fellini, Federico, 5:63
felting, 7:51
feminism, 7:173
fencing, 3:72, *72*
feral animals, 2:25, 166
fermentation, 1:32, 137, *137*
Fermi, Enrico, 8:85
Fernández de Lizardi, José, 4:141
ferns, 3:72, *72*; 5:*176*; 6:179, *179*
Ferre, Maurice, 4:33
Ferrer, José, 33
ferries, 6:*132*; 6:10, *10*
Ferris, George Washington, 1:49; 4:65
Ferris wheels, 1:*49*
fertilization, 3:104; 5:185; 6:65, 127
fertilizers, 3:72; 3:62, 64; 5:103
  and **pollution,** 1:23
  seaweed as, 6:121
festivals and holidays, 3:73–74, *73, 74*; 3:113
  in **Christianity,** 2:55, 56, 57, *57*, 180, *180*
  dancing in, 2:132; 3:106, *106*; 7:63
  eid, 2:191; 3:74, *74*
  Halloween, 4:11, *11*
  Hanukkah, 4:13
  Hispanic, 4:34
  Indian, 4:76, *76*
  of **Judaism,** 4:117, *117*
  Mardi Gras, 2:15; 4:167, *167*, 168
  national dress for, 2:78, *78, 79*
  New Year, 4:*139*; 7:30
  Passover, 5:157
  Quinceañera, 4:33
  Thanksgiving, 3:73, 113; 4:14

Tulip Festival, Holland, Michigan, 5:*24*

fetus, 6:18, *18*

feudal system, 3:75; 4:128; 5:27–28, 80, 160

FGD (Flue Gas Desulphurization) equipment, 1:10

fiber, in **food**, 3:111

fiberglass, 5:178

fiber optics, 3:75, *75*; 1:178; 4:141; 7:38, 39

fibers, 3:76, *76*; 6:92; 7:176, *176*

  cellulose, 7:29

  cotton, 2:118–119

  knitting, 4:128

  paper, 5:151, *151*

  silk, 6:138, *138*

  spinning, 6:178

  synthetic, 7:29

  textiles, 7:50–51, *51*

  weaving, 7:154, *154*

fibrous root systems, 6:91, *91*

Field, Cyrus W., 1:178

Field, Marshall, 4:65

field hockey, 4:35, *35*

Fielding, Henry, 3:29

field studies (archaeology), 1:70

fighters, jet, 1:27, *27*

Fiji, 3:76, *76*; 2:95; 5:121

filaments, 3:7

Fillmore, Millard, 8:85–86, *86*; 5:100; 7:101

films, *see* **movies**

filter feeders, 3:87

finches, 1:139, *139*

fine arts, 3:77

  in **museums**, 5:66

  and **Renaissance**, 4:104, 105; 6:63–64

  see also art; *specific genres*

fingerprints, 3:77, *77*; 2:147

Finland, 3:78, *78*; 3:41; 5:156; 6:107; 7:179

fire, 3:78–79; 4:20, 21

  Chicago, 3:79, 80; 4:65

  myths and legends of, 5:77

firearms, 7:150–151, *150*

fire fighting, 3:79–80, *79*

fireflies, 3:80, *80*

fireworks, 3:80, *80*

first aid, 3:81, *81*

  hypothermia, 4:56

first ladies, 3:82–83, *82, 83*; 7:101

Fischer, William, 3:172

fish, 3:84–87, *84–85, 86–87*; 7:120, *120*

  in **aquariums**, 1:67

  evolution of, 3:43–45, *44–45*

  in **oceans and seas**, 5:123, *123, 124*

  and **parasites**, 5:153

  in **rivers**, 6:72

  senses of, 3:86–87

  sharks, 6:130, *130*

  spawning of, 3:84–85, 89

  in **streams**, 7:12–13, *12*

  swimming, 7:24

  in winter, 4:57

fishing, 3:88–89, *88, 89*; 4:91

fishing industry, 3:90–91, *90–91*; 6:10

Fisk Jubilee Singers, 6:178, *178*

fission, 1:96, 149; 5:115

fitness, 3:92; 4:18

Fitzgerald, Ella, 1:19; 4:112

Fitzgerald, F. Scott, 8:86–87, *86*; 1:40, 41; 5:36

five-and-ten-cent stores, 7:9

fixed-action patterns, 1:55–56

fjords, 3:92, *92*; 5:114; 6:107; 7:112

Flag Day, 8:208

Flagg, James Montgomery, poster by, 7:104, *104*

Flagler, Henry M., 3:99

flags, 3:93, *93*; 3:*131*; 4:*187*

flak jackets, 1:85

flamingos, 1:*139*

flashlights, 3:94, *94*

flatbed trucks, 7:82–83, *82*

flatworms, 7:182, *182*

Flaubert, Gustave, 8:87; 3:41; 5:15

fleas, 3:94; 8:*118*

fleece, 7:176, *176*

Fleischer, Dave and Max, 2:18

Fleming, Alexander, 1:63

Fleming, Ambrose, 3:13

flesh-eaters, 1:57; 2:184, 185; 3:94, *94*; 5:12

  fish, 3:87

  food chains and webs, 3:114, *114*

flies, 3:95, *95*; 4:87

  fossils of, 3:124, *124*

  mosquitoes, 5:56, *56*

flight, 3:96–97, *96*; 3:167

  aircraft, 1:25–27

  balloons and airships, 1:112–113, *112, 113*

  bats, 1:122, *122*

  birds, 1:139–140, *139, 140*

  butterflies, 1:176

  feathers and, 3:70

  of **flies**, 3:95, *95*

  hang gliders, 4:13, *13*

  kites, 4:127, *127*

  and **parachutes**, 5:152, *152*

  and **skydiving**, 6:145, *145*

Flintstones, the, 2:19

floating, 3:97, *97*

  ice, 4:57, *57*

flood-plains, 7:159

floods, 3:98–99, *98, 99*; 1:88, 116; 2:85, 131, 187–188, 190; 6:75

  and **dams**, 2:131

  Johnstown, Pennsylvania, 5:163

floor coverings, 6:93, *93*

Florence, Italy, 1:64; 4:105

  cathedral, 6:64, *64*

  Ponte Vecchio, 1:*160*

  sculpture in, 6:*112*

florets, 3:104

Florida, 3:99–100, *100*; 2:67, 109; 7:100, 102, *160–161*

flowering plants, 3:101–102, *101, 102*; 5:175, *175*

  and **fruits**, 3:136–137

  gardens of, 3:147, *147*

  grasses, 3:175, *175*

  leaves of, 4:147, *147*

  orchids, 5:136, *136*

  pollination of, 5:185

  seeds, 6:122, *122*

  shrubbery, 6:136, *136*

  trees, 7:78–80, *80*

  see also **flowers**; **plants**

flowers, 3:103–104, *103, 104*; 3:101–102, *101, 102*

  in **gardens**, 3:147, *147*

  language of, 7:26

  pollination of, 1:126, *126, 176*; 5:185

tulip festival, 5:*24*

flu, *see* **influenza**

Flue Gas Desulphurization (FGD) equipment, 1:10

flukes (of whales), 7:162

fluorescence, 3:105

fluorescent tubes, 4:*157*

fluorine, 3:105; 7:148

flutes, 5:70, *70*

fly fishing, 3:88, *88*, 89

flying buttresses, 1:76, *76–77*

foehn winds, 7:168

fog, 3:105, *105*; 5:187

Fogo, Mount, 2:9

foil (sword), 3:72

folk art, 3:77, 107

folk dance, 3:106, *106*; 2:132–133, *132*

folklore, 3:107, *107*; *see also* **myths and legends**

folk medicine, 1:39

folk music, 3:108, *108*; 5:68; 6:141

 ballads, 1:109

 country and western, 2:119

 of ethnic choirs, 2:53, *53*

folktales, 3:109, *109*

 Arabian Nights, 1:68

 in ballets, 1:111

 in **children's books**, 2:44–45

 fairy tales, 3:58, *58*

Fon people, legends, 1:21

Fonteyn, Margot, 1:111

food, 3:110–113, *110–111*, *112*

 additives, 3:*112*, 115

 beans, 1:123

 bread, 1:157, *157*

 cannibalism, 2:8, *8*

 cheese, 2:39, *39*

 chickens, 2:42, *42*

 chocolate, 2:53, *53*

 cooking of, 2:114; 3:113

 and **diets**, 2:151

 digestion of, 2:152, *152*

 and **eating disorders**, 2:180

 energy from, 1:158; 3:20, *20*, 110

 farming, 3:60–64

 fats in, 3:67, *67*, 110

 germs in, 2:158

 grain, 3:173, *173*

 and **health**, 4:18

honey, 4:38, *38*

and **malnutrition**, 4:177

meat, 5:12

milk, 5:32

and nitrogen cycle, 5:103, *103*

and nutrition, 3:110–111; 4:18

pasta, 5:158, *158*

poultry, 7:87

pyramid, 3:*111*

rice, 6:70, *70*

salt, 6:104–105, *104*, *105*

seaweeds, 6:121

seeds, 6:122

spices, 6:176, *176*

staples, 3:111

sugar, 7:17, *17*

tasting, 6:123

vegetables, 7:116, *116*

of **vegetarians**, 7:117

vitamins in, 7:131

wheat, 7:163

yogurt, 7:188

Food and Drug Administration (FDA), 3:112

food chains and webs, 3:114, *114*; 2:182, 184–85

 flesh-eaters, 3:94, *94*

 growth and, 3:188, *188*

 in the ocean, 5:123, *123*

 photosynthesis, 5:168

food processing, 3:115, *115*; 2:114; 3:112, 113

food vacuole, 1:*47*

football, 3:116, *116*

footprints, *see* **animal tracks and signs**

forces, 3:117, *117*; 3:179; 5:157

 levers, 4:151, *151*

 pressure, 6:24, *24*

Ford, Gerald R., 8:87, *87*; 5:88; 7:101

Ford, Henry, 8:88; 1:102; 4:190; 5:24, 36

forecasting, weather, 7:152–153

forests, 3:118–121, *118*, *119*, *120*, *121*; 4:*171*; 7:175, *175*

 conservation of, 2:110

 destruction of, 3:19, 30, 121, *121*, 186

 and **endangered species**, 3:19

 timber from, 7:59

formic acid, 1:64

Formosa (**Taiwan**), 7:30, *30*

formwork, 1:73

Forrest, Nathan Bedford, 4:131

Forster, E. M., 3:29

forts, 3:122, *122*; 2:20; 5:*112*; 6:33

Fort Ticonderoga, 1:44

Fort Union Trading Post, 5:*112*

fossil fuels, 2:10; 3:21, *21*, 22, 138

fossils, 3:123–124, *123*, *124*; 4:58, 123; 5:51; 6:18–19, *19*

 and **coal**, 2:81

 dinosaurs, 2:153–156, *153*

 evolution and, 3:43–49, *43*, *44–45*, *46*, *47*

 geological time and, 3:152, *153*

 geologists and, 3:154

 of **mosses**, 5:56

Foster, Stephen, 8:88; 5:68, 162

foster children, 3:125

foundations, building, 1:169, 170, *170*

4-H clubs, 3:125, *125*

Fox, George, 8:88; 6:41

Fox, Terry, 2:38

foxes, 3:126, *126*; 2:*175*; 3:140

fractals, 3:126, *126*

fractional distillation, 5:129, *129*

fractions, 3:127; 1:*149*; 2:137; 5:164

fractures, 3:127, *127*; 1:149

 first aid for, 3:81

frames, television, 7:41

France, 3:128–132, *128*, *129*; 3:39

 African colonies of, 1:18, 130, 174, 186; 2:34, 105; 5:8, 101; 6:122; 7:63

 and Algeria, 1:34–35

 American colonies of, 1:82, 190; 2:14; 6:164; 7:45

 and American Revolution, 1:45

 and **Andorra**, 1:51

 armies of, 1:84

 Asian colonies of, 1:183; 7:124

 auto racing in, 1:103

 cave paintings in, 2:28–29, *28–29*; 6:18, *18*

 Celts in, 2:31

 Channel Tunnel, 2:38

 colonies of, 3:40, 132, 190; 4:106, 148, 167, 177

and **Crimean War,** 2:124
early settlers in, 1:53
Eiffel Tower in, 3:23, *129*
vs. **England,** 3:26, 39
in EU, 3:41
explorers from, 3:51, 130; 7:103
flag of, 3:*131*
Giverny garden in, 3:*147*
history of, 3:39–40, 130–132
Huguenots in, 4:47
Impressionism in, 5:144, *145,* 146
languages of, 2:31
law and legal systems in, 4:143
literature of, 3:41
map, 3:*129*
medals of, 5:12, *12*
medieval legends of, 5:14
and **Mediterranean,** 5:16
Middle Ages in, 5:29
monasteries in, 5:45–46, *45*
Mont Blanc in, 5:59
Napoleonic wars in, 5:79–80, *79,*
    80
national anthem of, 5:80
Normandie bridge in, 1:161
Pacific territories of, 5:121
prehistoric people in, 6:*20–21,* 21
presidents of, 6:24
as a **republic,** 6:66
revolution in, 1:45, 84; 3:39, 131,
    131; 4:52; 5:79
theater in, 7:54
wars and warfare, 7:136
in **World War I,** 3:132; 7:177–178,
    178
in **World War II,** 3:40, 132;
    7:179–181, *179, 181*
Franciscan monks, 5:46
Francis of Assisi, St., 8:88–89, *99;*
    2:57; 5:46; 6:102
Franco, Francisco, 8:89; 2:150; 6:174
Franco-Prussian War, 7:136
Frank, Anne, 8:89, *89;* 5:92
Frankenstein (Shelley), 3:29; 5:51;
    6:110
Frankfurt, Germany, 3:158, *158*
frankincense, 2:57
Franklin, Aretha, 7:44
Franklin, Benjamin, 8:90, *90;* 1:36,
    40, 43, 45, 136; 2:112, 138; 3:167;
    4:89, 127, 152; 5:162; 6:32

Franks, 1:53
freckles, 6:143
Frederick I, Holy Roman emperor,
    8:90; 2:126
Frederick II, Holy Roman emperor,
    8:90–91, *91;* 3:159
Fredericksburg, Battle of, 2:68
Freedom Riders, 2:66
freefall (**skydiving**), 6:145
free-market system, 2:183
Freetown, Sierra Leone, 6:137
freeways, 6:77, *77*
freezers, 6:58, *58*
Frémont, John C., 8:91; 2:67, 92;
    3:156; 5:93, 185; 7:184
French and Indian War, 3:132; 1:29,
    43; 3:122; 5:127; 7:118
French horns, 5:71, *71*
French knots, 3:18, *18*
frequency, 6:47, 161; 7:149
    and **radiation,** 6:45–46, *45*
    and **vibration,** 7:121
frequency modulation (FM) radio,
    6:47, 48
frescoes, 3:133, *133;* 4:105; 5:*23,* 140
Freud, Sigmund, 8:91, *91;* 2:171
friars, 5:46
Frick, Henry Clay, 5:163
friction, 3:134; 3:117
Friedan, Betty, 7:173
Friedman, Milton, 2:183
Frigg/Freya (Norse goddess), 5:107
Frisians, 1:53
Froelich, John, 3:65
frogs, 3:134–135, *134–135;* 1:47–48;
    6:*142;* 7:118
    cannibalism of, 2:*8*
    larvae of, 4:140
    mating of, 5:*7*
    metamorphosis of, 1:47, 48, *48*
    nests of, 5:92
    and **toads,** 7:62
frost, 3:135, *135*
    and **snow,** 6:153
Frost, Robert, 8:92, *92;* 1:40, 41;
    5:94, 181
fructose, 7:17
fruit, 3:136–137, *136, 137*
    nuts, 5:119
    seeds of, 6:122
    of **trees,** 7:78–79, *80*

fruit growing, 3:137, *137*
fuel, 3:138, *138;* 3:78, 148
    and **acid rain,** 1:10
    alcohol as, 1:32
    automobile, 1:102
    biotechnology and, 1:137
    coal, 2:81–82, *81, 82*
    and **conservation,** 2:110
    and **energy,** 3:20–21, *21*
    for **engines,** 3:23, 149
    from **forests,** 3:120
    fossil, 2:10
    and **greenhouse effect,** 3:186, *186*
    for **jet engines,** 4:114
    in **nuclear power,** 5:115
    oil, 5:128–129
    power stations, 6:16–17, *16*
    rocket, 6:80
    wood for, 7:59
Fuentes, Carlos, 4:142
Fugitive Slave Act (1850), 2:67
Fujeirah, 7:90
Fuji, Mount, 4:109, *110;* 5:60, *60*
fulcrum point, 4:170
Fuller, R. Buckminster, 1:171
Fulton, Robert, 8:92–93; 5:162; 6:191
    steamboat of, 8:*93*
funerals, 3:139
    burial mounds, 1:174
    cemeteries, 2:33
    clothing for, 2:79
    and **tombs,** 7:63
fungi, 3:139, *139;* 2:30; 5:175; 6:179
    classification of, 2:70
    and **fermentation,** 1:137
    in **forests,** 3:120
    lichens, 4:154
    mushrooms, 5:67, *67*
    yeasts, 7:187
fur, 3:140, *140;* 6:144, *144*
    of **cats,** 2:24, 25, *25*
    clothing from, 4:*91*
furniture, 3:141–142, *141, 142*
    carpentry, 2:16–17
    of **Shakers,** 6:129, *129*
fur trade, 1:125
fuse boxes, 3:10, *10*
fusion, 1:96, 149; 5:115

Gable, Clark, 5:*63*
Gabriel, archangel, 1:52
Gagaku, 5:134
Gagarin, Yuri, 8:93; 1:93
Galapagos Islands, 2:185; 3:42; 4:103;
  5:161; 7:66, 165
galaxies, 3:143, *143*; 5:32, *32*, 89;
  6:42; 7:108, *108*
  Big Bang theory, 1:134; 2:177
  black holes, 1:145
  and **cosmic rays,** 2:117
  and **gravity,** 3:179
  Milky Way, 5:32, *32*; 5:89
  space between, 4:158
Galen, 3:183
Galilei, Galileo, 8:93–94, *93*; 1:93;
  2:75; 4:26; 5:161, 171; 6:63; 7:40,
  55
Galileo spacecraft, 6:171
Galland, Antoine, 1:68
Gallaudet, Thomas Hopkins, 2:137
galleons, 6:*101*
gall wasps, 7:142
galvanizing, 7:191
Gama, Vasco da, 8:94; 4:73; 5:64;
  6:11
Gambia, 3:144; 2:95; 3:60; 6:122
Gambia, River, 3:144
gambling, 3:144; 6:30
  in Las Vegas, 2:12; 5:93, 94
  lotteries, 4:166
gamelans, 5:*135*
games, 3:144–146, *145*
  card, 2:11–12, *11*, *12*

computer, 2:99, *99*
  darts, 2:135, *135*
  gambling on, 3:144
  sports, 6:180
  and **toys,** 7:68–69
Gamma rays, 6:*45*, 46
gamma waves, 1:96
Gamond, Thomé de, 2:38
Gandhi, Indira, 8:94, *94*; 4:72; 6:25
Gandhi, Mohandas, 8:94–95, *95*;
  3:67; 4:73
Ganges, 3:146; 1:88; 3:139; 4:31, 70;
  5:169; 6:*62*
gangsters, 3:146
gannets, 2:71, *71*; 4:8
garam masala, 6:176
garbage trucks, 7:*82*
Garbarek, Jan, 4:112, 113
Garcia, Andy, 4:33
Garcia, Hector P., 4:33
Garcia Lorca, Federico, 3:41
García Márquez, Gabriel, 8:95;
  4:142
Garden of Eden, 1:132
Garden of the Gods, Colorado, 2:*93*
gardens, 3:147, *147*
  flowers in, 3:103–104, *104*
  grasses in, 3:175–176, *176*
  Persian style, 4:73
Garfield, James A., 8:96, *96*; 5:127,
  128; 7:101
Garfunkel, Art, 3:108
Garibaldi, Giuseppe, 8:96; 4:105
Garland, Judy, 5:36, *36*, 62, 76
Garlin, Hamlin, 1:40
Garrison, Jimmy, 4:112
Garrison, William Lloyd, 8:96–97
Garvey, Marcus, 1:19; 6:52, *52*; 8:153
gases, 3:148, *148*; 5:8
  in acid rain, 1:10
  in the **air,** 1:24, *24*
  in the **atmosphere,** 1:94, *94*
  in **balloons and airships,**
    1:112–113
  and **Big Bang theory,** 1:134
  in **bubbles,** 1:164
  greenhouse, 3:186, *186*
  inert, 3:148
  neon, 5:90, *90*
  oxygen, 5:139
  ozone, 5:139

gas lamps, 4:157, *157*
gasohol, 1:137
gasoline, 3:138; 5:129
gasoline and diesel engines, 3:149,
  149; 4:164–165, *164–165*
Gates, Bill, 7:137
Gates, Horatio, 1:45
GATT (General Agreement on Tariffs
  and Trade), 7:73
gauchos, 1:79; 2:120; 3:62; 7:109
Gaudí, Antonio, 1:74
Gauguin, Paul, 8:97
  painting by, 8:*97*
Gautama, Siddartha, *see* **Buddha**
Gaye, Marvin, 5:25
gays and lesbians, 6:128
geese, 1:141–142; 2:166
Gehrig, Lou, 1:120
gelignite, 3:52
Gemini spacecraft, 6:169
gems, 3:150, *150*; 2:128, 150, *150*;
  4:115, *115*; 5:34, *34*
general stores, 7:9, *9*
generators, electric, 3:8
genes, 3:150, *150*, 151, *151*; 4:26, *26*,
  51
genetic codes, 2:86
genetic engineering, 3:150, *150*;
  1:137; 2:76, 150
genetics, 3:151, *151*; 4:26, *26*
  DNA, 2:160
  and **proteins,** 6:31
Geneva Convention (1864), 6:56
Genghis Khan, 8:97–98; 5:48
  map, 8:*98*
genitals, 6:128
Genji monogatari (*Tale of Genji*), 1:90,
  90
Gennep, Arnold van, 6:71
geography, 3:151
geological time, 3:152–153, *152*,
  153; 2:153, 177
  absolute dating in, 3:152
  evolution in, 3:43–46, *44–45*
  fossils from, 3:123–124
  ice ages, 4:58, *58*; 6:107
  prehistoric animals, 6:18–19, *18*,
    19
  prehistoric people, 6:20–23,
    20–21, *22*, *23*
  relative dating in, 3:152

geologists, 3:154
geometry, 3:154–155, *154, 155*; 5:7
    fractals, 3:126, *126*
    shapes, 6:129, *129*
geomorphology, 4:136
George I, king of England, 7:91
George II, king of England, 7:91
George III, king of England, 8:98;
    1:43; 2:138, 139; 4:125; 6:69;
    7:91–92
George IV, king of England, 7:92
George V, king of England, 7:93
George VI, king of England, 7:94, *94*
George, Jean, 2:45
George, St., 2:167, *168*; 6:102, *103*
Georgia (C.I.S.), 3:155; 1:88; 6:98,
    168
Georgia (U.S.A.), 3:156–157, *157*;
    2:67, 69, 70; 7:56, 100
geostationary orbits, 5:87; 6:106, *106*
geothermal energy, 3:22
geothermal power stations, 6:17, *17*
gerbils, 3:157, *157*; 6:86
geriatrics, 5:13
Germany, 3:158–160, *158, 159*; 6:168
    African colonies of, 1:186; 5:78;
        7:32, 63
    Anglo-Saxons, 1:53
    autobahn in, 6:*77*
    cities and states of, 3:158, *158*
    in EU, 3:41
    Fasching in, 2:15
    fascism in, 3:66
    history of, 3:159–160, *160*
    incinerator in, 7:*77*
    literature of, 3:41
    medals of, 5:12, *12*
    medieval legends of, 5:15, *15*
    mining in, 5:35, *35*
    Nazis in, *see* **Nazis**
    and pollution, 2:64, *64*
    Purity Order (1516) in, 1:125
    toys made in, 7:*68*, 69
    U-boats of, 7:178, 180
    valley in, 7:*112–113*
    wars and warfare, 7:136
    in **World War I**, 3:132, 160;
        7:177–178, *178*
    in **World War II**, 3:40, 132, 160;
        7:179–181, *179, 181*

germs, 3:161; 1:63, 107; 2:158; 4:56,
    68; 7:131, *131*
Geronimo, 8:98; 1:81
Gershwin, George, 8:98–99; 5:67, 75,
    100, 132
Gettysburg, Battle of, 2:68, 69; 7:136
Gettysburg Address, 3:161, *161*;
    2:67, 69
Getz, Stan, 4:112
geysers, 3:162, *162*; 4:61, *61*
Ghana, 3:162; 2:95, 132, *132*; 7:63
Ghazzali, Al, 4:102
Ghent, Treaty of, 7:135
ghettos, 4:118
Ghirlandaio, Domenico, portrait by,
    6:*8*
ghosts, 3:163
giants, 3:163; 3:*184–185*; 5:51
Gibbon, Edward, 3:29
gibbons, 1:65, 66, *66*
Gibbs, Michael, 4:112
Gibraltar, 3:163, *163*; 6:174
Gibson, Althea, 1:19; 7:47
Gibson, Josh, 1:120
Gilbert, W. S. (Gilbert and
    Sullivan), 8:99; 5:132
Gillespie, Dizzy, 4:112–113
gin, 1:33
ginger, 6:176, *176*
Ginsburg, Ruth Bader, 8:99; 4:145,
    145; 5:100
Giotto, 8:99; 4:105
    painting by, 8:*99*
giraffes, 3:164, *164*; 2:26
Girl Scouts, 3:164, *164*
Glacier National Park, 5:52, *52*
glaciers, 3:165, *165*; 4:57, 59–60, *59*;
    5:52
    fjords, 3:92
    glacial **lakes**, 4:134, *135*
    ice ages, 4:58, *58*
    and **valleys**, 7:112–113, *114*
gladiators, 2:61; 6:88
Gladstone, William, 6:25
glands, 3:165
    and **hormones**, 4:40, *40*
Glasgow, Scotland, 6:111
glass, 3:166, *166*
    photochromic, 4:191
    prisms, 1:136; 2:91
    recycling of, 6:55, *55*

safety, 1:101
    stained, 6:183, *183*; 2:*22*
glasses, 3:167; 4:150; 5:133
glaucoma, 1:145
Glenn, John, 8:100; 5:127, 128
gliders, 3:167, *167*; 1:27; 3:96, 97
    hang gliders, 4:13, *13*
Global Positioning System (GPS),
    5:87; 7:22
global warming, 3:168, *168*; 2:85,
    110; 3:186
globular star clusters, 6:187
Gloyn Lyn, North Wales, 1:*163*
glucose, 7:17
glue, 3:168; 2:33
gluons, 5:157
gneiss, 6:84, *84*
Goa, 4:73
goats, 3:169, *169*; 1:*14*; 2:39, 166;
    5:*90*
    farming, 3:62
    leather from, 4:146, *146*
    wool from, 7:176
Gobi Desert, 1:88; 2:47; 5:38, 48
goblins, 3:56, *56*
God, 3:169; 2:57; 6:61, 138
    Allah, 4:100–102; 5:76
    Christianity and, 2:54–56
    and **heaven**, 4:22
    and **Hinduism**, 4:30–31
    and **Judaism**, 4:117–118
Goddard, Robert, 6:80
Godey's Lady's Book, 3:66
Goethe, Johann von, 8:100; 3:41;
    5:15
Gogol, Nikolai, 3:41
gold, 3:170, *170*; 1:17
    in Alaska, 1:31
    in Australia, 1:99
    and **banks**, 1:116
    in California, 1:182
    coins, 2:87, *87*; 5:46
    in Colorado, 2:92, 93
    discovery of, 5:137
    as gift to **Jesus**, 2:57
    jewelry, 4:115, *115*
    legends of, 5:77, 97
    mining of, 5:35
    in Nevada, 5:93
    from South America, 2:90
Goldbach, Christian, 5:117

Golden Rule, 3:34

Golding, William, 8:100; 3:29

Goldsmith, Oliver, 3:29

golf, 3:170–171, *170, 171*

Gone With the Wind (movie), 5:*63*

Gonzales, Pancho, 7:47

Gonzalez, Henry B., 4:33

Gonzalez, Rodolfo, 4:33

Goodall, Jane, 8:100–101, *101*

Good Friday, 2:56

Goodman, Benny, 1:*114–115*; 4:65, 112

Goodrich, B. F., 5:127

Goodyear, Miles, 7:109

Goofy (Disney), 2:19

Gorbachev, Mikhail, 8:101; 2:94; 6:168

Gordimer, Nadine, 1:18

Gordy, Berry, 5:25

Gore, Al, 7:*105*

gorges, 7:113, *114*

gorillas, 3:171, *171*; 1:65–66, *65*; 3:47, *48*; 5:*77*; 6:25

Gorman, Carl, 7:181

gospel music, 3:172; 2:53; 6:141, *141*, 178

gospels, 1:131–132, *131*

Gould, Chester, 2:18

Gounod, Charles, 5:15, 132

gout, 6:68

government, 3:172

    Congress, U.S., 2:106–107

    Constitution, U.S., 2:112

    Declaration of Independence, 2:138–139

    democracy, 2:141

    elections and, 2:192

    parliaments of, 5:156

    political parties, 5:185

    presidents, 6:24

    republics, 6:66

    and **revolutions,** 6:68

    and separation of powers, 2:112

    state and local, 6:190

    and **taxes,** 7:34

Goya, Francisco, 8:101

GPS (Global Positioning System), 5:87; 7:22

graffiti, 3:172

Graf, Steffi, 7:*46*

Graham, Rev. Billy, 5:109, 110

Graham, Martha, 8:102, *102*; 2:133; 5:162

Grahame, Kenneth, 2:45

grain, 3:173, *173*, 175

    bread from, 1:157, *157*

    corn, 2:116, *116*

    farming, 3:63, *63, 64*

    rice, 6:70, *70*

    wheat, 7:163, *163*

    whiskey from, 1:33

    winnowing of, 7:*32*

Granada, 6:174

Grand Canyon of the Colorado River (Arizona), 1:81, 82; 2:71; 3:*152*; 4:136, *183*; 5:109; 6:73, 125; 7:98, *98*, 113

Grand Canyon of the Yellowstone River (Wyoming), 7:113, *114*

Grand Coulee Dam, 7:138

Grand Ole Opry, 7:*44*, 45

Granger movement, 4:93

granite, 6:82, *82*

Grant, Ulysses S., 8:102, *102*; 2:68–70; 4:65; 5:127, 128; 7:101, 107, 128

grapes, 7:170, *170*

graphic design, 2:146–147

graphics, 7:176

graphite, 2:10, 40, 171; 3:150

graphs, 3:174, *174*; 6:190

Grass, Günter, 3:41

grasses, 3:175–176, *175, 176*; 3:101, *102*, 173, *173*, 177, *178*; 6:56

    leaves of, 4:147, *147*

    rice, 6:70, *70*

grasshoppers and crickets, 3:176, *176*; 4:86–87

    locusts, 4:166, *166*

grasslands, 3:177–178, *177, 178*

Grateful Dead, 6:81

gravestones, 2:59

gravity, 3:179; 3:117

    center of, 3:179

    force of, 5:157, 168

    and **space exploration,** 6:172

gravure printing, 6:26, *27*

Gray, Robert, 7:137

Great Adventure, Virginia, 1:49

Great Awakening, 8:79

Great Barrier Reef, 2:115; 5:81; 6:125

Great Britain, *see* **British Isles; United Kingdom;** *specific countries*

Greater Antilles, 7:157

Great Lakes, 1:192; 4:66, 134, 135; 7:98

Great Salt Lake, 7:110

"Great Society," 8:131

Great Wall of China, 3:179, *179*; 2:49, 50; 6:125

Greece, 3:180–182, *180, 182*; 3:41

    alphabet, 1:37, *37*

    in **ancient world,** 1:50

    architecture of, 1:74, 75–76

    armor in, 1:85, *85*

    coins of, 2:87, *87*

    and **Cyprus,** 2:130

    democracy and, 2:141

    folk dance in, 3:*106*

    harbor of Skiathos, 6:*10*

    history of, 3:180–182, *182*

    icons from, 4:62

    marathons, 4:184

    medicines in, 2:172

    and **Mediterranean,** 5:16

    Olympic Games in, 5:131, *131*

    Parthenon in, 7:*43*

    slavery in, 6:146, *146*

    statue of Zeus, 6:124, *125*

    theaters in, 7:53, *53*

    Trojan War, 7:82

    wars and warfare, 7:136, 179

Greek and Roman literature, 3:183; 4:26, 64

    Aenead, 1:13

    biography and autobiography, 1:136

    drama, 2:169, *169*

    Iliad, 3:183; 4:26, 64; 5:126

    Odyssey, 3:183; 4:26, 64; 5:126

Greek and Roman mythology, 3:184–185, *184–185*; 3:163; 4:26, 64; 5:77

    art and, 5:142

    monsters in, 5:51

Greek theater, 5:134; 7:53, *53*

Greek chorus, 2:169, *169*

greenbelts, 2:65

greenhouse effect, 3:186, *186*; 3:22, 121, 168

Greenland, 3:187, *187*; 1:78, *78*; 2:71, 144; 3:92; 4:59, 60, 103; 5:108, 109

fjords in, 7:112

Inuit in, 4:91, *91*

Green Mountain Boys, 7:119

green movement, 3:187, *187*; 3:63, 64

in architecture, 1:74

in farming, 1:23; 4:73

Greenpeace, 3:*187*

greenrooms, 7:53

greenstick fractures, 3:127

Greenwich Mean Time (GMT), 7:60

Greenwood, Chester, 4:174

Greer, Germaine, 7:173

Gregory XIII, Pope, 1:181

Grenada, 7:157; 2:95

Grenadines, 7:157, *157*; 2:95

Grieg, Edvard, 2:103

Griffith, D. W., 5:63

Grimaldi, Joseph (Joey the Clown), 2:61

Grimm, Jakob and Wilhelm, 8:103; 2:44, 45; 3:41, 58, 109

Grinnell, George Bird, 1:142; 5:52

griots (storytellers), 1:22, *22*

Gropius, Walter, 1:74, 77

grounding wires, 3:10

groundnuts (peanuts), 5:119, *119*

growth, 3:188, *188*

grubs (larvae), 3:95

Guadalupe Hidalgo, Treaty of (1821), 1:81, 182; 7:109

Guadeloupe, 7:157

Guam, 3:189; 5:121; 6:175; 7:100

Guanches, 2:7

Guangzhou, China, 2:48

Guatemala, 3:189, *189*; 1:129; 2:34–35; 7:*154*

Guernsey, 2:37

guillemots, 2:71, *71*, 186

Guinea, 3:190

guinea pigs, 3:190, *190*; 6:86

guitars, 5:72, *72*

Gujarati Rovers, 5:170

Gulf War (1991), 1:27; 4:95

Gulliver's Travels (Swift), 2:44; 3:29

illustration, 8:*225*

gulls, 1:139, 140; 2:71

gunpowder, 2:8, 21, 50; 3:52; 7:150, 151

guns, 3:190; 2:27; 7:150–151, *150*, 180

cannons, 2:8, *8*

and **tanks**, 7:31, *31*

Gunther, Fritz, 2:148

Guru Granth Sahib, 6:138

gurus, 6:138

Gutenberg, Johann, 8:103; 1:131, 151; 2:50; 6:27

Guthrie, Woody, 3:108; 5:130

Guyana, 3:190; 2:95; 6:164

Guys and Dolls, 5:75

Gwinnett, Button, 2:139

gymnastics, 3:191–192, *191–192*

gymnosperms, 7:78

gypsies, 4:7, *7*; 5:104

gyroscopes, 4:7, *7*; 2:98

Haakon VII, king of Norway, 5:114

habitats, 4:8, *8*

conservation of, 2:109–110

deserts, 2:144–145, *144–145*

ponds, 5:188–189, *188–189*

streams, 7:12–13, *12*, *13*

wetlands, 2:110, *110*; 7:161

Habsburg empire, 1:100; 3:159–160

Hades (Greek god), 3:184, 185

Hadrian's Wall, 3:27; 6:111

Hagia Sofia, Istanbul, 1:73, 177, *177*; 6:125; 7:*86*

Hague, The, Netherlands, 5:92

haiku, 1:90; 5:181

Haile Selassie, 8:103; 6:52

hailstones, 4:8

Haines, Jackson, 4:61

hair, 4:9–10, *9*, *10*

albino, 1:32

animal fur, 3:140, *140*

dreadlocks, 6:52

wigs, 4:15

Haiti, 4:10, *10*; 2:14; 7:157

hajj (pilgrimage), 5:169

Hale, Nathan, 8:103–104; 1:43; 2:108

Haley, Bill, 6:81

halftones, 6:26, *26*

Halicarnassus, Mausoleum of, 6:125, *125*

Halifax, Nova Scotia, 1:189

Halley, Edmond, 8:104; 2:94

Halley's Comet, 2:94

Halloween, 4:11, *11*; 3:163; 4:188; 7:172

halls of fame, 4:12

baseball, 1:118; 5:100; 8:59

basketball, 1:121

bowling, 1:152

country music, 7:45

cowboy, 5:130

football, 3:116; 5:128

rock and roll, 5:128; 6:81

tennis, 6:70

halothane, 1:52

Hamilton, Alexander, 8:104; 1:40; 2:83, 112

Hamilton, Bermuda, 1:130

Hamlisch, Marvin, 5:75

Hammarskjöld, Dag, 8:104–105; 7:95

Hammerstein, Oscar II, 5:75

hammer throw, 7:71, *71*

Hammurabi, Code of, 4:144

Hammurabi, king of Babylon, 5:19

hamsters, 4:12, *12*; 6:86

Hancock, George, 6:156

Hancock, John, 8:105, *105*; 2:138, *139*; 4:189

Handel, George Frideric, 8:105;
1:63; 5:67
Handley Page HP42 (aircraft), 1:*25*
hands, 3:71, *71*
Handy, W. C., 8:106; 1:19, 29, 147;
7:45
hang gliders, 4:13, *13*; 1:27
Hanging Gardens of Babyon, 6:124,
125
Hanna, Mark, 8:162
Hanna-Barbera, 2:19
Hannibal, 8:106; 5:166; 7:85
Hanno (explorer), 3:50
Hansberry, Lorraine, 1:20, 41
Hanukkah, 4:13
Harald V, king of Norway, 5:114
Harappa, 1:50
harbors, *see* **ports and harbors**
Harding, Warren G., 8:106–107, *106*;
5:127, 128; 7:101
hardwood, 7:59, 80
Hardy, Thomas, 3:29
hares, 4:14, *14*; 2:*175*
Hargreaves, Allison, 5:59, *59*
Hargreaves, James, 4:78; 6:178
Harlem Renaissance, 8:122
harmony, 4:14; 5:17, 68
Harpers Ferry, West Virginia, 7:158,
158
Harris, Joel Chandler, 1:40; 3:156
Harrison, Anna, 3:82
Harrison, Benjamin, 8:107–108, *107*;
2:138; 3:82; 5:127, 128; 7:101
Harrison, John, 2:75
Harrison, William Henry, 8:108,
108; 2:138; 3:82; 4:74; 7:101, 128,
135
Hart, Lorenz, 5:75
Harte, Bret, 1:40, 182
harvest, 4:14
harvest festivals, 3:73, 113
Harvey, William, 8:108
Harz mountains, 5:61, *61*
Hass, Robert, 5:182
Hastings, Battle of, 7:136
hats and headdresses, 4:15, *15*
Hausa (language), 1:16
Havana, Cuba, 2:*128*
Havel, Vaclav, 8:109; 2:130

Hawaii, 4:16–17, *17*; 5:187; 7:96,
100, 104, 165
cliffs in, 2:71
Keck telescopes in, 7:40
lava tunnels and caves, 2:29
Mauna Loa in, 5:60, *60*, 61; 7:132,
132
Pearl Harbor in, 2:107; 4:16, 111;
5:159–160, *159*; 7:180
surfing in, 7:20, *20*
volcanoes in, 7:132, *132*, 133
Hawking, Stephen, 8:109, *109*
Hawkins, Coleman, 4:112
hawks, 1:*142*; 6:*123*
Hawthorne, Nathaniel, 8:109–110,
110; 1:40; 4:189; 7:110
Hayden, Palmer, 1:19
painting by, 1:*42*
Haydn, Franz Joseph, 8:110; 2:36;
5:67; 7:28
Hayes, Rutherford B., 8:110–111,
111; 5:127, 128; 7:101
hay fever, 4:17; 5:185
hazelnuts, 5:119
HDTV (high-definition television),
7:41
headaches, 4:17
headdresses, 4:15, *15*
heads, 4:17
ears, 2:175, *175*
eyes, 3:54, *54*
noses, 5:114
and **senses,** 6:123
health, 4:18; 4:44, 56; 5:13, *13*
in **developing countries,** 2:149
and **diets,** 2:151
epidemics, 3:31
and **fitness,** 3:92
food and, 3:111–112, *111*, *112*
mental illness, 5:18
quarantine, 6:41
hearing aids, 2:137, *137*
Hearst, William Randolph, 8:111;
1:182; 6:175
heart attacks, 4:19
hearts, 4:19, *19*; 4:50, *50*
and **blood,** 1:146
cardiac muscles of, 5:66
and **pulse,** 6:35
transplants of, 7:75

valves of, 7:115
heat, 4:20, *20*; 3:20, 78; 5:168; 7:43,
43, 55
cooking with, 2:114
fire, 3:78–79
and **insulation,** 4:88–89
and **pollution,** 5:187
and **power stations,** 6:17
and **radiation,** 6:45–46, *45*
solar power for, 6:158, *158*
thermostats, 7:55, *55*
heathers, 6:136
heating systems, 4:21, *21*
heaven, 4:22; 2:54, 104
Hebrew alphabet, 1:37, *37*
Hebrews, 4:22; 4:117–118; *see also*
Jews; **Judaism**
Hebrides Islands, 6:111
Hector of Troy, 4:26, 64
hedgehogs, 4:22, *22*
hedges, 6:136, *136*
Heidi (Spyri), 2:45
Heimdall (Norse god), 5:107
Heinkel He-178 (aircraft), 1:25; 4:114
Heinlein, Robert, 6:110
Helena, Montana, 5:51
helicopters, 4:23, *23*; 1:27; 5:86;
7:*151*
Heliopolis, 1:50
helium, 4:24; 3:14, 148, *148*
atoms, 1:134
in **balloons and airships,**
1:112–113
hell, 4:24; 2:149
helmets, in **armor,** 1:*54*, 85, *85*; 2:*32*
Helsinki, Finland, 3:78
Hemingway, Ernest, 8:111; 1:40, 41;
4:65; 6:34
hemoglobin, 1:51, 146
Hendrix, Jimi, 6:81
Henry I, king of England, 5:10
Henry II, king of England, 4:97, 125
Henry VII, king of England, 3:26
Henry VIII, king of England, 8:112,
112; 2:60; 3:26; 4:97, 125; 5:46;
6:57
Henry, John, 1:*42, 42*
Henry, Marguerite, 5:189
Henry, O., 5:109, 110

Henry, Patrick, 8:112–113; 1:43; 7:128

Henry the Navigator, 3:50

Henson, Jim, 6:*38*

Henson, Matthew, 8:113; 1:19

Hephaestus (Greek god), 3:185

Hepplewhite, George, 3:141

heptathlons, 7:71

Hepworth, Barbara, **sculpture** by, 6:116, *116*

Hera (Greek goddess), 3:185

heraldry, 4:24–25, *24–25*; 3:26; 4:128
    flags, 3:93

Herbert, George, 3:29

Herbert, Victor, 5:132

herbivores, 1:57; 2:184, 185; 3:94, 114

herbs, 4:25, *25*; 1:39

Hercules, 4:26

heredity, 4:26, *26*
    genetic engineering, 3:150, *150*
    and **genetics,** 3:151, *151*

heretics, 4:26

Hergé (Remi), 2:18

hermaphroditic animals, 4:148; 6:127, 150

Hermes (Greek god), 3:185

Hero (Greek), 6:191

Herod, King, 7:44

Herodotus, 2:187; 3:38, 181, 183

heroes and heroines, 4:26
    medals for, 5:12, *12*
    in **medieval legends,** 5:14–15, *14*
    in **myths and legends,** 5:77
    in *Odyssey*, 5:126

heroin, **addiction** to, 1:11

herons, 1:139

Herschel, William and Caroline, 8:113; 5:174

Hertz, Heinrich, 6:46

hertz (Hz), 3:7; 6:45, 161

Herzegovina, *see* **Bosnia and Herzegovina**

Hesiod, 3:183

Hess, Victor, 2:117

Hesse, Hermann, 8:113–114; 3:41

heterosexuals, 6:128

Heyerdahl, Thor, 8:114; 3:50

hibernation, 4:27, *27*; 2:88; 6:152; 7:134

Hickok, James B. "Wild Bill," 8:114; 1:42; 4:65, 120; 6:167

Hicks, Edward, *Noah's Ark* by, 1:*132*

hieroglyphics, 4:28, *28, 29*; 1:105; 2:187; 4:34; 5:9; 7:183

highland guan, 3:19

highlife (music), 1:21

highways, *see* **roads and highways**

Hijuelos, Oscar, 4:33

Hillary, Edmund, 8:114

Hillier, Lejaren, 3:11

Himalayas, 4:29, *29*; 1:88, 103, 130, 160; 4:70, 71; 5:60, *60*, 61, 90, *90*; 7:57, *127*

Hinduism, 4:30–31, *30–31*; 3:73–74, 169; 6:61–62, *62*, 102
    and **ethics,** 3:34
    funerals in, 3:139
    and **Ganges,** 3:146
    in **India,** 4:71, 72, 73, 76
    initiation ceremonies in, 4:85
    monasteries, 5:45–46
    and **music,** 4:75
    in **Nepal,** 5:90
    pilgrimages of, 5:169
    reincarnation, 6:60
    temples of, 7:43–44, *44*

Hindu Kush, 1:14

Hines, Earl "Fatha," 4:112

Hinton, S. E., 2:45

Hippocrates, 8:114–115, *115*; 5:13

hippopotamuses, 4:32, *32*; 6:72

Hirohito, emperor of Japan, 8:115, *115*

Hiroshige, Ando, wood-block print by, 6:*28*

Hiroshima, 4:32, 111; 5:159; 7:181

Hispanics, 4:32–34, *33*; 7:99

Hispaniola, 7:157

histograms, 3:174, *174*; 6:190

history, 4:34
    African, 1:17–18
    ancient world, 1:50
    art, 3:77
    European, 3:38–40
    United States, 7:102–105
    world, timeline of, 9:12–17
    see also **Dark Ages; Middle Ages;** *specific states and countries*

History of Plimouth Plantation (Bradford), 1:40

Hitchcock, Alfred, 5:63

Hitler, Adolf, 8:115–116, *116*; 2:150; 3:66, 160, *160*; 5:87; 7:70, 179–181

Hittites, 4:34

HIV (human immuno-deficiency virus), 1:23, *23*; 2:158

Hobbit, The (Tolkien), 2:45
    illustration, 8:*231*

hobgoblins, 3:56

Ho Chi Minh, 8:116, *116*; 7:124

hockey, field, 4:35, *35*

hockey, ice, 4:35–36, *35, 36*

Hockney, David, painting by, 5:*146*

Hodgkin, Dorothy, 8:117

Hoffmann, E. T. A., 3:41

Hokusai, 8:117
    print by, 8:*117*

holdfast, 6:121

Holiday, Billie, 1:19, 147; 4:114, *115*

holidays, *see* **festivals and holidays**

Holland, *see* **Netherlands**

Holland, John, 7:15

Holliday, Doc, 1:81

Holly, Buddy, 6:81

Hollywood, 4:36, *36*; 1:182
    movies in, 5:62–64, *62, 63*

Holi (spring festival), 3:74

Holmes, Oliver Wendell, Jr., 4:145, 189

Holmes, Oliver Wendell, Sr., 1:40; 4:189

Holocaust, 4:37; 2:103; 4:7, 118; 5:87; 6:43

holograms, 4:37, *37*; 4:141

Holst, Gustav, 3:108

Holy Land, 5:148, 169

Holy Roman Empire, birth of, 3:159

homeopathy, 1:39; 5:13

Homer, 8:117; 3:183; 4:64; 5:126; 7:82

Homer, Winslow, 8:118; 3:144; 4:189
    paintings by, 3:*145*; 5:*145*; 8:*118*

home range, of animals, 4:8

Homo erectus, 3:48, *49*

Homo habilis, 3:48, *48*

Homo sapiens, **evolution** of, 3:47–49, *48–49*
homosexuals, 6:128
Honduras, 4:38; 2:34–35; 5:9, *9*
honey, 4:38, *38*; 7:17
honeybees, 1:126; 4:38
honeycombs, 4:38, *38*
Hong Kong, 4:39, *39*; 2:51; 7:94
  airport, 1:29
  monsoons in, 5:50
Honolulu, Hawaii, 4:16, *17*
Honshu, Japan, 4:110
Hood, Mount, 5:*137*
Hooke, Robert, 8:118–119; 2:75
Hooker, Joseph, 2:69
Hoover Dam, 2:*131*; 7:98
Hoover, Herbert, 8:119–120, *119*; 3:82; 4:93
Hoover, J. Edgar, 8:120; 3:69
Hoover, Lou, 3:82
Hopkins, Gerard Manley, 3:29
Hopkinson, Francis, 2:99
Hopper, Edward, 8:120–121
  painting by, 8:*120*
hops, 4:40; 1:125
Horace, 3:77, 183
hormones, 4:40, *40*; 1:146; 5:91
  and **glands,** 3:165
  in **metamorphosis,** 5:21, *21*
  and **proteins,** 6:31
  and **puberty,** 6:33
Hornbook, 2:45
horns and antlers, 4:41, *41*; 1:149; 2:26, *26, 140*
  reindeer, 6:60, *60*
  rhinoceroses, 6:68, *68*
horoscopes, 1:92
horse collars, 1:22; 2:50
horses, 4:42–43, *42–43*; 4:122, *122*
  in battles, 2:27, *27*
  and **cowboys,** 2:120, *120*
  domestication of, 2:165–166
  and **polo,** 5:187
  ponies, 5:189, *189*
  prehistoric, 6:*18*
  ranches, 6:52, *52*
  show-jumping, 6:134, *134*
Horseshoe Bend, Battle of, 1:30
hospitals, 4:44, *44*; 5:13
  doctors in, 2:161

electronics used in, 3:12
  nurses in, 5:118
  surgeons in, 7:21, *21*
Hottentots, 6:162
Houdin, Robert, 4:173
Houdini, Harry, 4:173, *173*
hourglasses, 2:*75*
House of Representatives, *see*
  Congress, U.S.
housing, 4:45–46, *45, 46*
  in ancient Greece, 3:*182*
  Anglo-Saxon, 1:53
  architecture, 1:*77*
  Chinese, 2:48, 50
  in **cities,** 2:63, *63,* 64
  and **Civil Rights Movement,** 2:66
  heating systems in, 4:21, *21*
  in **Mongolia,** 5:*48*
  Native American tepees, 5:*84*
  roofs, 1:170
  yurts, 3:*178*
Houston, Sam, 8:121; 7:49
hoverflies, 3:95, *95*
Howe, Elias, 8:121; 4:189; 6:126–127
Howe, Julia Ward, 5:100
Howells, William Dean, 1:40
Hoyle, Edmond, 2:11
Hoyle's Rules, 2:11
HPAs (human powered aircraft), 1:27
HPV (human-powered vehicle), 1:133, *133*
Huang He (Yellow River), 1:50, 88, 89; 2:49; 3:98; 6:73, 74
Hubble, Edwin, 8:122
Hubble space telescope, 6:106, 169, 172; 7:40; 8:122
Hubble's Law, 8:122
Huckleberry Hound, 2:19
Hudson, Henry, 8:122, *122*; 5:99; 7:103
Hudson's Bay Company, 1:190
Hughes, Charles Evans, 4:145; 5:100
Hughes, Langston, 8:122–123; 1:20, 41
Hughes, Ted, 5:182
Hugo, Victor, 8:123; 3:41
Huguenots, 4:47; 3:130; 6:59
human beings, 4:47
  behavior of, 1:56
  communication of, 2:96

eating disorders of, 2:180
evolution of, 3:47–49, *47, 48–49*
population of, 5:191–192, *191, 192*
and **primates,** 6:25
study of, 1:63
human body, 4:48–51
  acids in, 1:11
  arteries of, *19*; 4:19
  blood, 1:146, *146*
  bones, 1:149, *149*
  brains, 1:154–155, *155*; 4:17, 51, *51*
  breathing, 1:158
  cells in, 2:30
  chiropractic for, 1:39
  circulatory system, 4:50, *50*
  colds and coughs, 2:88
  decoration of, 2:117, *117*
  digestive system, 2:152, *152*; 4:49, *49*
  excretory system, 4:50, *50*
  feet and hands, 3:71, *71*
  first aid for, 3:81, *81*
  fitness of, 3:92
  glands, 3:165
  head, 4:17
  heart, 4:19, *19*
  hormones, 4:40, *40*
  immune system, 4:68
  kidneys, 4:50, *50,* 124
  liver, 4:160, *160*
  lungs, 4:168, *168*
  muscles, 5:66
  nervous system, 4:51, *51*; 5:91, *91*
  noses, 5:114
  oxygen in, 1:51
  puberty, 6:33
  pulse, 6:35, *35*
  reproductive system, 4:51, *51*
  respiratory system, 4:49, *49*; 6:67, *67*
  senses of, 6:123
  sex and sexuality, 6:127–128, *128*
  skeleton and muscular system, 4:48, *48*; 6:142, *142*
  skin, 6:143, *143*
  stomach, 7:7, *7*
  surgery on, 7:21, *21*
  teeth, 7:36–37, *37*

tonsils, 7:63
voice, 7:131, *131*
water in, 7:143
human immuno-deficiency virus
    (HIV), 1:23, *23*; 2:158
human rights, 4:52; 6:43
Humboldt, Alexander von,
    8:123–124, *123*
hummingbirds, 1:138, *138*, 139, 140;
    2:186
Humperdinck, Engelbert, 5:132
Humphrey, Doris, 2:133
Humphrey, Hubert, 5:36
humus, 6:157, *157*
Hundred Years' War (1337–1453),
    3:26; 7:136
Hungary, 4:52–53, *53*; 6:168;
    7:177–178, 179
hunter-gatherers, 4:53, *53*; 1:9, 175;
    6:21, 39, 162
hurdling, 7:70–71
Hurley, Frank, 1:61
Huron, Lake, 4:135
hurricanes, 4:54, *54*; 1:116
Hurston, Zora Neale, 1:20, 41
Hussein, king of Jordan, 4:116
Hussein, Saddam, 4:95
Hutchinson, Anne, 6:69
Huxley, Aldous, 3:29; 8:124
Huxley, Thomas, 8:124; 3:45
Huygens, Christian, 8:124; 2:75
hybrids, 5:136
hydraulics, 4:54, *54*
    in **brakes**, 1:155, *155*
    cranes, 2:123
    in **elevators**, 3:17, *17*
hydrocarbons, 2:10
hydrochloric acid, 1:11
hydroelectric power, 4:55, *55*; 2:131,
    188
    power stations, 3:9; 6:16–17, *17*
hydrogen, 3:14, 148
    in atoms, 1:95, 96, 134
    in balloons and airships, 1:112,
        113
hydrogen bomb (H-bomb), 1:96, 149
hydroplanes, 7:14
hydrosphere, 3:30
hydrotherapy, 1:39
hyenas, 4:55, *55*

hygiene, 4:56; 4:18
hymns, 4:56; 8:244
    Bay Psalm Book, 1:40
hypnosis, 4:56; 1:39
hypothermia, 4:56; 2:88
Hyracotherium, 4:42, *42*

Ibert, Jacques, 2:36
Ibn Batuta, 4:102
Ibn Sina, 4:102
Ibsen, Henrik, 3:41
ice, 4:57, *57*
    Antarctica, 1:60–61
    Arctic, 1:78, *78*
    asteroids, 1:91
    and **erosion**, 3:33
    frost, 3:135, *135*
    glaciers, 3:165, *165*
    hailstones, 4:8
    in harbors, 3:*187*
    in **refrigerators**, 6:58
    and **snow**, 6:153, *153*
ice ages, 4:58, *58*; 1:38; 2:28; 3:92,
    165; 6:107
icebergs and ice caps, 4:59–60, *59*,
    60; 3:165; 5:125
ice climbing, 5:59
ice fishing, 3:89
ice hockey, 4:35–36, *35*, *36*
Iceland, 4:61, *61*; 3:92; 6:*82*, 107
    literature of, 3:41
    mosses in, 5:*56*
    parliament of, 5:156

ice skating, 4:61–62, *61*, *62*; 4:57;
    7:170
I Ching (The Book of Changes), 1:90;
    2:104
ichthyosaurs, 3:124
Ichthyostega, 3:44–45
icons, 4:62, *62*; 1:177; 2:56, 59; 7:26
Idaho, 4:63–64, *63*, *64*; 7:100
ideograms, 7:183, *183*
idiom, 3:27, 28
Iditarod Trail Sled Dog Race, 1:31
igneous rocks, 6:82–83, *82*
Iguanadon, 2:155
iguanas, 7:165
Iliad, 4:64; 3:183; 4:26; 5:126
Illinois, 4:65–66, *65*, *66*; 2:116; 7:100
illuminated manuscripts, 4:66;
    1:*150*, 151, *181*; 2:*21*, 22, *52*;
    3:*130*, 172; 5:*28*
Imhotep, 5:13
immersive systems, 7:130
immigration, 4:67–68, *67*; 5:31, 99,
    100, 109, 110, 111; 6:59
    to British Isles, 2:95
    and **passports**, 5:158
    to **United States**, 7:104
immune system, human, 4:68
immunity, 4:68; 3:161
    and **transplants**, 7:75
    and **vaccinations**, 7:111
impalas, 1:62, *62*; 3:*178*
impeachment, 8:130
imports, 7:73
Impressionists, 5:144, *145*, 146
impressment, 7:135
inaugurations, 7:100
Incas, 4:69, *69*; 1:50, 148; 2:109;
    5:82, 164; 6:77
inchworms, 2:22
incinerators, 7:77
incisors, 7:36, *36*, *37*
income tax, 2:112; 7:34
incubation, 2:186
indenture, 4:67
India, 4:70–73, *70*, *71*, *72*; 1:88;
    7:177–178
    Bharatpur marshes, 7:161
    Buddhism, 1:*166*, 167
    colonial, 3:40
    and the Commonwealth, 2:95

dance in, 2:132–33, *132*
Ganges in, 3:146; 3:139
Hinduism in, 4:30–31, *30–31*;
 4:71, 72, 73, 76
irrigation in, 4:99
literature, 1:90
monsoons in, 5:50, *50*
music of, 4:75, 113
myths and legends of, 4:76, *76*;
 4:30–31, *30*
and **Pakistan**, 5:147
partition of, 4:73
people of, 4:71, *115*
puppets in, 6:38
sculpture of, 6:*114*, 115
Sikhism in, 6:138
Taj Mahal in, 4:*71*, 73
Varanasi, 5:169
vegetarians in, 7:117
villages in, 7:127
Indiana, 4:74–75, *74*; 7:100
Indianapolis 500 ("Indy 500"), 1:103,
 103
Indian music, 4:75; 4:113
Indian myths and legends, 4:76, *76*;
 4:30–31, *30*
Indian Ocean, 5:8, 122, *125*
indicators (chemistry), 1:11
Indo-China, 7:124
 French colonies in, 3:132
Indonesia, 4:77, *77*; 1:88, 151; 4:*53*;
 5:121, 152; 6:*70*; 7:51
induction, cooking by, 7:11
Indurain, Miguel, 2:129
Indus River, 1:50; 4:70; 5:147
industrial design, 2:146–147
Industrial Revolution, 4:78, *78*;
 2:119; 3:39; 4:189; 7:91, *92*
children working in, 2:44
and **mass production**, 4:190
and **socialism**, 6:156
steam engines and, 6:191, *191*
industry, 4:78, 79–80, *79*, *80*
factories, 3:56, *56*
and **labor unions**, 4:133
and **land use**, 4:138
mass production in, 4:190
inertial navigation, 5:87
infamy, 5:160
infantile paralysis, 5:184–185
infantry units, army, 1:84

infinity, 4:81, *81*
inflation, 2:183
influenza, 4:81; 3:31
information technology, 4:82–83,
 82, *83*; 7:176
computers, 2:100–102
fax machines, 3:68, *68*
Internet, 4:90, *90*
lasers, 4:140–141
infrared telescopes, 7:40
infrastructure, 7:75
infringement, **trademark**, 7:74
initiation ceremonies, 4:84–85, *84*,
 85
ink:
 drawings, 2:170, *171*
 squid, 6:182
innate behavior, 4:88
Innsbruck, Austria, 1:100
Inquisition, 6:174
insects, 4:86–87, *86–87*; 4:92; 7:149
ants, 1:64, *64*
beetles, 1:127, *127*
biological control of, 5:153
bugs, 1:168
butterflies, 1:176, *176*
camouflage of, 1:186, *186*
cockroaches, 2:85
in **deserts**, 2:145
and **disease**, 2:158
dragonflies, 2:167, *167*
eyes of, 3:54, *54*
fireflies, 3:80, *80*
fleas, 3:94
flies, 3:95, *95*
flight of, 3:95, 96
grasshoppers and crickets, 3:176,
 176
larvae of, 4:87, 140
lice, 4:153, *153*
locusts, 4:166, *166*
metamorphosis of, 5:21, *21*
moths, 5:57
nests of, 5:92
and **parasites**, 5:153
as pollinators, 3:104, *104*
and **ponds**, 5:188, *188*
pupae of, 6:37, *37*
stick, 6:192, *192*
in stream habitats, 7:12–13, *12*, *13*
wasps, 7:142, *142*

instinct, 4:88
 migration, 5:31
insulation, 4:88–89, *88–89*; 3:70, *70*,
 138
insulators (electricity), 3:7
insulin, injection of, 2:*150*
insurance, 4:89
Intel Corporation, 2:102
intelligence, 4:89; 1:155
Intelsat, 6:106
intercourse, sexual, 6:128
interior designers, 2:146
Internal Revenue Service (IRS), 7:34
International Court of Justice,
 4:144–145
International Date Line, 7:61
international law, 4:143
Internet, 4:90, *90*; 2:96; 4:83
Interpol, 5:184
intertidal zone, 6:119, *119*
intestines, 2:*152*; 1:66
Intolerable Acts (1774), 1:44; 2:138
Inuit, 4:91, *91*; 1:30, 31, 78, 190;
 3:187; 4:53; 5:104
inventors, 4:92; 5:158; 7:37, 38, 39,
 40, 42, 104
invertebrates, 4:92, *92*; 1:57; 3:44,
 71; 6:119; 7:159
amoebas, 1:*47*
centipedes, 2:*33*
coral, 2:*115*
crustaceans, 2:*127*
earthworms, 2:179, *179*
insects, 4:86-87
jellyfish, 4:113, *113*
leeches, 4:148, *148*
millipedes, 5:*32*
mollusks, 5:44, *44*
scorpions, 6:110, *110*
sea anemones, 6:65, 116, *116*
and **skeletons**, 6:142
slugs and snails, 6:*67*, 150, *150*
spiders, 6:177, *177*
sponges, 6:179, *179*
squid, 6:182, *182*
starfish, 6:185, *185*
tapeworms, 7:33, *182*
worms, 7:182
ionosphere, 1:94
ions, 1:95
Iowa, 4:93–94, *93*; 2:116; 7:100

IQ (Intelligence Quotient), 4:89
Iqbal, Muhammad, 1:90
IRA (Irish Republican Army), 5:112;
    7:48
Iran, 4:94, *94*; 1:84; 4:131; 5:30; 7:87
    Bahaism in, 1:108
    mosaic in, 5:54
    mosques in, 5:55, *55*
    revolutions, 6:68
Iraq, 4:95; 1:84; 4:131, 132; 5:30
    Gulf War, 1:27
    and Mesopotamia, 5:19, *19*
Ireland, Republic of, 4:95–97, *96*;
    3:41; 7:94
    Celts in, 2:31–32
    coast of, 2:*84*
    in the Commonwealth, 2:95
    famine in, 3:60, 139
Irish Republican Army (IRA), 5:112;
    7:48
iron (dietary), and anemia, 1:51
iron and steel, 4:98, *98*; 1:36; 5:20,
    20
    bridges of, 1:160, *161*
    discovery of, 6:23
    magnets, 4:173–174, *174*
    recycling, 6:55
    rusting of, 5:139
Iron Age, 6:23
Iron Curtain, 2:88
Irrawaddy River, 5:76
irrigation, 4:99, *99*; 1:22; 5:119
    in ancient world, 1:50
    canals for, 1:191
    and drought, 2:172
Irtysh River, Russia, 6:74
Irving, Washington, 8:124–125;
    1:40; 5:100
Isaacs, Jorge, 4:141
Isaacson, Leonard, 3:11
Isis, 2:190, *190*
Islam, 4:100–102, *100–101, 102*;
    3:169; 5:30, 76; 6:61–62, *62*
    in Africa, 1:16, 17, *17*, 18, 34
    and alcohol, 1:33
    Arabs and, 1:69
    architecture of, 1:73, 76
    and crusades, 2:126
    eid in, 2:191; 3:74, *74*
    in Europe, 3:38

festivals and holidays, 3:73–74,
    74
Five Pillars of, 4:100–101
funerals in, 3:139
in India, 4:72, 73
initiation ceremonies of, 4:84
in Iran, 4:94
in Iraq, 4:95
Koran of, 1:*150*; 2:191; 4:130
law of, 5:147
in Lebanon, 4:148
mosques of, 1:*17*; 5:55, *55*
pilgrimages of, 5:169
prophets of, 6:30
in Saudi Arabia, 6:107
see also Muhammad; Muslims
Islamabad, Pakistan, 5:147
islands, 4:103
    Caribbean, 2:13–14
    Hawaii, 4:16–17, *17*
    Indonesia, 4:77, *77*
    Japan, 4:109–111
    Madagascar, 4:171, *171*
    New Zealand, 5:101
    Oceania, 5:121, *121*
    West Indies, 7:157, *157*
Isle of Man, 7:90
isotopes, 1:96; 3:14
Israel, 4:103, *103*; 1:50; 4:116, 118,
    148; 5:30
    flag, 3:93
    kibbutzim in, 4:124
    Knesset of, 5:156
    and Palestine, 5:148
Istanbul, Turkey, 5:139; 7:86, *86*
    architecture in, 1:76
    as Byzantium, 1:177; 2:*54*
    Hagia Sofia in, 1:73, 177, *177*;
    6:125
Italy, 4:104–105, *104*; 3:41
    cathedrals in, 6:64, *64*
    Etruscans in, 3:35
    fascism in, 3:66
    frescoes in, 3:133, *133*
    Leaning Tower of Pisa, 6:125
    and Libya, 4:153
    literature of, 3:41
    medieval legends of, 5:14
    and Mediterranean, 5:16
    in Middle Ages, 5:27
    pasta in, 5:158, *158*

Ponte Vecchio in, 1:*160*
    Renaissance in, 6:63–64, *63, 64*
    in World War I, 7:177–178
    in World War II, 7:179–181
Ivan the Terrible, 8:125, *125*; 6:97
Ives, Charles, 8:125; 3:11; 5:67
ivory, 4:106; 3:15, *15*, 16
Ivory Coast, 4:106

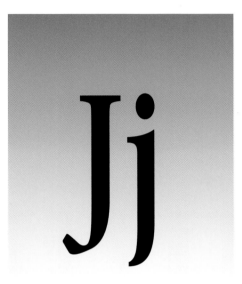

jackals, 4:106, *106*
jack-o'-lanterns, 4:11
jackrabbits, 4:14, *14*
Jackson, Andrew, 8:126,*126*; 1:30;
    3:99; 4:167; 5:109, 110, 185; 7:45,
    101, 135
Jackson, Jesse, 1:19, 20; 2:66; 6:165
Jackson, Mahalia, 1:19; 3:172
Jackson, Michael, 6:81
Jackson, Mississippi, 5:39
Jackson, Thomas "Stonewall",
    8:126; 2:68, 69; 7:107, 158
Jacobites, 7:91
jaguars, 4:107, *107*
Jahan, Shah, Taj Mahal of, 4:*71*, 73
jails, 6:29, *29*
Jains of India, 7:117
Jakarta, Indonesia, 4:77
Jamaica, 4:107; 2:95; 7:157
    independence of, 2:14
    Rastafarians in, 6:52, *52*
    reggae in, 6:60, *60*; 6:52
jamborees, Scout, 1:153, *153*
James I, king of England, 6:111
James II, king of England, 3:27; 7:91

James VI, king of England, 3:27
James, Henry, 1:40, 41; 5:100
James, Jesse, 8:126–127, *127*; 1:42; 3:146; 5:41
James, William, 5:100
Jamestown, 4:108, *108*; 7:56
Janamashtami, 3:74
Janssen, Zacharias, 5:26
Japan, 4:109–111, *110, 111*; 1:88, 89; 3:*63*
   Akashi-Kaikyo bridge in, 1:161
   alphabet, 1:37
   architecture of, 1:*77*
   armor in, 1:*85*
   atomic bombs dropped on, 1:96; 5:159
   and **China**, 2:52
   clothing of, 2:*79*
   drama in, 4:188, *188*
   flag, 3:93
   gardens in, 3:147, *147*
   Hiroshima, 4:32, 109, 111
   history of, 4:111
   kabuki theater in, 2:*117*
   literature, 1:90
   medals of, 5:12, *12*
   monsoons in, 5:50
   pottery of, 6:13
   printing in, 6:27
   printmaking in, 6:28, *28*
   puppets in, 6:38
   royal family of, 4:126
   Shintoism in, 6:131
   stock exchange in, 6:192
   territories of, 5:113, 165
   war with **China**, 4:111
   in **World War I**, 7:177–178
   in **World War II**, 1:96; 2:52, 107; 4:16, 32, 111; 7:179–181, *180*
Japanese beetles, 1:127
Jarre, Jean-Michel, 3:11
Jarrett, Keith, 4:112, 113
Jason, 4:26
javelin throw, 7:71, *71*
Jawara, Dawda, 3:144
Jay, John, 8:127; 1:40, 45; 4:145; 5:100
jazz, 4:112–113, *112–113*; 5:68
   and **blues**, 1:147
   in New Orleans, 4:168
   singing, 6:141

Jazz Singer, The (movie), 5:64, 76
jeans, 2:*79*
Jeddah, Saudi Arabia, 6:107, *107*
Jefferson, Thomas, 8:127–128, *128*; 1:45; 2:138, *139*; 3:82; 4:152; 5:185; 6:167; 7:101, 102, 128, 139
Jefferson City, Missouri, 5:41
Jefferson Memorial, 7:140, *141*
jellyfish, 4:113, *113*; 5:91; 6:116, *116*; 7:118
Jenner, Edward, 8:128
Jennings, Waylon, 2:119
Jericho, 1:50; 5:148
Jerusalem, 2:56; 4:*102, 103*, 116, *118*
   and **Crusades**, 2:126; 5:28, 105
   Dome of the Rock in, 1:73; 5:55, 148
   pilgrimages to, 5:169
   Western Wall in, 7:44
Jesuit monks, 5:46
Jesus, 8:128–129; 1:*177*; 2:54–56, *54*; 3:73, 74; 4:*62*, 100; 5:169, 190; 6:30, 61–62, 102
   apostles of, 1:66; 2:54
   baptism of, 2:55
   in the **Bible**, 1:131
   birth of, 2:57, *57*; 5:148
   death of, 2:54
   resurrection of, 2:180
   teachings of, 2:54, 56
jet engines, 4:114, *114*; 1:24, 26, 27; 3:96–97
jewelry, 4:115, *115*; 3:150, *150*
   beans used in, 1:123
   gold, 3:170
   pearls, 5:160, *160*
Jews, 4:22, 117–118
   Bar/Bat Mitzvah of, 4:85, 118
   in **concentration camps**, 2:103, *103*; 5:87
   diaspora of, 4:118
   persecution of, 3:160
   prejudice against, 5:87
   refugees, 6:59
   see also **Hebrews**; **Judaism**; **Moses**
"Jim Crow" laws, 2:65; 5:40
Jimmu, emperor of Japan, 4:111
Joan of Arc, 8:129; 3:130; 4:26; 6:102
jobs, affirmative action in, 2:66
Johanson, Donald, 3:48

John XXIII, Pope, 5:190
John of the Cross, St., 3:41
John Paul II, Pope, 8:129; 5:*190*
Johnson, Andrew, 8:130, *130*; 1:30; 5:109, 110; 7:45, 101
Johnson, James Weldon, 8:130–131; 1:19; 3:99
Johnson, Lyndon B., 8:131, *131*; 7:49, 101, 124
Johnson, Magic, 1:121
Johnson, Philip, 1:77
Johnson, Robert, 1:147
Johnson, Samuel, 8:131–132, *132*; 2:151; 3:29; 5:16
Johnson, Walter, 1:120
Johnson Memorial Tunnel, Colorado, 7:85
Johnstown Flood, 3:98; 5:163
John the Baptist, St., 2:55; 6:30
joints, 6:68, *142*
jokers, 2:11
jokes, in **cartoons and comics**, 2:17–18
Joliet, Louis, 4:65, 93; 5:41; 7:103
Jolson, Al, 5:76
Jonah and the whale, 1:132
Jones, Chipper, 1:*119*
Jones, Elvin, 4:112
Jones, John Paul, 8:132, *132*
Jonson, Ben, 3:29
Joplin, Janis, 6:81
Joplin, Scott, 8:133; 1:19
Jordan, 4:116, *116*; 4:126; 5:30, 148
Jordan, Michael, 1:19, 20, 121
Jorvik, 7:125
Joseph, Chief, 8:133, *133*; 4:63; 5:136
Joseph (father of **Jesus**), 2:57
joules, 3:20
journals, 4:172, *172*
jousting, 2:*52*
Joyce, James, 8:133–134; 3:29
Joyner-Kersee, Jackie, 1:19; 3:*20*
Judah Maccabee, 4:13
Judaism, 4:117–118, *117, 118*; 3:169; 4:22; 5:30; 6:61–62
   festivals and holidays, 3:73–74, *74*
   funerals in, 3:139
   Hanukkah, 4:13
   and Old Testament, 1:131

Passover, **5:**157
prophets of, **6:**30
synagogues in, **7:**28, *28*
temples of, **7:**43–44
see also Jews; **Hebrews; Moses**
Judiciary Act (1789), **4:**144
judo, 4:119; **4:**186
Judson, Whitcombe, **7:**191
jugglers, **5:**37
jujitsu, **4:**186
Julia, Raul, **4:**33
Julian, Percy, **1:**20
Julian, St., **5:**15
Julius Caesar: *see* **Caesar, Julius**
Jung, C. G., 8:134
Jungle Book, The (Kipling), **2:**45; **3:**55;
    illustration of, **8:***141*
junks, **6:**100, *101*
Jupiter, **5:**171–174, *173*; **6:**159, *159,*
    160, 170, 171
Just, Ernest, **1:**19
Justinian, **1:***177*
Jutes, **1:**53

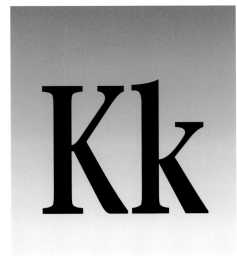

K2 (mountain), **4:**29; **5:**147
Kafka, Franz, 8:134; **3:**41
Kafkaesque, **8:**134
Kahlo, Frida, 8:135, *134–135*
Kalahari Desert, **1:**16, 151, 175;
    2:145; **5:**78
Kamehameha I, king of Hawaii, **4:**16
Kampuchea, People's Republic of,
    1:183
Kandinsky, Wassily, 8:135

painting by, **8:***135*
Kane, Paul, painting by, **5:***84*
Kanem, **2:**36
kangaroos, 4:119, *119*; **4:**178, *185*
Kansas, 4:119–120, *120*; **2:**67; **7:***66,*
    100
Kansas City, Missouri, **5:**41, 42
Kansas-Nebraska Act (1854), **2:**67
karate, 4:121; **4:**186
Karenga, Maulana, **4:**132
karma, **6:**60
Karsavina, Tamara, **1:**111
Kashmir, **4:**71
Kasparov, Gary, **2:**41
Kathina Day, **3:**73
Katsina, Emir of, **5:***102*
Kaufman, George S., **5:**75
Kaunda, Kenneth, **7:**189
Kay, John, **4:**78
kayaks, **2:**9, *9*
Kazakhstan, 4:121; **1:**88–89; **6:**168
Kearny, Stephen W., **5:**97
Keats, John, 8:135; **3:**29
Keita, Salif, **6:***140*
Keller, Helen, 8:136, *136*; **1:**29
Kellogg, W. W., **3:**173
Kelly, Gene, **5:**76
Kelly, Grace, **5:**44
Kelly, Ned, **3:**146
Kelly, Walt, **2:**18
Kelvin, William, 8:136
Kelvin scale, **7:**43
kendo, **4:**186, *186*
Kennedy, Anthony, **4:***145*
Kennedy, Jacqueline, **3:**82, *83*
Kennedy, John F., 8:136–137,
    136–137; **2:**33; **3:**82; **4:**189; **5:**158;
    7:101
kente cloth, **3:***162*
Kentucky, 4:122–123, *122*; **2:**81;
    7:100
Kenya, 4:123, *123*; **2:**95; **5:***104,* 156
Kenya, Mount, **1:**15
Kenyatta, Jomo, 8:137, *137*; **4:**123
Kepler, Johannes, 8:138
keratin, **5:**77
Kern, Jerome, **5:**75
kernels, **5:**119
kerosene, **5:**129
kestrels, **1:**140
Kevlar, **5:**177

Key, Francis Scott, 8:138; **4:**186;
    6:189
keyboard instruments, **5:**74, *74*
keyhole surgery, **7:**21
Keynes, John Maynard, **2:**183
keystones, **1:**72–73, *73*
Khartoum, Sudan, **7:**16
Khayyam, Omar, **5:**30
Khmer people, **1:**183
Khmer Rouge, **1:**183
Khomeini, Ayatollah, **4:**94, 101; **6:**68
Khrushchev, Nikita, 8:138–139, *138*;
    3:83
Khrushchev, Nina, **3:***83*
Khufu (Cheops), **6:**40
Khyber Pass, **1:**14
kibbutz, 4:124; **4:**103
Kidd, Captain (William), **5:**170
kidneys, 4:124, *124*; **4:**50, *50*
Kiel Canal, **1:**192
Kiev, Ukraine, **7:**89
Kilimanjaro, Mount, **1:**15; **7:***32,* 82
Killander, Maj. Ernst, **5:**138
kilns (wood), **7:**174
kilohertz (kHz), **6:**45, 47
kilojoules, **3:**110
Kilwa, Africa, **1:**17
kindling, **3:**78
kinetic energy, **3:**20
King, B. B., **5:**39
King, Martin Luther, Jr., 8:139–140,
    140; **1:**19, 20; **2:**66; **3:**156
King, Thomas J., **2:**76; **5:**85
King and I, The, **7:**52
kings and queens, 4:125–126, *126*
    feudal system, 3:75
    palaces of, **5:**147–148, *147, 148*
Kings Island, Ohio, **1:**49
Kingsley, Mary, 8:140, *140*
Kingston, Jamaica, **4:**107
Kipling, Rudyard, 8:141; **2:**45; **3:**29,
    55
    illustration by, **8:***141*
Kiribati, **2:**95; **5:**121
Kiswahili language, **1:**16
kitchen ranges (stoves), **7:**11, *11*
kites, 4:127, *127*
kiwis, **1:**143
Kleban, Edward, **5:**75
knights, 4:128, *128*; **2:**27; **3:**75;
    5:27–29, *28*

armor of, 1:85, *85*
Arthurian legends, 1:86–87, *86*
chivalry, 2:52, *52*
crusades of, 2:126
heraldry of, 4:24–25, *24–25*
horses of, 4:42
Knights Hospitaller, castles of, 2:*20*, 126
Knights of the Round Table, 1:86–87, *86*
Knights Templar, 2:126
knitting, 4:128; 7:51
knots, 4:129, *129*
Know-Nothings, 8:86
Knox, John, 8:141, *141*
koalas, 4:130, *130*; 4:178, *185*
Kobe, Japan, earthquake in, 2:179
Kobo, Abe, 1:90
Koko the Clown, 2:18
Konigsburg, E. L., 2:45
Kon-Tiki, 8:114
Kooris (Aborigines), 1:9
Koran, 4:130; 1:*150*; 2:191; 4:*84*, 100–102, *101*; 5:37, 55; 6:*62*
Korea, 1:88; 4:111, 131; 5:113; *see also* **North Korea; South Korea**
Korean War, 4:131; 2:88; 6:168; 7:136
Kossuth, Lajos, 4:52
kotos, 5:72, *72*
kouprey, 3:19
Kraftwerk (musical group), 3:11
Krak castle, Syria, 2:*20*
Kraken (giant octopus), 5:51
Krakow, Poland, 5:183
Kuala Lumpur, Malaysia, 4:176
Kublai Khan, 8:142; 2:50
Ku Klux Klan (KKK), 4:131, *131*; 1:19
kung fu, 4:186
Kurds, 4:131
Kurosawa, Akira, 5:63
Kuwait, 4:132; 4:95, 126; 5:30
Kwanza, 4:132, *132*
Kyrgyzstan, 4:132; 6:168

Laban dance notation, 2:134
laboratories, 4:133, *133*; 5:13
labor unions, 4:133; 4:78, 122
La Brea Tar Pits, 6:19
lace, 4:134, *134*; 7:51
lacrosse, 4:134
lactic acid, 1:11; 6:67
lactose, 7:17
ladybugs (ladybirds), 1:127, *127*; 7:166
Ladysmith Black Mambazo, 1:21
Lafayette, Marquis de, 8:142; 1:45
La Follette, Robert, 7:171
La Fontaine, Jean de, 3:41, 55
Lagerkvist, Pär, 3:41
Lagerlöf, Selma, 3:41
lagoons, 4:134
Lake District, England, 1:*163*
Lake Erie, Battle of, 7:135
lakes, 4:134–135, *135*
  fishing in, 3:88, 89
  Great Lakes, 4:66, 134, 135
  oxbows, 3:98
  pollution of, 5:186
Lambert Glacier, 1:60
lamps, 2:74–75; 4:*156*, 157, *157*
landforms, 4:136–137, *136*, *137*; 3:30
  geologists and, 3:154
  glaciers, 3:165, *165*
  islands, 4:103
  mountains, 5:60–61, *60*, *61*
  and **plate tectonics**, 5:179, *179*
  valleys, 7:112–114, *112–113*, *114*

Landon, Margaret, 7:52
landscape designers, 2:146
landscape painting, 5:*143*
land use, 4:138, *138*
  farming, *see* **farming**
  open range, 6:52
  reclamation, 7:77
  wetlands and, 7:161, *161*
Lane, Harriet, 3:82
Lang, Andrew, 3:109
Lange, Dorothea, photography by, 2:*143*
Langland, William, 3:29; 5:14
languages, 4:138–139
  African, 1:16; 2:34
  alphabets, 1:37, *37*
  Anglo-Saxon, 1:53
  of Arabs, 1:69
  of Aztecs, 1:105
  in Belgium, 1:128
  Bible translations, 1:131
  and bilingual people, 4:138
  body, 1:56; 2:96
  of the Caribbean area, 2:14
  Celtic, 2:31
  of chimpanzees, 2:46
  Chinese, 2:47, 50, *50*, 51
  in church services, 1:63
  and **communication**, 2:96
  computer programming, 2:102
  Creole, 2:124
  dialects, 3:27
  and **dictionaries**, 2:151
  English, 3:27–28
  grammar, 3:28
  Hebrew, 4:22, 117
  hieroglyphics, 4:28, *28*
  idiom in, 3:27, 28
  of Inca people, 1:148
  of **India**, 1:90; 4:71, 73
  Latin, 1:54, 63; 4:105
  and **names**, 5:78
  Navajo code talkers, 7:181
  in **North America**, 5:109
  Sanskrit, 4:73
  sign language, 6:137, *137*
Lansing, Michigan, 5:24
Laos, 4:139, *139*; 1:89
Lao-tzu, 1:90; 7:32
La Paz, Bolivia, 1:148, *148*

Lapland, 7:23

larvae, 4:140, *140*; 1:127; 2:127, 167; 3:95; 5:175, *175*
  of **insects**, 4:87
  metamorphosis of, 5:21, *21*

larynx, 7:131, *131*

la Salle, Sieur de, 4:120, 167; 5:127; 7:103

La Scala (Milan), 8:232

lasers, 4:140–141, *140, 141*; 7:123
  and bar codes, 4:83, *83*, 141
  and **compact discs**, 2:97
  fiber optics, 3:75, *75*
  holograms, 4:37, *37*, 141
  recording with, 6:54
  surgery with, 7:21

Las Vegas, Nevada, 2:12; 5:*90, 93*, 94

lateral line system, 3:87

Latin, 1:54, 63

Latin America, 4:141; 6:163
  beans in, 1:123
  developing countries in, 2:148–149
  dictators in, 2:150
  see also **Central America; South America**

Latin American literature, 4:141–142; 7:157

Latinos (**Hispanics**), 4:32–34, *33*

latitude and longitude, 4:142, *142*; 2:72; 5:183
  Equator and, 3:32
  maps, 4:180–183, *180*

Latrobe, Benjamin Henry, 1:74

Latvia, 4:142; 6:168

Laurens, Henry, 1:45

lava, 6:82, *82*; 7:132, *132*

Lavinium, *see* **Rome and the Roman Empire**

Lavoisier, Antoine, 8:142–143; 6:158

law and legal systems, 4:143–145, *145*
  affirmative action, 2:66
  Bill of Rights, 1:135–136
  and **Civil Rights Movement**, 2:65–66
  Code Napoléon, 5:80
  code of Hammurabi, 5:19
  Code of Roman Law, 1:177
  copyrights, 2:115

  courtroom, 4:*143*
  detectives and, 2:147
  and **government**, 3:172
  "Jim Crow" laws, 2:65
  legislative process, 2:106, *106*
  Roman, 6:91
  U.S. **Congress**, 2:106–107
  U.S. **Constitution**, 2:112
  U.S. Supreme Court, 2:65, 66, 112; 4:144, 145, *145*

Lawrence, D. H., 8:143; 3:29; 5:181

Lawrence, Jacob, 1:19

LCDs (liquid-crystal displays), 1:*27*, 179; 4:192

lead, 4:146

Leadbelly (Huddie Ledbetter), 1:147

League of Nations, 6:59; 7:95

Leakey family, 8:143, *143*; 7:32

Leaning Tower of Pisa, 6:125

leap years, 1:181

Lear, Edward, 5:182

leather, 4:146, *146*

leaves, 4:147, *147*; 3:101–102, *101*
  fossils, 3:123–124, *123*
  and **photosynthesis**, 5:168
  of **trees**, 7:78–80, *78, 80*

Lebanon, 4:148, *148*; 5:30; 6:*105*

Le Corbusier, 8:144; 1:74, *77*
  buildings designed by, 1:*77*; 2:58

Led Zeppelin, 3:11; 6:81

Lee, Mother Ann, 6:129

Lee, Richard Henry, 2:138; 7:128

Lee, Robert E., 8:144, *144*; 2:67–70; 4:187; 7:107, 128, 141

leeches, 4:148, *148*

Leeuwenhoek, Anton van, 8:144–145

Leeward Islands, 7:157

legends, *see* **myths and legends**

legions, Roman, 6:88

legislature, 3:172

legumes, 1:123

Leif Ericsson, 8:145; 7:126

Leigh, Vivien, 5:*63*

lemmings, 4:149; 7:133

lemurs, 4:149, *149*; 3:*19*; 4:171

Lena River, Russia, 6:96

L'Enfant, Pierre Charles, 7:138–139

L'Engle, Madeleine, 2:45

Lenglen, Suzanne, 7:*47*

Lenin, 8:145; 2:97; 6:98, *98*; 7:*63*

Lennon, John, 2:99

lenses, 4:150, *150*; 3:167; 5:133
  in **binoculars**, 1:136, *136*
  in **cameras**, 1:184, *185*
  in **lighthouses**, 4:158
  in **microscopes**, 5:26, *26*
  in **telescopes**, 7:40, *40*

Lent, 2:15; 3:67

Leonard, Buck, 1:120

Leonardo da Vinci, 8:145–146; 2:17; 6:63
  drawings by, 1:*170*; 6:*63*; 8:*146*

leopards, 4:150, *150*; 2:24–25, *25*

Leopold and Loeb case, 8:66

Lepanto, Battle of, 7:136

leprechauns, 3:56, *56*

Lerner, Alan Jay, 5:75

Les Misérables, 5:75; 8:123

lesbians, 6:128

Lesotho, 4:151; 2:95; 4:126

less developed countries (LDCs), 7:55

Lesser Antilles, 7:157

Les Troyens (Berlioz), 1:13

letterpress, 6:26, *27*

Leutze, Emanuel Gottlieb, 1:45

levers, 4:151, *151*; 4:169, 170, *170*; 6:34, *34*

Lewis, C. S., 8:146; 1:35; 2:45; 3:29

Lewis, Jerry, 2:38

Lewis, Jerry Lee, 6:81

Lewis, Meriwether (Lewis and Clark), 8:146–147, *210*; 3:51; 4:63, 120; 5:51, 88, 112, 136; 6:166; 7:103, 128

Lewis, Sinclair, 1:40, 41; 5:36; 6:34

Lexington, Battle of, 1:44

Lexington, Massachusetts, 4:189

Lhasa, Tibet, 7:57, *57*

Libby, Willard F., 1:71

Liberia, 4:152

Liberty Bell, 4:152; 5:163; 7:*104*

libraries, 4:152

Library of Congress, Washington, D.C., 4:152

Libya, 4:153, *153*; 5:16

lice, 4:153, *153*; 4:87; 5:*26*

lichens, 4:154, *154*; 5:175

Lie, Trygve, 7:95

Liechtenstein, 4:154; 4:126

lie detectors, 4:154
lieder, 8:213
lifeboats, 4:155, *155*
life expectancy, 2:137; 4:18
light, 4:156–157, *156–157*; 3:20;
    5:168
    bulbs, 4:*157*; 8:*78*
    candles, 2:7
    and color, 2:91
    and electricity, 3:7–10
    fiber optics, 3:75, *75*
    fireflies, 3:80
    flashlights, 3:94, *94*
    fluorescence, 3:105
    holograms, 4:37, *37*, 141
    lasers, 4:140–141, *140, 141*
    lenses and, 4:150
    and mirages, 5:38, *38*
    and mirrors, 5:38, *38*
    northern lights, 5:113, *113*
    optics, 5:133
    and radiation, 6:45, *46*
    rainbows, 6:51
    solar power, 6:158, *158*
    spectrum of, 4:156
    speed of, 6:46, 61; 7:108
    wavelength of, 4:157
lighthouses, 4:158, *158*; 4:*175*
    Pharos of Alexandria, 6:125, *125*
lightning, 3:*7*; 7:57
light-years, 4:158; 6:42
lignin, 6:136; 7:80
lignite, 2:81
lignocaine, 1:52
Lilienthal, Otto and Gustav, 3:167
Liliuokalani, queen of Hawaiian
    Islands, 4:16
Lima, Peru, 5:164
limelight, 7:54
limericks, 5:182
limestone, 2:33; 6:184, *184*
limestone caves, 2:29
Limon, José, 4:33
Lincoln, Abraham, 8:147–148, *147*;
    3:82; 4:65, 123; 5:185; 6:167;
    7:45, 101, 119
    and Civil War, 2:67–70, *69*
    and Emancipation Proclamation,
       2:67, 68–69, 70

Gettysburg Address of, 2:67, 69;
    3:161, *161*
    and slavery, 6:148
Lincoln-Douglas Debates, 8:73
Lincoln, Mary Todd, 3:82, *83*
Lincoln, Nebraska, 5:88, 89
Lincoln Memorial, 7:140, *141*
Lind, Jenny, 8:21
Lindbergh, Anne Morrow, 8:148
Lindbergh, Charles, 8:148
    plane of, 1:*25*
Lindsay, Vachel, 8:122
Lindstrand, Per, 1:113
linen, 7:51
Linnaeus, Carolus, 8:148; 2:70;
    6:175; 7:23
lintels, 1:72
lions, 4:159, *159*; 2:24–25, *24*; 7:*36*
Lipinski, Tara, 4:*61*
Li Po, 1:90
liposuction, 5:178
Lippershey, Hans, 7:40
liquid-crystal displays (LCDs), 1:*27*,
    179; 4:192
liquids, 4:160; 5:8
    air changed into, 1:24
    bubbles, 1:164, *164*
liquor, proof of, 1:33
Lisbon, Portugal, 6:11, *11*
Liszt, Franz, 8:148–149, *149*; 5:67
literature, 4:160; 3:77
    African, 1:18
    American, 1:40–41
    Asian, 1:90; 2:104; 4:76, *76*
    Bible, 1:132
    biography and autobiography,
       1:136
    for children, 2:44–45
    classical, 3:183
    English, 1:86; 3:29
    European, 3:41, 183
    folktales, 3:109, *109*
    heroes and heroines in, 4:26
    Latin American, 4:141–142
    of Middle East, 5:30
    Nobel Prize in, 1:18, 90; 5:30
    novels, 5:114
    oral tradition of, 1:18, 90
    poems and poetry, 5:181–182
    proverbs and sayings, 6:32

Pulitzer Prize, 6:34
    science fiction, 6:110
    see also Greek and Roman
       literature
lithography, 6:26, 27, *27*
Lithuania, 4:160; 6:168
litmus, 1:11
littering, 5:186, *186–187*
Little Bighorn, South Dakota, 2:27
Little League baseball, 1:118, *119*
Little Rock, Arkansas, 1:82, 83
Little Women (Alcott), 2:45
Live Aid (charity), 6:81
livers, 4:160, *160*
Livingston, Robert, 2:138
lizards, 4:161, *161*; 6:66, *66*
    chameleons, 2:37, *37*
    dinosaurs, 2:153–156
    eggs of, 2:186
Ljubljana, Slovenia, 6:150
llamas, 4:161, *161*; 2:166; 4:69, *69*;
    7:176
Lloyd-George, David, 6:25
Lloyd Webber, Andrew, 5:75, 76
lobsters, 4:162, *162*; 4:*140*; 5:*77*
local anesthetic, 1:52
locater maps, 4:181, *181*
Locke, John, 8:149; 2:138
locks (canals), 4:163, *163*
locks and keys, 4:164, *164*
locomotives, 4:164–165, *164–165*;
    6:49–51, *49*, 191
locusts, 4:166, *166*
lodestone, 2:98
loess, 2:47; 6:157
Loewe, Frederick, 5:75
logarithms, 1:179, 180
logic gates, 3:13
logos, 2:146, *146, 147*; 7:74, *74*
Loire River, 3:128
Loki (Norse god), 5:107
London, England, 2:*177*; 3:24, 25, 26,
    37, 80; 7:90, *92, 93*
    flood defenses for, 2:85
    Globe Theatre, 2:169
    greenbelts in, 2:65
    marathon, 4:184
    stock exchange ("the City") in,
       6:192
    theaters in, 7:53, *53*, 54

Tower Bridge in, **1**:*160*
London, Jack, **1**:182
Long, Earl, **4**:167
Long, Huey "Kingfish," **4**:167
Long, Stephen H., **2**:92; **4**:120
Longfellow, Henry Wadsworth, **1**:40, 41; **8**:202
longitude, *see* **latitude and longitude**
longshore drift, **2**:84, *84*
looms, for **weaving**, **7**:154, *154*
Lope de Vega Carpio, Felix, **3**:41
Lopez, Nancy, **4**:33
Lorenz, Konrad, **4**:88
Los Angeles, California, **1**:182, *182*, 183; **2**:64, 179; **6**:*77*; **7**:98
lotteries, **4**:166; **3**:144
loudspeakers, **4**:166, *166*; **5**:25
Louis, Joe, **1**:19, 152
Louis XIV, king of France, **8**:149; **1**:84, 110–111; **3**:72, 130–31, *131*; **4**:167
Louis XVI, king of France, **8**:150, *150*; **3**:131
Louisiana, **4**:167–168, *167*; **2**:67, 124; **7**:100
Louisiana Purchase, **1**:82; **2**:67, 92; **4**:167; **7**:*102*
Low, Juliette Gordon, **8**:150; **3**:156, 164
Lowell, James Russell, **1**:40
Luanda, Angola, **1**:55
Lucifer (Satan), **1**:52
Lucy (fossil), **3**:48, *48*
Lucy, Autherine, **8**:*156*
luges, **7**:170
Lugosi, Bela, **7**:*115*
Lujan, Manuel, Jr., **4**:33
lullabies, **5**:182
Lunar Rover, **6**:170
Luna spacecraft, **6**:169, *170*
lung cancer, **1**:87
lungs, **4**:168, *168*; **4**:48, *48*
    breathing, **1**:158
    respiration, **6**:67, *67*
Luther, Martin, **8**:150–151; **6**:31, 57
Luthuli, Albert, **8**:151, *151*
Luxembourg, **4**:169; **3**:41; **4**:126
Lyme disease, **1**:85; **7**:58
lymph nodes, **4**:68

MacArthur, Douglas, **8**:151; **1**:82
Macbeth (Shakespeare), **6**:111
MacCready, Paul, **3**:96
mace, **6**:176, *176*
Macedonia, **4**:169; **6**:124, 148; **7**:188
Mach, Ernst, **6**:161
Machado de Assis, Joaquim María, **4**:142
machines, **4**:169, *169*, 170
    computers for control of, **4**:82–83, *83*
    farm, **3**:65, *65*
    levers, **4**:151, *151*, 169, 170, *170*
    motors, **5**:58, *58*
    pulleys, **6**:34, *34*
    robots, **6**:78–79, *78*, *79*
    see also **engines; farm machinery**
Machu Picchu, Peru, **1**:70; **4**:69, *69*
macramé, **4**:129, *129*
macroeconomics, **2**:183
Macy's department store, **7**:9
Madagascar, **4**:171, *171*; **1**:15; **4**:149
Madison, Dolley, **3**:82; **5**:109, 110
Madison, James, **8**:151, *151*; **1**:40; **2**:112; **3**:82; **7**:101, 128
Madison, Wisconsin, **7**:171, 172
Madonna (performer), **6**:81
Madrid, Spain, **6**:173
madrigals, **2**:53
Maelzel, Johann, **2**:74
Mafia, **4**:171, *171*; **4**:104, 105
magazines, **4**:172, *172*; **5**:13

Magellan, Ferdinand, **8**:152–153; **3**:50
    map, **8**:*153*
maggots (larvae), **3**:95
magicians, **4**:173, *173*
magic metal, **4**:192
magma, **5**:34; **6**:82, 84; **7**:132, *132*
Magna Carta, **3**:26, 27
magnesium, **5**:20
magnetic north, **4**:182
magnetic poles, **5**:183
magnetrons, **5**:26
magnets, **4**:173–174, *174*; **7**:19, *19*; **3**:117; **5**:168; **7**:149
    compasses, **2**:98, *98*
    electromagnets, **3**:7, *8*
    in **motors**, **5**:58, *58*
Mahfouz, Naguib, **5**:30
mail:
    electronic (e-mail), **4**:90; **6**:12
    postal services, **6**:11–12, *11*
    stamps and, **6**:184, *184*
    ZIP codes, **7**:191
Maiman, Theodore, **4**:141
Maine, **4**:174–175, *175*; **2**:67; **7**:100
Maine (battleship), **6**:175
maize: *see* **corn**
Major, John, **7**:94
malaria, **4**:176; **5**:56
Malawi, **4**:176; **2**:95
Malawi, Lake, **1**:16
Malaysia, **4**:176; **1**:151; **2**:95; **6**:139, 145
Malcolm III, king of Scotland, **6**:111
Malcolm X, **8**:153–154, *153*; **1**:19, 20; **5**:88
Maldives, **2**:95
Mali, **4**:177; **1**:17, 22; **7**:127
Malinke language, **1**:16
Mall of America, **7**:*10*
malls, shopping, **7**:10, *10*
malnutrition, **4**:177; **3**:111; **6**:189
Malory, Thomas, **1**:86, 136; **3**:29
Malta, **4**:177, *177*; **2**:95; **7**:*27*, 43
maltose, **7**:17
mammals, **4**:178, *178*; **7**:120, *120*
    evolution of, **3**:46–49, *46*, *47*, *48–49*
    extinction of, **3**:52–53, *52–53*
    hair of, **4**:9–10, *9*

human beings, 4:47
marsupials, 4:185, *185*; 4:178
prehistoric animals, 6:18–19, *18, 19*
warm- and cold-bloodedness, 7:134
see also animals
Managua, Nicaragua, 5:101
Manassas, Battles of, *see* Bull Run, Battles of
manatees, 6:72; 7:162
Manchuria, 2:51
Mandarins, 2:50
Mandela, Nelson, 8:154, *154*; 2:95; 6:162
Mandelbrot, Benoit B., 3:126
Manet, Edouard, 8:154
mangrove swamps, 7:159–160
Manhattan Project, 1:96
Manila, Philippines, 5:165
Mann, Horace, 8:154–155; 6:109
Mann, Thomas, 8:155; 3:41
manners, "good", 3:35
Mansa Musa, king of Mali, 1:17
Mantle, Mickey, 5:130
mantras, 5:15
manuscripts:
   Anglo-Saxon, 1:54
   musical, 2:99
   see also illuminated manuscripts
Maori, 4:179, *179*
Mao Zedong, 8:155, 256; 2:52
maps, 4:180–183, *180, 181, 182, 183*
   Africa, 1:15, *16*, 18
   American Revolution, 1:43
   ancient world, 1:50
   Anglo-Saxons, 1:53
   Antarctica, 1:60
   Arctic Circle, 1:78
   Asia, 1:88, 89
   Australia, 1:97
   British Isles, 1:162
   Buddhism, 1:167
   Caribbean, 2:13
   Central America, 2:13
   cities, 2:63
   continents, 2:113
   Eurasia, 1:88, 89; 3:36
   Europe, 3:36, 37
   Europe in Middle Ages, 5:29
   of explorers, 3:50, *50, 51*
   and geography, 3:151
   of ice age, 4:58
   latitude and longitude, 4:142, 142
   Mediterranean, 5:16
   Native Americans, 5:83
   North America, 5:108
   Oceania, 5:121
   in orienteering, 5:138
   South America, 6:163
   symbols on, 4:182, 182
   United States, formation of, 7:102
   see also specific nations, states and explorers
marathons, 4:184, *184*; 6:94; 7:72, 72
marble, 6:41
Marbury v. *Madison*, 8:156
Marceau, Marcel, 5:33
March on Washington, 2:66; 8:140
Marciano, Rocky, 1:152
Marconi, Guglielmo, 8:155–156; 4:92; 6:48
Marcos, Ferdinand, 5:165
Mardi Gras, 2:15; 4:167, *167*, 168
Marie Antoinette, queen of France, 3:131
Mariner space probes, 6:170, *170*, 171
Marines, U.S., 7:106, *106*, 107
marionettes, 6:37
Marley, Bob, 6:60, *60*
Marlowe, Christopher, 3:29; 5:15
Marne, Battle of, 7:136
Marquette, Jacques, 4:65, 93; 5:24, 41; 7:103
marriage, 4:184; 6:71; 7:155, *155*
   and divorce, 2:159
   polygamy, 7:110
Mars, 5:171, 172, 174; 6:159, *159*, 160, 170, *170–171*, 171
Marsalis, Wynton, 4:112
Marseilles, France, 5:16; 1:77
Marshall, George C., 5:162; 7:181; 8:233
Marshall, James, 3:170
Marshall, John, 8:156; 4:145, 152; 7:128
Marshall, Thurgood, 8:156–157, *157*; 1:19, 20; 2:66; 4:145
Marshall Plan, 7:104, 181: 8:233
marsupials, 4:185, *185*; 4:178
   kangaroos, 4:119, *119*
   koalas, 4:130, *130*
   opossums, 5:132, *132*
Martel, Charles, 3:38, 39; 7:136
Martí, José, 8:157, *157*; 4:142
martial arts, 4:186, *186*
   judo, 4:119
   karate, 4:121
Martinez, Bob, 4:33
Martinez, José P., 7:181
Martinez, Maria, 5:85
Martinez, Vilma, 4:33
Martinique, 7:132, 157
martyrs, 6:102
Marx, Karl, 8:157; 2:97, 183; 6:98, 156
Mary (mother of Jesus), 8:158, *158*; 1:177; 2:56, 57; 4:62
Mary Celeste, 5:170
Mary I, queen of England, 8:158; 4:125
Mary, Queen of Scots, 8:158–159, *158*; 6:111
Maryland, 4:186–187, *187*; 7:56, 100
   Naval Academy at Annapolis, 7:107, *107*
Mary Magdalene, St., 6:102
Mary Poppins (Travers), 2:45
masers, 2:74; 4:140
masks, 4:188, *188*; 2:169, *169*
   in mime, 5:33
   of mummies, 5:65, *65*
Mason, George, 7:128
Mason-Dixon Line, 5:162; 7:103
masques, 7:54
mass, 4:188; 1:95; 6:61
Massachusetts, 4:189–190, *189*; 7:56, 100, 172
   and American Revolution, 1:43–45
   and Maine, 4:174
   Minute Men in, 1:44
   Pilgrims in, 5:169–170, *169*, 170
Massachusetts Bay Colony, 8:251
mass-energy equation (E = mc²), 3:32; 6:61
mass extinctions, 3:53
mass production, 4:190; 2:183; 4:78

robots for, 6:78–79, *78, 79*
see also **Industrial Revolution**
Masterson, Bat, 4:120
matadors, 1:173, *173*
materials, 4:191–192
alloys, 4:98, 191, 192
bricks, 1:159, *159*
ceramics, 4:192
composites, 4:192, *192*
plastics, 4:192
recycling of, 6:55, *55*
smart, 4:191
mathematics, 5:7; 4:81
algebra, 1:34
arithmetic, 1:80
calculators, 1:179–180, *179*
chaos theory, 2:38
decimals, 2:137
equations, 3:32
fractals, 3:126, *126*
fractions, 3:127
geometry, 3:154–155, *154, 155*
infinity, 4:81, *81*
models in, 2:38
numbers, 5:116–117, *117*
percentages, 5:164
sets, 6:124, *124*
trigonometry, 7:81, *81*
Mather, Increase and Cotton, 8:159;
1:40
Mathieu, Albert, 2:38
mating, 5:7
and **reproduction**, 6:65, *65*
sex and sexuality, 6:127–128
Matisse, Henri, 8:160
painting by, 8:*160*
matter, 5:8
liquids, 4:160
molecules, 5:43
particles of, 5:157, *157*
Matterhorn, 6:125
Mauldin, Bill, 2:18
Mauna Kea Observatory, 4:16; 5:120,
120
Mauna Loa, Hawaii, 5:60, *60*, 61;
7:132, *132*
Maupassant, Guy de, 3:41
Mauritania, 5:8
Mauritius, 5:8; 2:95
maxims, 6:32
Maxwell, James Clerk, 8:160

Maya, 5:9, *9*; 1:41, 50, 104; 2:34;
3:189, *189*; 4:28, 38; 5:22, 82;
6:21; 7:*154*
Maya Mountains, 1:129
Mayflower, 5:*169*
Mayo Clinic, Rochester, Minnesota,
2:74
Mays, Willie, 1:29
mbalax (music), 1:21
McAdam, John, 6:77
McAuliffe, Christa, 5:94; 6:169
McCartney, Paul, 2:99
McClellan, George, 8:160–161; 2:68,
69
McClintock, Barbara, 8:161
McCormick, Cyrus, 8:161; 3:65; 4:65
McCoy, Elijah, 1:19
McCulloch v. *Maryland*, 8:156
McDowell, Irvin, 2:68
McGillivray, James, 1:42
McIndoe, Archibald, 5:178
McKay, Donald, 6:100
McKinley, Mount, 1:31, *31*; 5:108,
109
McKinley, William, 8:161–162, *162*;
5:88, 127, 128; 6:175; 7:101
Mead, Margaret, 8:162; 1:46
Meade, George, 2:69, 70
mean (average), 1:104
meanders (**rivers**), 6:73, 74
measurement, 5:10–11, *10, 11*
decimals, 2:137
light-years, 4:158
mass, 4:188
meat, 5:12
Mecca, 1:17, 68, 69; 4:100–102, *100,
102*; 5:55, 169; 6:107
Meccano construction sets, 7:*68*
medals, 5:12, *12*; 2:124, *124*
media, 5:13
magazines, 4:172, *172*
multimedia, 5:65
newspapers, 5:99
see also **television**
median (average), 1:104
medicine, 2:172; 5:13, *13*
alternative, 1:38–39; 5:15
anesthetics, 1:52
antibiotics, 1:63
biotechnology, 1:137
doctors and, 2:161

folk, 1:39
hospitals, 4:44
nurses and, 5:118
plastic surgery, 5:178
surgeons, 7:21, *21*
training in, 7:*130*
vaccinations, 7:111
see also **diseases**
medieval legends, 5:14–15, *14, 15*;
3:29; 5:77
medieval times, see **Middle Ages**
Medina, 1:69; 4:100, 101, *102*; 6:107
meditation, 5:15; 5:37
in **Buddhism**, 1:165, 166, 167
Mediterranean, 5:16; 3:61; 5:170;
6:173
Medusa, the Gorgon, 5:51
megahertz (MHz), 6:45, 47
megaliths, 7:7–8, *8*
megalopolis, 2:62
Megalosaurus, 2:153
Mehmed II, Sultan, 5:139
Meir, Golda, 8:162–163, *163*; 6:25
Mekong River, 1:183; 4:139; 6:74
Melanesia, 5:121
melanin, 1:32; 6:143
Melbourne Cathedral, Australia, 2:23
Melcher, Frederic, 2:45
melody, 5:17
Melville, Herman, 8:163; 1:40; 5:100
memoirs, 1:136
memory, 5:17; 1:155
Memphis, Tennessee, 7:45
Mencius, 2:104
Mendel, Gregor, 8:164
Mendeleev, Dimitri, 8:164
Mendelssohn, Felix, 8:164–165;
2:36, 103; 5:67
Menelik, emperor of Ethiopia, 3:34
Menem, Carlos, 1:79
Menes, king of Egypt, 2:187
Mennonites, 1:46
Menotti, Gian-Carlo, 8:165; 5:132
menstruation, 5:17, *17*; 4:51; 6:33
mental illness, 5:18; 2:158; 5:13;
6:32
Mercator's projection, 4:180, *180*
merchant marine, 5:18
ports and harbors, 6:9–10, *9*
Merckx, Eddy, 2:129
mercury, as solid, 4:160

mercury barometer, 1:117

Mercury (planet), 5:171; 6:159, *159*, 160, 170, 171

mercury (quicksilver), 5:18

Meredith, James, 2:66

Merlin, 1:86–87; 2:32, 168

Merlin, Joseph, 6:86

mermaids and mermen, 5:19, *19*

Mesa Verde National Park, 2:92

Mesmer, Franz, 4:56

Mesopotamia, 5:19, *19*; 4:95; 5:30; 7:76

  in **ancient world**, 1:50

  Sumerians in, 7:17, *17*

mestizos, 3:16; 4:33

metals, 5:20, *20*; 4:191–192, *192*; 5:18

  alloys, 1:36

  aluminum, 1:39; 1:10; 2:40

  copper, 2:114

  discoveries of, 6:23

  gold, 3:170, *170*

  iron and steel, 4:98, *98*

  lead, 4:146

  magnets, 4:173–174, *174*

  melting of, 4:160

  recycling of, 6:55, *55*

  sculpture of, 6:112–113, *113*, 115, *115*

  smelting of, 6:23

  tin, 7:62

  welding of, 3:*148*

metamorphic rocks, 6:82, 84

metamorphosis, 5:21, *21*; 1:47, 48, *48*, 127, 168, 176; 4:87, *87*, 140; 6:37, *37*

metaphors, 5:182

meteorologists, 7:153

meteors and meteorites, 5:21, *21*; 3:134; 6:125

methanol, 1:32

metric measurements, 5:10–11, *11*

metronomes, 2:74

Metropolitan Museum, New York City, 5:66

Metropolitan Opera, New York City, 5:132

Meuse River, 1:128

Mexico, 5:22–23, *22*, *23*; 5:108, 109

  Aztecs of, 1:104–105; 1:41

  and **California**, 1:182

  Cinco de Mayo, 4:34

  conquistadores in, 2:109

  Day of the Dead, 4:11, *11*

  Hispanics from, 4:32–34, *33*

  immigration from, 4:68

  land ceded to U.S. from, 5:93, 97

  literature of, 4:141–142

  Maya in, 5:9, *9*, 22, 82

  and NAFTA, 7:73, 101

  poverty in, 6:15

  prehistoric people in, 6:21

  pyramids in, 6:40, *40*

  Spanish rule of, 1:81, 105, 182

  and **Texas**, 7:49–50

  and Treaty of Guadalupe Hidalgo, 1:81, 182; 7:109

  and U.S. territory, 1:81

  volcanoes in, 7:132

Mexico City, 2:64

  archaeology in, 1:104, *104–105*

  and Tenochtitlán, 1:104, 105; 2:65

mica, 6:84, *84*

mice, 5:23, *23*; 3:*137*; 6:86

Michael, archangel, 1:52

Michaux, Ernest and Pierre, 5:58

Michelangelo, 8:165–166; 2:23; 3:133

  frescoes by, 3:*133*

  sculpture by, 6:*112*; 8:166, *173*

Michigan, 5:24–25, *24*; 7:100

Michigan, Lake, 4:135; 7:171, 172

Mickey Mouse, 2:18–19

microbes, 1:107

microbiology, 5:26

microchips, 7:19

microeconomics, 2:183

microhabitats, 4:8

microlight aircraft, 1:27; 4:13

micrometer gauges, 5:*10*

Micronesia, 5:121

microphones, 5:25, *25*; 4:166; 6:54

microprocessors, 2:100, 101, *101*, 102

microscopes, 5:26, *26*; 4:133, 150; 5:133; 7:21, *21*

microsurgery, 7:21, *21*

microwaves, 5:26; 7:121

  radar, 6:44

  and **radiation**, 6:45, *45*

  stoves and ovens, 7:11

Middle Ages, 5:27–29, *28*, *29*; 5:106

  apprentices in, 2:44

  armies in, 1:84

  armor in, 1:85, *85*

  in **Belgium**, 1:128

  biography and autobiography in, 1:136

  Black Death in, 1:144

  bridges in, 1:*160*

  canals in, 1:191

  carnival in, 2:15

  castles of, 2:20

  cavalry in, 2:27

  chivalry in, 2:52, *52*

  clothing, 2:*77*

  convents in, 2:114

  cosmetics in, 2:117

  crusades in, 2:126

  dolls in, 2:164

  drama in, 2:169

  in **England**, 3:26

  fables of, 3:55

  fairs in, 3:57

  feudal system of, 3:75

  fine arts in, 3:77

  frescoes painted in, 3:133, *133*

  furniture in, 3:141

  Gothic architecture in, 2:59

  guilds in, 2:122

  headdresses in, 4:15, *15*

  heraldry of, 4:24–25, *24–25*

  horses in, 4:42

  Hungary in, 4:52

  illuminated manuscripts in, 3:172; 4:66

  in **Italy**, 4:105

  knights in, 4:128, *128*

  light in, 4:*156*

  map of Europe in, 5:*29*

  medieval legends of, 5:14–15, *14*

  minstrels in, 5:37

  monasteries in, 5:45–46, *46*

  monks in, 4:10

  names in, 5:78

  paper made in, 5:151

  peasants in, 5:29, 160

  slavery in, 6:146, *146*, 148

  stained glass in, 6:183, *183*

middle colonies, 7:56

Middle East, 5:30, *30*; 1:89; 7:29

in **ancient world**, 1:50
Arabian Nights, 1:68
Arabs in, 1:69, *69*
Bahrain, 1:109
conflict in, 1:190
cosmetics in, 2:117
Cyprus, 2:130
Egypt, 2:187–189
European colonies in, 5:131
Gulf War in, 1:27
Iran, 4:94
Iraq, 4:95
Israel, 4:103, *103*
Jordan, 4:116, *116*
Kurds in, 4:131
Kuwait, 4:132
Lebanon, 4:148
Libya, 4:153, *153*
literature of, 5:30
monarchies in, 4:126
mosques in, 5:55, *55*
nomads in, 2:145, *145*
Oman, 5:131, *131*
Ottoman Empire, 5:139
prehistoric people and farming in,
    6:22
Qatar, 6:40
Saudi Arabia, 6:107, *107*
Syria, 7:29, *29*
terrorism in, 7:48
Turkey, 7:86, *86*
United Arab Emirates, 7:90, *90*
Yemen, 7:187
Midnight Sun, 5:31, *31*; 1:31, 78;
    5:114
midwives, 1:144
Mies van der Rohe, Ludwig, 8:166;
    1:74, 77
migration, 5:31; 4:27, 88; 7:84
    of **birds**, 1:138, 140; 4:27, 88; 5:31;
        7:159
    of **butterflies**, 1:176
    of people, 2:63
Milan, Italy, 4:104, 105
militia, Minute Men, 1:44
milk, 5:32; 2:26, 39, *39*, 121; 3:65;
    7:188
Milky Way, 5:32, *32*; 5:89
Mill, John Stuart, 8:167
Mill, Harriet Taylor, 8:167

Miller, Arthur, 8:167; 1:41; 2:169
Miller, Dorie, 1:19; 7:181
Miller, Glenn, 4:93
millet, 3:173, *173*
Millet, Kate, 7:173
millipedes, 5:32, *32*; 2:33; 3:*120*
Milne, A. A., 8:167, *167*; 2:45; 4:160
Milne, Christopher Robin, 8:*167*
Milton, John, 8:168, 93; 3:29
Milwaukee, Wisconsin, 7:171, 172
mime, 5:33, *33*
mimicry, in camouflage, 1:186
minerals, 5:34, *34*; 3:154
    crystals, 2:128
    diamonds, 2:150, *150*
    gems, 3:150, *150*
    mining of, 5:35, *35*
    Mohs scale of hardness of, 5:34
    rocks, 6:83, 84
    in **Russia**, 6:96
minesweepers, 5:86
Mingus, Charles, 4:112
mining, 5:35, *35*; 4:137; 5:36–37, 93;
    6:*22*, 23
    coal, 2:81–82, *81*, *82*
    in **deserts**, 2:145
    gold, 3:170, *170*
    quarries, 6:41
    salt, 6:104–105, *104*
    strip, 2:81
Minneapolis, Minnesota, 5:36, 37
Minnesota, 5:36–37, *36*; 7:100
Minoan civilization, 1:50
Minsk, Belarus, 1:128
minstrels, 5:37; 1:109
mint, 4:25, *25*
Mint, U.S., 2:87, 93
Minute Men, 1:44
miracle plays, 2:169
miracles, 5:37
mirages, 5:38, *38*
mirrors, 5:38, *38*; 5:133
Mir space station, 1:93; 6:170, *172*
miscarriages, 6:18
Mishima, Yukio, 1:90
missiles, 5:39, *39*; 6:80; 7:151
missionaries, 2:54, 55, *55*
Mississippi, 5:39–41, *40*; 2:67; 7:100
Mississippi River, 2:68, 84; 4:93, 167;

    5:*36*, 40, 41, 42, 108, 109; 6:74,
        75; 7:97, 171
Missouri, 5:41–42, *42*; 2:67; 7:100
Missouri Compromise (1820), 2:67
Missouri River, 4:93; 5:41, 89, 108,
    109, 111; 6:74, 167; 7:97
mistletoe, 5:153
Mistral, 7:168
Mistral, Gabriela, 4:142
Mitchell, Margaret, 3:156
Mitchell, Maria, 8:169
mnemonics, 5:17
moats, 2:20
Mobile, Alabama, 1:30
Mobile Bay, Battle of, 2:68
mobile phones, 7:39
Mobutu Sese Seko, 2:105
Moby-Dick, illustration, 8:*163*
mode (average), 1:104
models:
    mathematical, 2:38
    scientific, 1:95
modems, 2:*101*, 102
modulation, broadcasting, 6:47
Mogadishu, Somalia, 6:160
Mohenjo-daro, 1:50
Moher, cliffs of, 1:*163*
Mohs, Friedrich, 5:34
Mohs' scale of hardness, 5:34
Mojave Desert, 1:183; 2:145
molars, 7:36
molasses, 7:17, *17*
Moldova, 5:42; 6:168
molecules, 5:43, *43*; 2:88; 3:151
    DNA, 2:160, *161*
    fat, 3:*67*
    in **liquids**, 4:160
    proteins, 6:31
moles (animals), 5:43, *43*; 4:*185*; 5:*77*
moles (on skin), 6:143
Molière, 8:168; 3:41, 131
mollusks, 5:44, *44*; 4:92, *92*
Momaday, N. Scott, 5:85
Monaco, 5:44; 4:126
monarchs, 4:125–126, *126*
monasteries, 5:45–46, *45*, *46*; 2:136
    Buddhist, 1:*172*
    and **Dark Ages**, 2:135
    illuminated manuscripts, 4:66
Mondale, Walter, 5:36

Monet, Claude, 8:168–169; 3:132, 147
  painting by, 8:169
monetarism, 2:183
money, 5:46–47, 46, 47
  and banks, 1:116
  coins, 2:87, 87
  decimal system of, 2:137
  and economics, 2:183, 183
Mongolia, 5:48, 48; 1:88; 3:108; 5:104
mongooses, 5:48, 48
Monitor and Merrimack, battle between, 1:68; 5:86
Monk, Thelonious, 4:112
monkeys, 5:49, 49; 6:25
"Monkey Trial," 7:45
monocoque construction, 1:26
monotremes, 5:180
Monroe Doctrine, 8:169
Monroe, James, 8:169, 169; 7:101, 128
Monroe, Marilyn, 5:63; 8:167
Monrovia, Liberia, 4:152
monsoons, 5:50, 50; 5:76
monsters, 5:51
Montaigne, Michel de, 3:41
Montana, 5:51–52, 52; 7:100
Mont Blanc, 5:59
Montcalm, Louis, 7:91
Montenegro, 6:124; 7:188
Monterey Bay Aquarium, 1:67
Montessori, Maria, 8:170, 170
Montevideo, Uruguay, 7:109
Montezuma II, 8:170; 1:105; 6:151
Montgolfier brothers, 8:170–171; 1:112, 113; 3:96
Montgomery, Alabama, 1:29, 30; 2:65–66, 67
Montgomery, Lucy Maud, 2:45
months, 1:181
Montoya, Joseph, 4:33
Montpelier, Vermont, 7:119
Montreal, Canada, 1:171, 171, 189
Montserrat, 7:157
Moody, Dwight, 3:172
Moon, 5:53, 53; 5:171, 173, 173, 174; 6:159
  astronauts and, 1:93
  and calendars, 1:181, 181

eclipses of, 2:181, 181
  and gravity, 3:179
  meteors and meteorites on, 5:21
  phases of, 5:53, 53
  and space exploration, 6:169–170
  and tides, 7:58, 58
moons, 5:171–174, 173, 174; 6:106
Moore, Clement, 8:171
Moore, Henry, 8:171
  drawing by, 2:171
  sculpture by, 6:115; 8:171
moose, antlers of, 4:41, 41
moraines, 3:165, 165; 4:60
Moravia, Alberto, 3:41
More, Thomas, 8:172; 7:110
Moreno, Rita, 4:33
Morgan, Henry, 5:170
Morgan, J. P., 2:108; 5:100; 8:42
Morgan, William, 7:133
Mormonism, 5:54; 7:109–110, 109
Morocco, 5:54; 4:126
Morris, William, 3:142
Morrison, Toni, 8:172, 172; 1:20, 40, 41; 5:127, 128; 6:34
Morse, Samuel F. B., 8:172–173; 2:86; 4:189; 7:37
Morse code, 2:86, 86; 7:37
mortar, 2:104
mosaics, 5:54, 54; 1:177, 177; 2:54, 59; 4:105; 6:89
Moscow, Russia, 1:129; 2:65; 3:37; 6:95, 95, 97
Moses, 8:173, 173; 4:100, 117; 7:28
Moses, Grandma, 8:174
  painting by, 8:174
mosques, 5:55, 55; 1:17, 174; 4:100–101, 102, 102; 5:147, 148; 6:125; 7:29
mosquitoes, 5:56, 56; 4:176
mosses, 5:56, 56; 5:175; 6:179; 7:160
Mother Goose rhymes, 2:44
Mother's Day, 3:74
moths, 5:57, 57; 2:22
  antennae of, 6:123, 123
  larvae of, 4:140
  pupae, 6:37
  and silkworms, 6:138, 138
motion, and forces, 3:117
motorcycles, 5:57–58, 57, 58; 3:149
motors, 5:58, 58; see also engines

Motown Sound, 5:25
Mott, Lucretia, 8:174; 5:100; 7:173
mountain climbing, 5:59, 59
mountain lions, 6:36, 36
mountains, 5:60–61, 60, 61; 6:125
  avalanches on, 1:103
  and climate, 2:72, 73
  and Continental Divide, 2:92, 113
  and continents, 2:113
  formation of, 5:179, 179; 6:84
  Himalayas, 4:29, 29
  of North America, 5:109
  on ocean floor, 5:122, 122
  oxygen on, 1:24, 94
  Rocky Mountains, 6:85, 85
  see also specific mountains
Mountbatten, Earl, 8:179
Mount Vernon, 7:128, 129, 141
mouths, 6:123
movies, 5:62–64, 62, 63; 1:182; 7:53
  cameras, 1:185, 185
  cartoons, 2:17–19
  censorship of, 2:33
  Hollywood, 4:36
  Indian, 4:75
  musicals, 5:75–76, 75
  science fiction, 6:110
  sound in, 5:64
Mozambique, 5:64; 1:18
Mozart, Wolfgang Amadeus, 8:175, 175; 2:99, 103; 5:67, 132
MRI (magnetic resonance imaging) scanners, 6:108
MTV, 5:65; 7:41–42
Muhammad, 8:175–176; 1:69; 2:191; 3:38, 74; 4:100–102, 130; 5:37, 169; 6:30, 61, 62, 107
Muir, John, 8:176–177, 176–177; 1:182
mulattos, 4:33
multimedia, 5:65; 4:90, 90; 5:13
multiplication, 1:80
  Egyptian, 1:80
  logarithms, 1:179, 180
mummies, 5:65, 65
Muñoz Marín, Luis, 8:177; 6:33
Muppets, 6:38
Murasaki Shikibu (Lady Murasaki), 1:90
Muscat, Oman, 5:131

muscle fibers, 2:30
muscles, 5:66; 4:48, *48*, 51
  connective tissue of, 5:12
  involuntary, 5:66
  rheumatism, 6:68
  and **skeletons**, 6:142
museums, 5:66; 3:77; 5:100
  and archaeology, 1:71, *71*
  collections of, 5:*85*
  design of, 1:*75*
  of dolls, 2:164
  furniture in, 3:*141*
  open-air, 5:66, *66*
  and **palaces**, 5:148
mushrooms and toadstools, 5:67,
  67; 3:139, *139*; 6:179
music, 5:67–69, *68*, *69*; 2:103
  African, 1:21, 22; 2:173, *173*
  anthems, 1:63
  ballads, 1:109; 2:119
  bands, 1:114–115, *114–115*
  blues, 1:147
  calypso, 2:14
  on **cassette players**, 2:19, *19*
  chamber music, 2:36, *36*
  choirs, 2:53, *53*
  classical, 5:67
  on **compact discs**, 2:97
  composers of, 2:98–99
  copyrights of, 2:115
  country and western, 2:119; 5:68
  electronic, 3:11, *11*
  folk, 3:108, *108*
  gospel, 3:172
  harmony, 4:14
  heavy metal, 6:81
  hymns, 4:56
  Indian, 4:75
  jazz, 4:112–113, *112–113*, 168
  manuscript, 2:*99*
  melody in, 5:17
  metronomes for, 2:74
  minstrels, 5:37
  musicals, 5:75–76
  national anthems, 5:80; 6:189,
  189
  operas, 5:132, *132*
  orchestras, 5:134–135, *134–135*
  reading, 5:*68*
  reggae, 6:60, *60*; 6:52

rock, 5:68; 6:81, *81*
singing and songs, 6:140–141,
  140, *141*
  spirituals, 6:178, *178*
  and storytelling, 1:22
  symphonies, 7:28
  tempo of, 5:69
  terms in, 5:69
  themes in, 5:17
musical instruments, 5:70–75,
  70–75; 5:134–135, *134–135*
  of Aborigines, 1:9
  African, 1:21, *22*; 2:173, *173*
  in **bands**, 1:114–115, *114–115*
  beans in, 1:123
  bells, 1:129, *129*
  brass, 5:71, *71*, 134
  drums, 2:173, *173*
  electronic, 3:11
  Indian, 4:75
  in Mongolia, 3:*108*
  percussion, 5:74, *74*, 75, 134
  steel drums, 2:15, *15*, 114–15, *115*
  stringed, 5:72–73, *72*, *73*, 134
  woodwinds, 5:70, *70*, 134
musicals, 5:75–76, *75*
music halls, 5:75
musk, 1:107
musk oxen, 7:84
muskrats, 6:53
Muslims, 5:76
  Black, 2:66; 5:76; 8:*153*
  Shiite, 4:102
  Sunni, 4:102
  see also **Islam**
muslin, 7:51
mussels, 6:118
Mussolini, Benito, 8:177, *177*; 2:150;
  3:66; 4:105
mutation, 2:160
Myanmar (Burma), 5:76, *76*; 1:88;
  2:95
Mycenae, 3:180, *181*
myrrh, 2:57
mystery plays, 2:169
myths and legends, 5:77; 3:109;
  4:26, 64; 5:36, 51
  of Aborigines, 1:9
  African, 1:21–22
  American, 1:41–42

ancestor, 1:21–22
  Arthurian, 1:86–87, *86*
  ballads of, 1:109
  in **Bible**, 1:131, 132
  Celtic, 2:32, *32*
  in **children's books**, 2:44–45
  Chinese, 2:49
  of **Christmas**, 2:57, *57*
  in constellations, 2:111, *111*
  cowboys, 2:120
  creation, 1:21
  dragons in, 2:167–168, *168*
  Egyptian, 2:189, 190, *190*
  Greek and Roman, 3:184–185,
  184–185
  in **Hinduism**, 4:30–31, *30*
  historical, 1:22
  Indian, 4:76, *76*
  medieval, 5:14–15, *14*, *15*
  Norse, 2:136, 168; 5:107
  oral tradition of, 1:22; 2:32
  religious, 6:62
  Romulus and Remus, 6:87
  of **saints**, 6:102, *103*
  see also **folktales**
myxomatosis, 7:166

NAACP (National Association for the
  Advancement of Colored People),
  1:19; 2:65–66; 8:75, 246
NAFTA (North American Free Trade
  Agreement), 5:22; 7:73, 101
Nagasaki, Japan, 4:32, 111; 7:181

nails and claws, 5:77, *77*; 2:25; 3:71
Nairobi, Kenya, 4:123
Naismith, James, 1:120
names, 5:78
   Asian surnames, 2:52
   of **Native Americans,** 5:78
Namib Desert, 1:16; 5:78
Namibia, 5:78; 1:175; 2:95
Nanking, China, Porcelain Tower of,
   6:125
nanotechnology, 7:35
Nansen, Fridtjof, 8:178
Napier, John, 1:180
Naples, Italy, 4:104
Napoleon I, 8:178–179, *178*;
   3:39–40, 131; 5:79–80; 6:97
Napoleonic wars, 5:79–80, *79*, *80*;
   7:136
Narayan, R. K., 1:90
NASA, 5:80
Nashville, Tennessee, 2:119; 7:44, *44*,
   45
Nassau, Bahamas, 1:108
Nasser, Gamal Abdel, 8:210
Nast, Thomas, 2:18
national anthems, 5:80; 6:189, *189*
national parks, 5:81, *81*; 5:52, *52*,
   155; 6:85, *85*; 7:110, 185
   and **conservation,** 2:109–110
   and **land use,** 4:138
Native Americans, 5:82–85, *82*, *83*,
   84, *85*; 5:109
   in **Alabama,** 1:29–30
   in **Alaska,** 1:30, 31
   in **Arkansas,** 1:82
   Aztecs, 1:104–105
   in **Bolivia,** 1:148
   burial mounds of, 1:174
   in **California,** 1:182
   in **Canada,** 1:189, 190
   and **cavalry,** 2:27
   in **Central America,** 2:34
   in **Chile,** 2:46
   code talkers, 7:181
   in **Colombia,** 2:90
   in **Colorado,** 1:81; 2:92
   in **Connecticut,** 2:107
   creation stories of, 1:41
   in **Delaware,** 2:140
   dugout canoe, *6:71*

   in **Florida,** 3:99
   French and Indian War, 3:132
   in **Georgia,** 3:156
   in **Guatemala,** 3:189, *189*
   in **Honduras,** 4:38
   hunter-gatherers, 4:53
   in **Idaho,** 4:63
   in **Illinois,** 4:65
   Incas, 4:69, *69*
   in **Indiana,** 4:74
   Inuit, 4:91, *91*
   in **Iowa,** 4:93
   in **Jamaica,** 4:107
   Kachina dolls of, 2:164
   in **Kansas,** 4:120
   in **Kentucky,** 4:122
   and **lacrosse,** 4:134
   in **Maine,** 4:174
   map of, *5:83*
   in **Maryland,** 4:186
   masks of, 4:188, *188*
   Maya, 5:9, *9*
   in **Michigan,** 5:24
   in **Minnesota,** 5:36
   in **Mississippi,** 5:39
   in **Missouri,** 5:41
   in **Montana,** 5:51
   names of, 5:78
   in **Nebraska,** 5:88
   in **Nevada,** 5:93
   in **New Hampshire,** 5:95
   in **New Mexico,** 5:97
   in **North Carolina,** 5:109
   in **North Dakota,** 5:111
   in **Ohio,** 5:127
   in **Oklahoma,** 5:129
   in **Paraguay,** 5:153
   and **Pilgrims,** 5:169–170
   in **Rhode Island,** 6:69
   rituals of, 1:123
   sign language used by, 6:137
   in **South America,** 6:164
   in **South Carolina,** 6:165
   in **South Dakota,** 5:85; 6:166–167
   sweat baths of, 1:39
   in **Tennessee,** 7:44–45
   in **Texas,** 7:49
   in **U.S.,** map, *5:83*
   in **Utah,** 7:109–110
   in **Vermont,** 7:118

   in **Virgin Islands,** 7:129
   in **Washington** state, 7:137
   in **West Virginia,** 7:158
   in **Wisconsin,** 7:171
   at **Wounded Knee,** 6:167
   in **Wyoming,** 7:184
nativity plays, 2:57, *57*
NATO, 3:93; 5:86
naturalists, 1:153
nature, balance of, 5:190
Nauru, 5:121; 2:95
Nautilus, U.S.S., 1:78; 2:108
Naval Academy, U.S., 4:186; 7:107
Navaratrami, 3:73
navies, 5:86; 6:133
   and **pirates,** 5:170
   submarines of, 7:14–15, *14–15*
   of U.S., 2:68, 83; 5:86; 7:107, *107*
navigation, 5:87, *87*; 2:181
   compasses, 2:98, *98*; 2:50; 3:50;
      4:173
   by **explorers,** 3:50–51, *50*, *51*
   gyroscopes, 4:7, *7*
   latitude and longitude, 4:142,
      142
   maps for, 4:180–183, *180*
   satellites, 6:106
Navratilova, Martina, *7:46*
Nazareth, 5:169
Nazis, 5:87; 3:66, 69, 160, *160*; 6:43
   and **concentration camps,** 2:103;
      4:7, 37, 118
   and **Holocaust,** 4:37, 118
N'Dour, Youssou, 1:21
Neanderthal humans, 3:48–49, *49*
neap tides, 7:58, *58*
Nebraska, 5:88–89, *88*; 2:67; 7:100
Nebuchadnezzar II, king of Babylon,
   6:124; 7:44
nebulas, 5:89, *89*; 6:35, *35*, 187, *188*
necropolis, 2:33
needles, **sewing,** 6:126–127
Negroes, *see* **African Americans**
Nehru, Jawaharlal, 8:179, *179*; 4:73;
   6:25
Nelson, Horatio, 8:179
Nemerov, Howard, 5:182
neolithic period, 1:22
neon, 5:90, *90*; 3:148
neo-Nazis, 5:87

NEOs (near-earth objects), 1:91
Nepal, 5:90, *90*; 4:29, *29*, 126; 7:*127*
    flag, 3:93
nephrons, 4:124
Neptune (planet), 5:171, 173, 174, *174*; 6:63, 159, *159*, 160, 171
Nero, 8:180
Neruda, Pablo, 4:142
nerve impulses, 1:154
nervous breakdowns, 5:18
nervous systems, 5:91, *91*; 4:51, *51*
Nesbit, E., 2:45
Ness, Eliot, 6:30
Nessie (Loch Ness monster), 5:51
Nestlé's instant coffee, 2:87
nests, 5:92; 1:59; 4:*8*
    of ants, 1:64
    of birds, 1:*142*; 2:*186*
Netherlands, 5:92, *92*; 3:41; 4:169
    and American Revolution, 1:45
    and **Belgium,** 1:128
    colonies of, 1:148; 2:14; 3:40; 4:77; 6:164; 7:22, 157
    dikes in, 4:137
    early clocks in, 2:75
    early settlers in, 1:53
    explorers from, 3:51
    monarchy of, 4:125, *126*
    painting in, 5:*142–143*
    reclaimed land of, 2:85
    Rotterdam harbor, 6:9, *9*
    windmills in, 7:169
    in **World War II,** 7:179
networks, **radio,** 6:47
Neumann, Johann Balthasar, 1:74
neurology, 5:13
neuroses, 5:18
neurosurgeons, 7:21
neutrons, 1:95, 96, 134; 5:157
Nevada, 5:93–94, *93*; 7:100
Nevis, 7:157
Newbery, John, 2:44, 45
New Caledonia, 5:121
Newcomen, Thomas, 4:78; 6:191
New Deal, 2:143; 8:207
New Delhi, India, 4:70
New England, 7:56
New Hampshire, 5:94–95, *95*; 7:56, 100, 118
New Harmony, Indiana, 7:110

New Jersey, 5:96–97, *96*; 7:56, 100
New Mexico, 5:97–98, *98*; 1:81; 2:67; 7:100, 103
New Order (musical group), 3:11
New Orleans, 4:167–168
    Battle of, 2:68; 4:167; 7:135
    jazz in, 4:112–113
    Mardi Gras in, 2:15; 4:167, *167*, 168
Newport, Rhode Island, 6:*69*, 70, 86
New South Wales, Australia, 1:99, *99*
newspapers, 5:99; 5:13
    censorship of, 2:33
    magazines, 4:172, *172*
Newton, Isaac, 8:180; 3:32, 117; 7:40
newtons (N), 3:117; 6:24
newts, 1:47–48
New Year celebrations, 3:73, *73*
New York (state), 5:99–100, *100*; 7:56, 100, 119
    Fort Ticonderoga in, 3:122, *122*
    West Point in, 7:107, *107*
New York City, 5:99, 100, *100*
    airports, 1:29
    alligators in, 1:42
    Broadway **theaters** in, 7:54, *54*
    Bronx Zoo in, 7:*192*
    Central Park in, 2:65; 5:155, *155*; 8:*183*
    children in, 3:*30*
    on the coast, 2:84–85
    Coney Island, 1:49
    Ellis Island, 4:*67*
    games in, 3:145, *145*
    Guggenheim Museum, 1:*75*
    harbor, 6:9
    Harlem, 1:20
    history of, 2:90
    housing in, 2:64
    marathons, 4:184, *184*
    Metropolitan Museum in, 5:66
    Metropolitan Opera in, 5:132
    Public Library in, 4:152
    Seagram Building in, 1:77
    skyscrapers in, 6:145, *145*
    South Street Seaport in, 7:10
    Statue of Liberty in, 7:99, *99*
    stock market in, 2:143; 6:192, *192*
    tunnels to, 7:85

United Nations headquarters in, 7:95, *95*
    as U.S. capital, 7:138
New York Yankees, 1:118, 119
New Zealand, 5:101; 3:*98*; 4:103; 5:121, 161, 187
    in the Commonwealth, 2:95
    fjords in, 3:92, *92*
    Maori, 4:179, *179*
    mountain climbing in, 5:59, *59*
    and **Oceania,** 5:121
    parliament of, 5:156
    and world wars, 7:177–178, 179
Niagara Falls, 7:145, *145*
Nicaragua, 5:101; 2:34–35
Nicholas, St., 2:57; 6:102
nickel, 5:20
nickelodeons, 5:62
Nicklaus, Jack, 3:*170*
nicotine, 7:62
Niepce, Joseph, 1:185; 5:167
Niger, 5:101; 2:36
Nigeria, 5:102, *102*; 1:84, 186; 2:36, *174*
    in the Commonwealth, 2:95
    sculpture of, 6:112, *112*
night, *see* **day and night**
Nightingale, Florence, 8:180–181, *181*; 2:124; 4:26; 5:118
nightmares, 2:171
Nijinsky, Vaslav, 1:111
Nile, 5:102, *102*; 1:50, 151; 2:84, 145, 187–188, 190; 5:30; 6:74, 75; 7:16, 76
    Aswan dam, 2:*188*
    floods of, 3:98
    irrigation, 4:99, *99*
Nineteen eighty-four (1984), 8:184
Nineveh, sculpture in, 5:19
ninjitsu, 4:186
nirvana, 1:165, 166; 6:61, 102, *103*
nitinol, 4:192
nitric acid, 1:11
nitrogen, 5:103, *103*; 1:94, 95, 102
nitrogen dioxide, in acid rain, 1:10
Nixon, Richard M., 8:181, *181*, 138; 1:182; 7:101, 105
Nkrumah, Kwame, 3:162
Nō (Japanese drama), 7:53
NOAA (National Oceanographic and

Atmospheric Administration), 6:106

Noah, 1:132

Noah's Ark (Hicks), 1:*132*

Nobel, Alfred, 8:181–182, *182*; 3:52; 5:104

Nobel Prize, 5:104; 1:18, 90, 190; 2:117; 3:13, 52; 4:142; 5:30; 6:56; 7:158

nomads, 5:104, *104*; 1:69, 175, 187; 2:47, 145, *145*; 5:30, 119; 6:99, *99*
  gypsies, 4:7, *7*
  homes of, 3:177; 3:*178*; 4:46
  hunter-gatherers, 4:53
  Inuit, 4:91, *91*
  Kyrgyz people, 4:132

noon (midday), 7:60

Normans, 5:105–106, *105*, *106*; 2:37, 77; 3:26
  castles of, 2:20
  feudal system of, 3:75
  Middle English, 3:27–28

Norris, Frank, 1:40

Norse mythology, 5:107; 2:136, 168; 3:163

North America, 5:108–109; 2:113
  Continental Divide, 2:113
  European colonies in, 4:33, 108, 167, 174, 189; 5:22, 94, 95, 110; 7:45, 49, 56, 137
  French and Indian War, 3:132
  grasslands in, 3:177, *178*
  map, 5:*108*
  Mexico, 5:22–23, *22*, *23*
  NAFTA in, 5:22
  Native Americans in, 5:82–85, *83*, *84*, *85*; *see also* **Native Americans**
  Rocky Mountains, 6:85, *85*
  slavery in, 6:146–148, *147*, *148*
  Spanish colonies in, 3:99
  Spanish explorers in, 5:77
  wildlife in, 7:166, *167*
  see also **Canada; United States of America**

North Carolina, 5:109–111, *111*; 2:68; 7:56, 100

North Dakota, 5:111–112, *112*; 7:100, *163*

Northern Ireland, 5:112, *112*; 3:25; 4:97; 7:90–94

northern lights, 5:113, *113*; 7:19

Northern Mariana Islands, 5:113; 5:121; 7:100

Northern Rhodesia, 7:189

North Korea, 5:113; 2:97; 4:131; 6:168

North Pole, *see* **poles**

Northwest Passage, 1:78

Norway, 5:114, *114*; 6:107
  fjords in, 3:92
  literature of, 3:41
  monarchy of, 4:126
  mythology of, 5:107
  parliament of, 5:156
  Vikings, 7:125
  in **World War II,** 7:179

nosebleeds, 5:114

noses, 5:114; 6:123

notions, household, 7:9

Notre Dame cathedral, 3:129, 130

novas, 6:35

Novello, Antonia C., 4:33

novels, 5:114

NPR (National Public Radio), 6:47

nuclear energy, 3:20

nuclear families, 3:59

nuclear fusion, 6:186, *186*

nuclear power, 5:115, *115*; 3:20, 138; 4:63
  accidents, 5:115, 163
  Chernobyl disaster, 7:89
  and **peace movement,** 5:159
  and **pollution,** 5:187
  power stations, 6:16–17, *16*
  and **radiation,** 6:45–46, *45*; 1:96
  ships, 6:133
  for **submarines,** 2:108; 7:14–15, *14–15*
  wars and warfare, 7:136

nuclear weapons, 1:96, *96*, 149

nucleus:
  of atoms, 1:95, 96, 134
  of cells, 2:30

nullification, 8:243

numbers, 5:116–117, *116*, *117*; 4:81
  algebra, 1:34
  arithmetic, 1:80
  averages, 1:104
  binary system, 1:179
  calculators, 1:179–180, *179*

  decimals, 2:137
  equations, 3:32
  fractions, 3:127
  logarithms, 1:179
  percentages, 5:164
  sets, 6:124, *124*
  statistics, 6:190, *190*

Nureyev, Rudolf, 1:111

nursery rhymes, 5:118, *118*; 2:44–45; 3:108

nurses, 5:118; 4:44

Nutcracker, The (Tchaikovsky), 1:*110–111*

nutmeg, 6:176, *176*

nutrition, 3:110–111; 4:18
  and **diets,** 2:151
  malnutrition, 4:177
  meat, 5:12
  sugar and, 7:17

nutritionists, 3:111

nuts, 5:119, *119*; 6:122

Nyerere, Julius, 7:32

nylon, 5:177; 7:29

oak trees, 2:31; 7:78–80, *78–79*, *80*

Oakley, Annie, 8:182, *182*

oases, 5:119; 1:*34*; 2:145; 6:99

oats, 3:173, *173*, 175, *175*

oboes, 5:70

Ob River, Russia, 6:74, 96

observatories, 5:120, *120*
  telescopes in, 7:40, *40*

Oceania, 5:121, *121*; 2:113; 3:132

developing countries in, 2:148–149
Fiji, 3:76, *76*
Hawaii, 4:16–17, *17*
Indonesia, 4:77, *77*
Japan, 4:109–111
Maori in, 4:179, *179*
map, 5:*121*
monarchies in, 4:126
New Zealand, 5:101
Papua New Guinea, 5:152
Polynesia, 5:187
Ryukyu Islands, 4:109
oceans and seas, 5:122–125, *122, 123, 124, 125*
    algae in, 1:33
    animals in, 5:122–123, *123, 124*
    basins of, 5:122, *122, 124*
    and **caves**, 2:29
    and **climate**, 2:73
    coasts, 2:84–85, *84*
    currents in, 5:125
    divers in, 2:159, *159*
    earthquakes in, 2:178–179
    evolution of life in, 3:43–45, *44–45, 153*
    fish in, 3:85, 86
    fishing in, 3:89, *89*
    fishing industry in, 3:90–91, *90–91*
    pirates on, 5:170
    plankton, 5:175
    and **plate tectonics**, 5:179, *179*
    pollution of, 5:186
    seashore, 6:118–119, *118, 119*
    seaweeds, 6:121, *121*
    waves in, 5:125, *125*
    zones of, 5:122–123, *124*
    see also specific oceans
O'Connor, Sandra Day, 8:182; 1:81; 4:145, *145*; 7:49
octopuses, 5:126, *126*; 5:44, *44*
O'Dell, Scott, 2:45
Odessa, Ukraine, 7:*89*
Odin (Norse god), 5:107
Odysseus, 4:26
Odyssey, 5:126; 3:183; 4:26, 64
Ōe, Kenzaburō, 11.90
Offa, king of Mercia, 1:*53*
Oglethorpe, James, 3:156

O'Hare International Airport, Chicago, 1:28, *28*
O'Higgins, Bernardo, 8:212
Ohio, 5:127–128, *128*; 7:100
Ohio River, 5:127
oil, 5:128–129, *129*; 3:138; 4:95, 132, 153; 5:30
    in Algeria, 1:35
    in Bahrain, 1:109
    crude, 2:40
    and **detergents**, 2:148
    drilling for, 5:35, 128
    in **Middle East**, 5:30
    as **symbol**, 7:26
    in Venezuela, 7:117, *117*
oil lamps, 4:*156*, 157, *157*
Ojibway tribe, 1:41
Okavango Swamp, Botswana, 1:151; 7:*160*
O'Keeffe, Georgia, 8:183; 5:97; 7:171
    painting by, 8:*183*
Okefenokee Swamp, 3:157
Oklahoma, 5:129–130, *130*; 7:100
Old Farmer's Almanack, The, 1:36
Oldfield, Mike, 3:11
Olds, William, 4:190
Oliver, King, 4:112, *112–113*, 113
Olmec people, 1:50, 104; 6:21
Olmos, Edward James, 4:33
Olmsted, Frederick Law, 8:183
Olympia, Washington, 7:137
Olympic Games, 5:131, *131*; 3:156; 6:173, 180
    in ancient Greece, 3:181
    archery, 1:72, *72*
    arena for, 3:*157*
    baseball, 1:118, 120
    basketball, 1:120
    boxing, 1:153
    canoeing, 2:9
    cycling, 2:129
    gymnastics, 3:191–192, *191–192*
    ice skating, 4:62
    marathons, 4:184
    medals awarded in, 5:12
    rowing, 6:92
    show-jumping, 6:134, *134*
    skiing, 6:143, *143*
    soccer, 6:154–155
    swimming, 7:24, *24*

tae kwon do, 4:186
tennis, 7:46–47, *47*
terrorists at, 7:48
track and field, 7:70–72, *70, 71, 72*
in **Utah** (2002), 7:110
water sports, 7:*146*, 147, *147*
winter sports, 7:170
women's softball, 1:118
wrestling, 7:182, *182*
Olympus, Mount, 2:130
Omaha, Nebraska, 5:88, 89
Oman, 5:131, *131*; 4:126; 5:30
omnivores, 1:57; 3:94, 114
O'Neill, Eugene, 8:184; 1:41; 2:169; 5:100
Onnes, Heika Kamerlingh, 7:19
Ontario, Lake, 4:135
operas, 5:132, *132*; 3:77; 5:135; 6:140–141, *140*
    and ballets, 1:111
    and **musicals**, 5:75
operettas, 5:132
ophthalmic surgery, 7:21
ophthalmologists, 5:133
opium, 2:50–51, 172, *172*
Opium War (1839–1842), 2:51; 6:151
Opoku Ware, 1:22
opossums, 5:132, *132*; 4:185, *185*
optical brighteners, 3:105
optical fibers, 7:38, 39
optical microscopes, 5:26, *26*
optical telescopes, 7:40
optics, 5:133
    fiber, 3:75, *75*
    rainbows, 6:51
    telescopes, 7:40, *40*
optometrists and opticians, 5:133, *133*
oranges, 3:137, *137*
orangutans, 5:133, *133*; 1:65, 151; 6:25
Orb, the, 3:11, *11*
orbits:
    of **planets**, 6:159–160, *159*
    satellite, 6:106, *106*, 169–172
orchestra (theater section), 7:53
orchestras, 5:134–135, *134–135*; 2:36
orchids, 5:136, *136*
Oregon, 5:136–137, *137*; 7:100

Oregon Trail, 5:*88*, 89, 136; 7:137; 8:247
ores, 1:39; 5:20, 35, 36–37
organs (tissue), 2:30
orgasms, 6:128
Oriental rugs, 6:93, *93*
orienteering, 5:138; 2:98; 4:182
origami, 5:138, *138*
"Origin of Corn, The," 1:41
Orinoco River, 7:117
Orkney Islands, 6:111
Ornithischia, 2:154–155, *155*
ornithologists, 1:142
Orozco, José, 8:184
    mural by, 8:*184*
Ortega, Katherine, 4:33
Orthodox churches, 2:55, 56, *56*, 57, 58–59, *58*
orthopedic surgeons, 7:21
Orwell, George, 8:184–185, *185*; 1:35; 3:29
Oscars (Academy Awards), 5:62
oscillation, 7:121
Osiris, 2:190, *190*
Oslo, Norway, 5:114
osteopathy, 1:39
ostriches, 1:138, *138*, 143; 2:186
Otis, Elisha G., 3:17
Otis, James, 1:43
otters, 5:138, *138*
Otto I, king of Franconia, 3:159
Ottoman Empire, 5:139; 1:32, 84, 172, 177; 3:38; 4:52; 5:30
    Croatia, 2:125
    Greece, 3:182
    Iraq, 4:95
    Jordan, 4:116
    Lebanon, 4:148
    Macedonia, 4:169
    Palestine, 5:148
    and **Roman Empire**, 6:91
    Romania, 6:87
    Serbia, 6:124
    Turkey, 7:86
    and **World War I**, 7:177–178
ovaries, 6:127
ovens, 7:11, *11*
Ovid, 3:183
Ovimbundu people, 1:55
Owen, Robert, 4:74; 7:110

Owens, Jesse, 1:19; 7:70
owls, 1:141, *143*; 3:54
oxbows, 6:73, *73*
oxen, 1:22
oxidization, 5:139
oxygen, 5:139; 3:14, 43, 121, 148; 6:67, *67*
    in **air**, 1:24, 158
    in the **atmosphere**, 1:94; 2:177
    in blood, 1:146
    in body, 1:51
    and **fire**, 3:78
    in **human body**, 4:48
    as **liquid**, 4:160
Ozark Mountains, 1:82
ozone, 5:139
    and **aerosol containers**, 1:14
    in **atmosphere**, 1:94
    and **greenhouse effect**, 3:186, *186*
ozone layer, 5:139, *139*

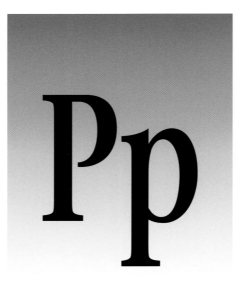

pacas, 6:86, *86*
Pachelbel, Johann, 5:67
Pacific Ocean, 5:122, *125*
    coral reef in, 2:*115*
    European colonies of, 5:113, 121, 165
    and Northwest Passage, 1:78
    Oceania in, 5:121, *121*
    and Panama Canal, 5:149, *149*
    Polynesia in, 5:187, *187*
    U.S. territories in, 5:121, 165

Padilla, Heberto, 4:33
Padua, Italy, 4:105
Pagliacci, 5:*132*
Pago Pago, Samoa, 1:46
Paige, Satchel, 1:120
Paine, Thomas, 8:185
paint, 5:140; 2:92
Painted Desert, Arizona, 1:82
painting, 5:140–146, *140*; 3:77; 5:*141*, *142–143*, *144*, *145*, *146*
    by Aborigines, 1:9
    abstract, 5:144
    by Bushmen, 1:175
    cave, 2:28–29, *28–29*; 5:140; 6:18, *18*
    frescoes, 3:133, *133*
    icons, 1:177; 4:62, *62*
    illuminated manuscripts, 4:66
    Impressionists, 5:144, *145*, 146
    portraits, 6:8, *8*
    Renaissance, 6:63, *64*
    on rocks, 1:175, *175*
    as self-expression, 5:143–144
    on tombs, 2:*189*; 3:35
Pakistan, 5:147, *147*; 1:50, 84; 3:*63*; 4:72, 73
    and **Bangladesh**, 1:116
    in the Commonwealth, 2:95
    Himalayas, 4:29
    Kashmir, 4:71
    mosques in, 5:55
palaces, 5:147–148, *147*, *148*
    castles, 2:20–21, *20–21*
Palestine, 5:148; 4:118; 5:30
    and Crusades, 1:177
    and **Israel**, 4:103, 124
    refugees from, 6:59
Palladio, Andrea, 1:74
    buildings designed by, 1:*75*, *76*
Palm Sunday, 3:74
palm trees, 5:149, *149*
Pamir mountains, 7:31
Panama, 5:149, *149*; 2:34–35
Panama Canal, 1:182, 192, *192*; 5:149, *149*; 6:175
Panavia Tornado (aircraft), 1:26
pancreas, 2:152
pandas, 5:150, *150*
pandemics, 3:31
Pangaea, 2:113, 153; 5:179, *179*

Pankhurst, Emmeline, 7:16
Paolo and Francesca, 5:14
paper, 5:151, *151*; 3:76; 6:27
    in books, 1:151
    invention of, 2:50, 170
    recycling of, 6:55, *55*
    from **wood**, 7:124
Papua New Guinea, 5:152; 2:95, *169*; 5:121
papyrus, 1:151; 2:188; 5:151; 6:56; 7:183
parables, 5:152; 1:165; 2:54
parachutes, 5:152, *152*
    and **skydiving,** 6:145, *145*
parades, 1:114, 115
Paradise Lost, 8:168
paraffin wax, 7:149
paragliding, 4:13, *13*
Paraguay, 5:153, *153*; 6:164
parakeets, 5:156
parasites, 5:153, *153*; 1:57, 107
    fleas, 3:94
    on **hedgehogs,** 4:22
    lice, 4:153, *153*
    plants, 3:102
    roundworms, 7:182
    tapeworms, 7:33
    wasps, 7:142
parchment, 1:151; 2:45
Paré, Ambroise, 7:21
parenthood, 5:154, *154*; 6:18, *18*
Paricutín, Mount (Mexico), 7:132
Paris, France, 2:62, 64, 72; 3:37, 128, 129
    Eiffel Tower in, 3:23, *129*
    fashion in, 3:66, *66*
    Louvre Museum in, 5:148
    Luxembourg Gardens in, 5:*154*
    Métro (subway) in, 7:*16*
Paris, Treaty of (1763), 1:190; 3:132
Paris, Treaty of (1783), 1:44, 45; 7:105
Parker, Charlie, 1:19; 4:112
Parker, Judge Isaac ("hanging judge"), 1:82
Parkes, Alexander, 5:177
parks, 5:154–155, *154, 155*
    and **land use,** 4:138
    national, 5:81, *81*; 5:52, *52*
Parks, Rosa, 2:65

parliaments, 5:156; 3:26
parrots, 5:156, *156*
parsley, 4:25, *25*
Parson, Charles, 7:86
Parthenon (Greece), 7:*43*
particle board, 7:174, *174*
particles, 5:157, *157*; 3:14; 5:168
    atomic, 1:95, 96
    Big Bang theory, 1:134
    in **comets,** 2:94
    in exhaust fumes, 1:102
    and **radiation,** 6:45
Parton, Dolly, 2:119; 7:44
parts of speech, 3:28
Pasarell, Charlie, 7:47
Pascal, Blaise, 8:185; 1:180
pascals (Pa), 6:24
Passover, 5:157; 3:74, *74*; 4:117, 118
passports, 5:158
Passy, Frédéric, 6:56
pasta, 5:158, *158*
paste, 2:33
Pasternak, Boris, 3:41
Pasteur, Louis, 8:186, *186*; 1:107
pasteurized milk, 5:32
Patagonia, 1:79
patents, 5:158
    and **trademarks,** 7:74, *74*
Paterson, Katherine, 2:45
Pathfinder spacecraft, 6:*170–171*, 171
Paton, Alan, 1:18
Patrick, St., 8:186; 4:97; 6:102
patrons (of artists), 1:13
patterns:
    mathematical, 1:80
    symmetry in, 7:27, *27*
    in **textiles,** 7:51, *51*
Patton, George S., ?:000
"Paul Revere's Ride," 8:202
Paul, St., 8:186–187; 2:54; 6:62, 102, *103*
Pauling, Linus, 8:187; 5:136
Pavlov, Ivan, 8:187
Pavlova, Anna, 1:110, *110*, 111
Paz, Octavio, 4:142
PCT (position computed tomography) scans, 6:108, *108*
Peace Corps, 5:158–159, *159*
peace movement, 5:159
peanuts, 5:119, *119*

"Peanuts" (Schulz), 2:18, *18*
Pearl Harbor, 5:159–160, *159*; 2:107; 4:16, 111; 7:180
pearls, 5:160, *160*; 3:150
pears, 3:136, *136*
Pearson, Lester B., 1:190
Peary, Robert, 8:187–188, *188*; 5:162
peasants, 5:160; 5:29
peat, 2:81
peat bogs, 5:65
peatlands, 7:160
Pedersen, Niels, 4:112
pediatrics, 5:13
Peel, Robert, 6:25
Pei, I. M., 1:74
Pelée, Mont, 2:13; 7:132
pelicans, 1:*139*, 140
Peloponnesian War, 7:136
Peña, Federico F., 4:33
pencil drawings, 2:171
pendulums, 5:161; 2:74, 75; 5:10, *10*
penguins, 5:161–162, *161*; 1:138, *139*, 140, 143
penicillin, 1:63, 137; 2:39
penis, 6:128
penitentiaries, 6:29, *29*
Penn, William, 8:188–189, *188–189*; 5:162
Penn and Teller, 4:173
Pennsylvania, 5:162–163, *163*; 7:56, 100; *see also* Philadelphia
Pennsylvania Dutch, 1:46
Pentagon, the, 7:141
pentagons, 6:129, *129*
Pentecost, 3:74
pepper, 6:176, *176*
Pepys, Samuel, 3:29
percentages, 5:164; 2:137; 3:127; 6:30
percussion instruments, 5:74, *74, 75*, 134
perennial plants, 3:102
Pérez de Cuéllar, Javier, 7:95
perfumes, 3:103
Pericles, 8:188–189; 3:181
periodicals, 4:172, *172*
periodic table of elements, 3:14
periodic waves, 7:149
periscopes, 7:14
Perkin, William, 2:174

Perlman, Itzhak, 2:*157*

Perón, Eva, 1:79

Perón, Isabel, 1:79

Perón, Juan, 1:79; 2:150

Perrault, Charles, 3:58

Perry, Matthew, 8:189; 4:111; 6:69

Perry, Oliver Hazard, 8:189; 5:128;
 6:69; 7:135

Persephone (Greek goddess), 3:184,
 184

Persepolis, 8:*254*

Perseus, 4:26

Pershing, John, 8:189–190, *190*;
 5:41, 88

Persia (Iran), 3:181; 4:94, *94*; 8:254

Persian Wars, 7:136; 8:254

Peru, 5:164, *164*; 6:164
 conquistadores in, 2:109
 desert oasis in, 5:*119*
 El Cañon de Colca in, 7:112
 Incas in, 4:69, *69*
 Machu Picchu, 1:70

pesticides, and **pollution**, 5:186, *186*;
 8:43

petals, 3:103, *103*

Peter the Great, 8:190, *190*; 6:97

Peter Pan, illustration, 8:*21*

Peter, Paul and Mary, 3:108

Peter, St., 8:191; 2:58; 5:190; 6:102,
 103

Peterson, Oscar, 4:112

Peterson, Roger Tory, 1:142

Petra, Jordan, 4:*116*

Petrarch, 3:41

petrels, 2:71

Petrified Forest, Arizona, 1:82

petroleum, 5:128–129, *129*

pets, 5:165
 birds, 1:141
 cats, 2:24–25
 chickens, 2:42
 dogs, 2:162–163, *162–163*
 and **endangered species**, 3:19
 gerbils, 3:157, *157*
 hamsters, 4:12, *12*
 mice, 5:23
 ponies, 5:189, *189*
 tropical fish, 1:67
 veterinarians and, 7:121

Phaethon (asteroid), 1:91

phagocytes, 1:146

pharaohs, 2:188; 4:28

pharmacists, 2:41

Pharos of Alexandria, 4:158; 6:125,
 125

Phidias, statue of Zeus by, 6:124;
 6:*125*

Phidippides, 4:184

Philadelphia, Pennsylvania, 5:162,
 163
 Constitutional Convention in,
  2:112; 5:96, 162
 Independence Hall in, 5:162, *163*
 Liberty Bell in, 4:152
 Mint in, 2:87
 as U.S. capital, 7:138

philately, 6:185, *185*

Philip II, king of Spain, 8:191; 3:27,
 181; 5:165; 6:174

Philippines, 5:165; 4:*138*; 6:175;
 7:104

philosophers, 5:165

phloem, 7:80

Phoenicians, 5:166; 1:37, *37*; 3:50

Phoenix, Arizona, 1:81

phonographs, 6:54

phosphates, 2:148

phosphorescence, 3:105

photocopiers, 5:166, *166*

photography, 5:167, *167*; 3:77
 aerial, 1:70
 cameras, 1:184–185, *184*, *185*
 halftones, 6:26, *26*
 portraits, 6:8
 silver in, 6:139
 special-effects, 7:*146*
 video, 7:123, *123*

photons, 4:156–157; 5:157

photosynthesis, 5:168; 1:24, 33, 107;
 2:*10*, 185; 3:43, 101, 114, 121;
 4:154; 5:188
 leaves, 4:147
 and **ozone**, 5:139
 plankton, 5:175
 and **respiration**, 6:67
 seaweed, 6:121
 trees, 7:78

pH scale, 1:11

Phyfe, Duncan, 3:141

phylum, 1:58

physicists, 5:168; 4:133

physiotherapy, 2:35

phytoplankton, 1:33; 5:175, *175*

pianos, 5:74, *74*

Piazzi, Giuseppe, 1:91

pica, 2:180

Picasso, Pablo, 8:192
 painting by, 8:*192*

Pickett, Wilson, 6:81

Pico Duarte, 2:166

pictograms, 7:183

pidgin languages, 4:139

Pierce, Franklin, 8:192–193, *193*;
 5:94; 7:101

Piero della Francesca, 8:193
 painting by, 8:*193*

Pierre, South Dakota, 6:166

piers, 1:73

pigeons and doves, 1:143

pigs, 5:168, *168*; 2:166; 3:62

Pike, Zebulon, 2:92, 93; 4:120

Pikes Peak, 2:*93*

pilgrimages, 5:169; 2:56; 4:101, 102;
 5:29

Pilgrims, 5:169–170, *169*, *170*; 2:90;
 6:39

Pilgrim's Progress, The (Bunyan), 1:35;
 2:44; 3:29

Pinard, A., 2:74

Pinchot, Gifford, 2:109

pineapples, 3:136, *136*

pine cones, 7:*80*

Pinel, Philippe, 5:18

Pinkerton, Allan, 2:147

Pinocchio (Collodi), 2:45

Pinsky, Robert, 5:182

Pioneer spacecraft, 6:170, 171

pipe tobacco, 7:62

Pippin, Horace, 1:19
 painting by, 5:*146*

Piradello, Luigi, 3:41

pirates, 5:170; 4:107

Pi Sheng, 6:27

pistils (flowers), 3:103, *103*

pitch:
 in singing, 6:140
 in sound, 6:161

Pitt, William, 6:25

Pittsburgh, Pennsylvania, 2:62

pixies, 3:56, *56*

Pizarro, Francisco, 8:194; 2:109; 4:69; 5:164

placental mammals, 4:178

placer mining, 5:35

place value, 5:117

plague, 1:144; 3:31

Planck, Max, 8:194

planes, *see* aircraft

planets, 5:171–174, *171, 172, 173, 174*; 6:*63*; 7:108, *108*
  asteroids, 1:91
  and astronomers, 1:93
  meteors and meteorites, 5:21
  and satellites, 6:106
  and solar system, 6:159–160, *159*
  and space exploration, 6:169–172, *171*
  see also Earth

plankton, 5:175; 1:33, 117; 3:87; 4:140; 5:122, 123, *123, 124*

plantations, 7:56

plants, 5:175–176, *176*; 7:165–167, *167*
  bulbs and corms, 1:172, *172*
  cacti, 1:178, *178*; 2:145, *145*
  carnivorous, 3:94, 102
  cells of, 2:30, *31*
  chlorophyll of, 2:30; 4:147; 5:168, 175; 6:121
  classification of, 2:70
  on cliffs, 2:71
  cloning of, 2:76
  corn, 2:116, *116*
  cotton, 2:118–119, *119*
  and ecosystems, 2:184–185, *184*
  endangered species of, 3:19, *19*
  and energy, 3:20–21, *20, 21*
  evolution of, 3:43, *43*, 44
  extinct, *see* extinct animals and plants
  ferns, 3:72, *72*
  flowering, 3:101–102, *101, 102,* 103–104, *103, 104*
  food chains and webs, 3:114
  in forests, 3:118–121
  fossils, 3:123–124, *123*
  growth of, 3:188, *188*
  habitats of, 4:8
  hormones of, 4:40
  hybrid, 2:116; 5:136
  leaves of, 3:101–102, *101*; 4:147, *147*
  lichens, 4:154, *154*
  mosses, 5:56, *56*
  new drugs from, 3:19
  in the oceans, 5:122, *124*
  and oxygen, 3:43
  parasites, 3:102; 5:153
  photosynthesis, 5:168
  plankton, 5:175
  pollination of, 5:185
  in ponds, 5:188–189, *188–189*
  reproduction of, 6:65
  respiration of, 6:67
  in rivers, 6:71, *72*
  roots of, 6:91, *91*
  seaweed, 6:121, *121*
  seeds, 6:122, *122*
  shrubbery, 6:136, *136*
  spores of, 6:179, *179*
  stream habitat for, 7:12–13, *12*
  trees, 7:78–80, *78–79, 80*
  vegetables, 7:116, *116*
  and water, 7:143

plasma, 1:146

plastic explosives, 3:52

plastics, 5:177–178, *177*; 4:192
  recycling of, 6:55, *55*
  synthetic fibers, 7:29

plastic surgery, 5:178; 7:21

plate (printing surface), 6:26

plateaus, 1:15

platelets, 1:146, *146*

plate tectonics, 5:179, *179*; 2:113, 177, 178–79; 4:29, 136; 5:60–61, *60, 61*, 122; 6:84; 7:133

platinum, 5:20

Plato, 8:194, *194*; 3:77, 181

Platte River, 5:89

platypuses, 5:180, *180*; 4:178, *178*

Plessy v. *Ferguson,* 2:66

Plimpton, James L., 6:86

Plimsoll marks, 3:97, *97*

PLO (Palestine Liberation Organization), 5:148

Plotinus, 3:183

ploughs, 1:23; 3:65; 4:65

plumbing, 5:180; 7:148

plums, 3:136, *136*

Plutarch, 1:136; 3:183

Pluto (Disney), 2:19

Pluto (planet), 5:171, 174; 6:159, *159*, 160, 169

plutonic rocks, 6:83

plutonium, 6:45

Plymouth, Massachusetts, 4:189; 7:56; 8:251

plywood, 7:174, *174*

p.m. (post meridiem), 7:60

pneumatic tools, 1:24

pneumonia, 5:180

Pocahontas, 8:195, *195*; 4:108; 7:128

pocket billiards, 1:135

Poe, Edgar Allan, 8:195, *195*; 1:40; 4:187

poems and poetry, 5:181–182; 3:29, 183; 4:141–142, 160
  ballads, 1:109
  Bible and, 1:132
  Iliad, 3:183; 4:26, 64; 5:126
  nursery rhymes, 3:108; 5:118, *118*
  Odyssey, 3:183; 4:26; 5:126

poets laureate, 5:182

pogroms, 4:118

poisons, 5:182

poker, 2:12, *12*

Poland, 5:183, *183*; 3:30, 160; 6:148, 168; 7:179

Polaris, 6:144

polar orbits, 6:106

polders, 4:137

poles, 5:183; 4:59–60, *60*; 5:31, *31*
  latitude and longitude, 4:142
  magnetic north, 4:182
  North Pole (Arctic), 1:78
  and seasons, 6:120, *120*
  South Pole (Antarctica), 1:60

pole vault, 7:71, *72*

police, 5:184, *184*; 5:*186*
  detectives, 2:147
  and fingerprints, 3:77
  lie detectors used by, 4:154

polio, 5:184–185, *184*

political parties, 5:185; 2:192

political prisoners, 6:29

Polk, James K., 8:196, *196*; 1:182; 5:110; 7:101

pollination, 5:185; 1:126, *126*, 176; 3:95, 101, 103, 104, *104*, 137; 5:119, 136

pollution, 5:186–187, *186, 187*; 3:30; 4:154; 7:*92*, 144
  acid rain, 1:10; 3:30
  aerosol containers, 1:14
  in air, 1:24
  and **asthma**, 1:91
  from **automobiles**, 1:10, 102; 2:64
  and **conservation**, 2:109–110
  and **detergents**, 2:148
  from factories, 2:64, *64*; 3:*30*
  in farming, 1:23
  and **green movement**, 3:187, *187*
  lead, 4:146
  in **Mediterranean**, 5:16
  and nitrogen cycle, 5:103, *103*
  nuclear waste, 5:115
  from **power stations**, 6:17
  sewage, 6:126, *126*
  smog, 3:105
  and **water supplies**, 7:148
polo, 5:187
Polo, Marco, 8:196–197; 2:50; 3:50; 5:77, 158
  map, 8:*196*
polonium, 6:46
Pol Pot, 1:183
poltergeists, 3:163
Polyakov, Valery, 1:93
polycarbonate, 5:177
polyester, 5:177; 7:29
polygamy, 5:54; 7:110
polymers, 5:178
Polynesia, 5:187, *187*; 1:46; 4:16, 179, *179*; 5:101, 121
polypropylene, 5:177
polyps, 2:115
polystyrene, 5:178
polythene, 2:40; 5:177
Pompeii, Italy, 1:70; 6:88; 7:133
Ponce de León, Juan, 2:109; 3:99; 7:103
ponds, 5:188–189, *188–189*; 3:88, 89
ponies, 5:189, *189*; 4:42–43, *42–43*
Pont du Gard, France, 1:68, *68*, 73
Ponte Vecchio, Italy, 1:*160*
Pontiac, Chief, 5:24
Pony Express, 5:42
pool and billiards, 1:135
Poor Richard's Almanac (Franklin), 1:36

popcorn, 2:116
Pope, Alexander, 3:29
Pope, John, 2:68
popes, 5:190, *190*; 2:23, 56, 135; 5:27, 147; 6:57; 7:116
Popeye the Sailor, 2:18
population, 5:190–192, *190, 191, 192*
  animal, 5:190–191, *190*
  in **cities**, 12.63, map, 2:*63*
  human, 5:191–192, *191, 192*
  patterns of, 5:192
  and **poverty**, 6:15, *15*
porcelain, 6:13
Porcelain Tower of Nanking, 6:125
porcupines, 6:7, *7*; 6:86
Porky Pig, 2:19
porpoises, 6:7, *7*
Port-au-Prince, Haiti, 4:10
Porter, Cole, 4:74; 5:75
Portland, Maine, 4:175
Portland, Oregon, 5:137
portraits, 6:8, *8*; 3:77; 6:115
  of **Native American** child, 5:*84*
  painting, 5:144, *144*
  photographic, 5:*167*
ports and harbors, 6:9–10, *9, 10*
  Dubai, 7:*90*
  in **Greenland**, 3:*187*
  in **Haiti**, 4:*10*
  Mediterranean, 5:16
  Newport, Rhode Island, 6:*69*
  in **Norway**, 5:114, *114*
  San Francisco, 2:*62*; 7:*96*
  ships and, 6:132–133
Portugal, 6:11, *11*; 3:41
  African colonies of, 1:17, 18, 55; 2:105; 5:64
  American colonies of, 1:156; 6:164
  explorers from, 3:50, 51; 4:73
  Pacific colonies of, 4:77
  and **World War I**, 7:177–178
Poseidon (Greek god), 3:184, *184*, 185
positrons, 5:157
possums, 5:132, *132*
postage stamps, 6:184–185, *184, 185*
postal services, 6:11–12, *11*; 6:184; 7:191
Post, Emily, 3:35

posters, 6:12, *12*; 2:146, *146*; 6:50, 98; 7:104, *104*; 8:*198*, 216, *220–221*
potassium chlorate, 3:80
potatoes, 7:83, *83*
Potter, Beatrix, 2:45; 3:55
pottery, 6:13–14, *13, 14*; 4:80
Poulenc, Francis, 2:36
poultry, 2:42, *42*; 7:87
poverty, 6:15, *15*; 5:160
  in Brazil, 1:*156*; 2:*63*
  and **Civil Rights Movement**, 2:66
  in **developing countries**, 2:148–149
  and **famine**, 3:60
  fighting, 6:105
  and **health**, 4:18
  and **starvation**, 6:189
Powell, Colin, 8:197, *197*; 1:19; 2:66; 5:100
power stations, 6:16–17, *16, 17*; 3:21, 23, 138
  electricity generated by, 1:102; 3:7–10
  and **greenhouse effect**, 3:186
  nuclear, 1:96; 5:115, *115*
  and **pollution**, 5:187
  solar power and, 6:158
  steam engines, 6:191
  tidal power and, 7:58
pozzolana, 2:9
Prague, Czech Republic, 2:130, *130*
prairie dogs, 3:177, *177*
praying mantises, 4:86, *87–88*
pregnancy, 6:18, *18*
  and **birth**, 1:144
  hormones and, 4:40
  and **menstruation**, 5:17, *17*
  see also **sex and sexuality**
prehistoric animals, 6:18–19, *18, 19*; 6:*22*
  dinosaurs, 2:153–156, *153, 154, 155, 156*
  and **evolution**, 3:44–49, *46, 47, 48–49*
  extinction of, 3:52–53, *52–53*
  fossils, 3:123–124, *123, 124*
  in ice ages, 4:58, *58*
prehistoric people, 6:20–23, *20–21, 22, 23*; 3:26, 173; 4:47

agricultural revolution of, 1:22
art of, 6:*114*
burial mounds, 1:174
cave paintings of, 2:28–29, *28–29*
Celts, 2:31–32
drama of, 2:169, *169*
and evolution, 3:44–49, *46, 47, 48–49*
hunter-gatherers, 4:53
in Ireland, 4:96
in Kenya, 4:123
and light, 4:156, *156*
Maya, 5:9, *9*
medicines of, 2:172
stone circles, 7:7–8, *8*
tools of, 7:65
prehistory, 6:20
premiers, 6:25
preservatives, 3:115
Presidential Medal of Freedom, 5:12, *12*
presidents, 6:24; 3:172
   and Congress, 2:106, *107*
   and Constitution, 2:112
   election of, 2:192
   and first ladies, 3:82–83, *82, 83*
   and separation of powers, 2:112
   terms of office, 2:112
   of U.S., 7:101
   see also specific presidents
Presley, Elvis, 1:42; 5:39; 6:81, *81*; 7:45
pressure, 6:24, *24*; 3:117
   air, 1:24
   and barometers, 1:117
   and brakes, 1:155
   and climate, 2:72, 73
   and vacuums, 7:111, *111*
Pretoria, South Africa, 6:162
Priestley, Joseph, 8:197
priests, 6:24; 2:23, 56, 60
   Buddhist monks, 1:*166*, 167
   voodoo, 7:134
primates, 6:25, *25*
   apes, 1:65–66, *65, 66*
   baboons, 4:178, *178*
   chimpanzees, 2:46, *46*, 96; 6:*123*
   evolution of, 3:47, 48, 49
   gorillas, 3:171, *171*
   lemurs, 4:149, *149*

monkeys, 5:49, *49*
   nests of, 5:92
   orangutans, 5:133, *133*
   parenthood of, 5:154
prime ministers, 6:25
prime numbers, 5:117
printer's devil, 6:27
printing, 6:26–27, *26, 27*; 2:50; 6:28, *28*
   books, 1:150–151, *150*
   design, 2:146
   magazines, 4:172
   newspapers, 5:99
   photocopiers, 5:166, *166*
   type, 7:88, *88*
printmaking, 6:28, *28*; 6:12, *12*
prisms, 1:136; 2:*91*; 4:156, *156*
prisons, 6:29, *29*
probability, 6:30; 6:190
production, 2:183
   factors of, 3:56
program, broadcast, 6:47–48, *47, 48*
Prohibition, 6:30; 2:112; 3:146; 7:104
prokaryotes, 2:70
Prokofiev, Sergei, 8:198; 5:67
Prometheus (Greek god), 3:184
prominences, 7:19
proof (liquor), 1:33
propaganda, 6:*98*
propellants, 1:14
prophets, 6:30; 2:54
proportion, 5:164; 7:81, *81*
proprietary colonies, 7:56
proprietors, 6:165
proscenium, 7:54
prosecutors, 4:143
prostheses, 1:87
protectionism, 7:73
proteins, 6:31; 3:43, 47, 110–111, 151
Protestant Christianity, 6:31; 2:54–56, *56*; 3:39; 6:39
   Church of England, 2:60, *60*
   churches of, 2:59, *141*
   gospel music of, 3:172
   Huguenots, 4:47
   and Reformation, 6:57, *57*
protists, 2:70
protons, 1:95, 96, 134; 5:157

prototypes, 2:147
Proust, Marcel, 3:41
proverbs and sayings, 6:32; 1:36, 132
   parables, 1:165; 2:54; 5:152
Providence, Rhode Island, 6:69, 70
psychiatrists, 5:13, 18
psychologists, 6:32
psychoses, 5:18
Ptah (Egyptian god), 2:190
Pteraspis, 3:44
pterosaurs, 3:42, *42, 46*
Ptolemy, 3:183
puberty, 6:33
   and adolescence, 1:11
   coming of age ceremonies, 4:84–85, *84, 85*
   as end of childhood, 2:43
   and menstruation, 5:17, *17*
public domain, 2:115
public health, 4:18
public television, 7:42
Puccini, Giacomo, 8:198; 5:132
Pueblo Indians, cliff-dwelling, 1:*81*
Puerto Rico, 6:33, *33*; 3:*118*; 4:32–34, 34; 6:175; 7:100, 104, 157
puffins, 1:140; 2:71, *71*
Pugin, A. W. N., 1:74
Pulitzer, Joseph, 5:41; 6:175
Pulitzer Prize, 6:34
pulleys, 6:34, *34*; 2:123; 4:169, 170, *170*
Pullman, George M., 4:65, 66
pulsars, 6:35, *35*; 6:188
pulse, 6:35, *35*; 4:19
pumas, 6:36, *36*; 2:24–25
pumice, 6:83
pumps, 6:36, *36*; 7:115
Punch (magazine), 2:170; 8:167
Punch and Judy, 6:38
Punic Wars, 7:136
pupae, 6:37, *37*
   and metamorphosis, 5:21, *21*, 57
   parasites, 5:153, *153*
pupils (of eyes), 3:54
puppets, 6:37–38, *37, 38*
Purcell, Henry, 1:63; 5:67
Puritans, 6:39; 3:27; 8:159
Pushkin, Aleksandr, 3:41

pygmies, 6:39, *39*; 1:174; 2:105; 4:53
Pyle, Ernie, **4:**74
Pyongyang, North Korea, **5:**113
pyramids, 6:40, *40*; 2:188; 6:124, *125*; 7:17, 63
Pyrenees Mountains, **6:**173
Pythagoras, 8:198

Qaddafi, Col. Muammar, **4:**153
Qatar, 6:40; 5:30
quaggars, **7:**190
Quakers, 6:41
quantum mechanics, **1:**96
quarantine, 6:41
quarks, **1:**95, 134; 5:157
quarries, 6:41; 5:35, *35*
quartz crystals, **2:***128*
quartz rocks, **6:**82, *82*
quasars, 6:42
Quaternary Period, **1:**38
Quebec, Canada, **1:**189, *189*
Queensberry, Marquess of, **1:**153
Quetzalcóatl, **1:**105; 2:109
quicksilver (**mercury**), **5:**18
quilts, **6:**127, *127*
Quinceañera, **4:***33*
Quinn, Anthony, **4:**33
Quintilian, **7:**35
Quito, Ecuador, **2:**185
quotas, trade, **7:**73
Qur'an, *see* **Koran**
Qu Yuan, **3:**113

Ra, **2:**190
Rabat, Morocco, **5:**54
rabbits, 6:42, *42*; 2:166, 175; 4:14; 7:166
Rabelais, François, **3:**41
rabies, **6:**41
Rabin, Yitzhak, 8:198–199
raccoons, 6:43, *43*
Rachmaninoff, Sergei, 8:199; 2:103; 5:67
racing:
  auto, 1:103, *103*; 3:129; 4:75
  chariot, **2:**61
  cycling, 2:129, *129*
  horses, 4:42–43
  ice skating, 4:62, *62*
  Iditarod, **1:**31
  marathons, 4:184, *184*
  motorcycles, 5:58, *58*
  Olympic Games, 5:131
  orienteering, 5:138
  roller skating, 6:86
  rowing, 6:92
  running, 6:94, *94*
  skiing, 6:143, *143*
  skydiving competitions, 6:145
  track and field, 7:70–72, *70*
  water sports, 7:146–147, *147*
  white-water, **2:**9
  yachts, 6:70; 7:186, *186*
racism, **6:**43
  apartheid, **6:**162

  and **Civil Rights Movement,** 2:65–66; 1:20
  and **Ku Klux Klan,** 4:131, *131*
Rackham, Arthur, **3:**58
racquetball, **6:**181
radar, 6:44, *44*; 5:26
radial-flow turbines, **7:**86
radiant energy, **3:**20
radiation, 6:45–46, *45*, *46*; 3:20, 105, 115
  in atmosphere, **1:**94, 134
  atomic, **1:**96
  and **heat,** 4:20, *20*
  and **light,** 4:156
  ultraviolet, **4:**156
radio, 6:47–48, *47*, *48*; 5:13
  and **electronics,** 3:12, 13, *13*
  microphones, 2:*107*; 4:166, *166*
  microwaves, 5:26
  radar, 6:44, *44*
  and **radiation,** 6:45–46, *45*
radioactive carbon dating, **1:**71; 2:10
radioactive materials, **6:**45–46, *46*
radioactive waste, **5:**187
radioactivity, **5:**115
radio signals, **1:**94
radio telescopes, **7:**40
radium, **6:**46
Raedwald, king of East Anglia, **1:**54
  helmet of, **1:***54*
Raffles, Stamford, **6:**139
railroads, 6:49–51, *49*, *50–51*; 4:187; 7:76
  bullet trains, **4:***110*
  Channel Tunnel, 2:38; 6:50; 7:85
  funicular, **7:**25
  locomotives, 4:164–165, *164*, *165*
  in **Russia,** 6:96
  steam engines in, **6:**191
  subways, 7:15–16, *15*, *16*
  toy model, **7:**68, 69
  transcontinental, **1:**182, 190; 7:103, *103*
rain, 6:51, *51*; 7:152–153
  and **climate,** 2:72–73
  and **clouds,** 2:80
  and **floods,** 3:98–99, *99*
  monsoons, 5:50, *50*
  and nitrogen cycle, **5:**103, *103*
  and **thunderstorms,** 7:57, *57*

in **water cycle**, 7:*143*, 144, *144*, 148

rainbows, 6:51; 2:91; 7:26, *26, 180*

Rainey, Ma (Gertrude), 1:147

rain forests, 1:156; 3:118–121, *118, 119, 120*; 4:53, *53*

Rainier, Mount, 7:138

Rainier III, prince of Monaco, 5:44

Raksha Bandham, 3:74

Raleigh, North Carolina, 5:110

Raleigh, Walter, 8:199

Ramadan, 2:191; 3:67

Ramses II, 8:199; 2:188

Ramirez, Martin, 4:33

Ramos, Fidel, 5:165

Ramphal, Shridath "Sonny," 2:95

ramps, 4:170, *170*

ranches, 6:52, *52*; 3:62; 7:50

Rand, John J., 5:141

Randolph, A. Philip, 1:19

ranges (stoves), 7:11, *11*

Rangoon, Burma (**Myanmar**), 5:76, *76*

Rankin, Jeannette, 5:51

rap, 6:81

Raphael, 8:200; paintings by, 6:*64;* fresco by, 8:*200*

Raphael, archangel, 1:52

rapid transits, 7:15–16, *15, 16*

Ras al-Khaimah, 7:90

Rastafarians, 6:52, *52*; 4:107; 6:60

rats, 6:53, *53*; 7:*37*; 6:86

rattles, 1:123

Ravel, Maurice, 2:36; 3:132

Rawlings, Marjorie Kinnan, 3:99

raw materials, 4:191

reactors, nuclear, 5:115

Reagan, Ronald, 8:200–201, *201*; 4:65; 7:101

rebirth, 6:60

receiver, **radio**, 6:47

reconnaissance planes, 1:27

recorders, cassette, 2:19, *19*

recording, 6:54, *54*

on **compact discs**, 2:97

microphones, 5:25, *25*

video, 7:123, *123*

rectangles, 6:129, *129*

recycling, 6:55, *55*; 3:56; 7:77, *77*, 148

aluminum, 1:39

and **conservation**, 2:110

of **glass**, 3:166, *166*

paper, 5:151

Red Cloud, Chief, 7:184

Red Cross, 6:56; 7:25

Redding, Otis, 6:81

red giants, 6:187, 188

reed instruments, 5:70, *70*

reeds, 6:56, *56*; 7:161

reflecting telescopes, 7:40, *40*

reflexes, 5:91

reflexology, 1:39

Reformation, 6:57, *57*; 2:23, 56; 3:26, 39; 4:47

refracting telescopes, 7:40, *40*

refrigerants, 6:58, *58*

refrigerators, 6:58, *58*; 3:115

refugees, 6:59, *59*

regattas, 6:92

reggae, 6:60, *60*; 6:52

Rehnquist, William, 4:*145*; 7:171

reincarnation, 6:60; 1:166, 167; 2:32; 4:30; 6:138

reindeer, 6:60, *60*; 2:39; 5:31

antlers of, 4:41, *41*

clothing from, 2:*79*

Reis, Dragut, 5:170

relativity, 6:61; 7:60

religions, 6:61–62, *61, 62*; 3:169

of Africa, 1:16, 17, *17*, 18, 34

Amish, 1:46, *46*

and **angels**, 1:52

anthems of, 1:63

apostles, 1:66; 2:54

of Arabs, 1:69

and **art**, 3:77; 5:142, *142*

of Aztecs, 1:105

Bahaism, 1:108

Bible in, 1:131–132

Buddhism, 1:165–167

Catholicism, Roman, 2:23

Celtic, 2:31–32

Christianity, 2:54–56

Christian Science, 2:57

Church of England, 2:60

Confucianism, 2:104

Druids, 2:31–32; 4:11

of Egypt, 2:189

in Europe, 3:37, 38, 39

festivals and holidays of, 3:73–74, *73, 74*

and **funerals**, 3:139

God, 3:169; 2:57; 6:61, 138

heaven in, 4:22

hell, 4:24

Hinduism, 4:30–31, *30–31*

icons, 4:62, *62*

of Incas, 4:69

in **India**, 4:71, 72, 73, 76

Islam, 4:100–102, *100–101, 102*

Judaism, 4:117–118, *117, 118*

of Maya, 5:9

in **Middle Ages**, 5:27–29

and **miracles**, 5:37

monasteries, 5:45–46, *45, 46*

Mormonism, 5:54; 7:109–110, *109*

Muslims, 5:76

pilgrimages, 5:169

priests, 6:24

prophets, 6:30

Protestant Christianity, 6:31

Quakers, 6:41

Reformation, 6:57, *57*

and **reincarnation**, 6:60

rites and rituals, 6:71

saints, 6:102, *102, 103*

Shakers, 6:129, *129*

Shintoism, 6:131

Sikhism, 6:138

singing and songs, 6:140, *141*

Taoism, 7:32

temples of, 7:43, *43*

voodoo, 7:134

REM (rapid eye movement) sleep, 6:149

Rembrandt, 8:201, *201*

Remembrance Day, 3:73

Remi, Georges (Hergé), 2:18

Remington, Frederic: paintings by, 2:*120*; 8:*210*

sculpture by, 6:*115*

remote sensing, 2:176

Renaissance, 6:63–64, *63, 64*; 3:39; 4:104, 105; 5:29

architecture, 1:76; 2:23, 59; 6:64

fine arts in, 3:77; 5:142–143

portraits in, 6:8, *8*, 115

rennet, 2:39

Reno, Nevada, 5:93, 94

Renoir, Pierre-Auguste, 8:201; 3:132
  painting by, 5:*145*

reproduction, 6:65, *65*; 6:128
  and **eggs,** 2:186, *186*
  of **flowers,** 3:103–104, *103*
  and **genetics,** 3:151, *151*
  human body and, 4:51, *51*
  mating and, 5:7
  and **menstruation,** 5:17, *17*
  pregnancy, 6:18, *18*
  and **puberty,** 6:33
  of **seaweeds,** 6:121
  of **spores,** 6:179

reptiles, 6:66, *66*; 3:71; 7:120, *120,*
  165–167, *165*
  alligators, 1:36, *36*
  chameleons, 2:37, *37*
  crocodiles, 2:125, *125*
  dinosaurs, 2:153–156
  endangered species, 3:19
  evolution of, 3:45–46
  lizards, 4:161, *161*
  snakes, 6:152, *152*
  tortoises and turtles, 7:66–67, *66,*
  67

Republican Party, 5:185

republics, 6:66

resistance, 7:19

resistors, 3:12

resonance, 6:140; 7:121

resources, economic, 2:183

respiration, 6:67, *67*; 1:24; 2:30;
  5:139
  human, 4:49, *49*
  see also **breathing**

Revere, Paul, 8:202; 4:189; 6:139
  bowl by, 6:*139*
  engraving by, 1:*44*

revolutions, 6:68; 6:98, *98*
  American, *see* **American**
    Revolution
  French, 1:45, 84; 5:79
  Russian, 6:68, 98, 168

"Reynard the Fox," 3:55

Reynaud, Emile, 2:18

Reynolds, R. J., 5:110

rheumatism, 6:68

Rhine River, 1:38; 3:159

rhinoceroses, 6:68, *68*; 3:19

Rhode Island, 6:69–70, *69*; 7:56, 100

Rhodes, Cecil, 8:202, *202*; 6:25

Rhodes, Colossus of, 6:125, *125*

Rhodes Scholars, 8:202

Rhône River, 1:38; 3:159

rhyme, 5:181–182

rhythm, 5:69, 181; 6:141

rice, 6:70, *70*; 3:63, 173, 176; 4:*138*;
  6:*160*

Rice, Jerry, 3:*116*

Richard I, king of England,
  8:202–203, *202*; 2:126; 3:26;
  4:125

Richard III, king of England, **8:**203;
  4:125

Richards, Michael, 5:181

Richardson, Samuel, 5:114

Richmond, Virginia, 2:68, 70, *70*;
  7:128

Richter scale, 2:178

rift-valley lakes, 4:135, *135*

rift valleys, 7:113

Riga, Latvia, 4:142

rigging, 6:100

Rights of Man, The, **8:**185

Riley, James Whitcomb, 4:74

Rilke, Rainer Maria, 3:41

Rio de Janeiro, Brazil, 1:156; 2:15, 64,
  84–85

Ripken, Cal, 1:120

Ritchie, Jean, 3:108

rites and rituals, 6:71; 6:62
  baptism, 1:116; 2:55–56, *55*
  beans used in, 1:123
  of **Buddhism,** 4:84–85, *85*, 139
  Christmas, 2:57, *57*; 2:56
  funerals, 3:139
  of **Incas,** 4:69
  initiation ceremonies, 4:84–85,
  84, 85
  of **Islam,** 4:100–102, *100, 102*
  of **Judaism,** 4:118, *118*
  of **Maori,** 4:*179*
  marriage, 4:184
  masks for, 4:188, *188*
  weddings, 7:155, *155*

Rivera, Diego, 8:203, *135*; 3:133;
  fresco by, 5:*23*
  painting by, 8:*203*

Rivera, Tomas, 4:33

rivers, 6:71–75, *71, 72, 73, 74, 75*;
  6:83, *83*, 119
  baptism in, 1:116
  and **canals,** 1:192
  dams of, 2:131, *131*, 188
  deltas of, 4:167
  entering the sea, 2:84
  fishing in, 3:88, 89
  and **floods,** 1:88, 116; 2:131,
  187–188, 190; 3:98–99, *98*
  mining in, 5:35
  Nile, 5:102, *102*
  of **North America,** 5:108, 109
  pollution of, 5:186
  valleys of, 7:112–114, *112–113,*
  114, 145, *145*
  see also specific rivers

Riviera resorts, 5:16

Riyadh, Saudi Arabia, 6:107

Roach, Max, 4:112

Roadrunner (Warner Bros.), 2:19

roads and highways, 6:76–77,
  76–77; 4:*74*; 7:76
  autobahns, 3:159
  beltways, 2:65
  and **bridges,** 1:160
  of **concrete,** 2:104
  freeways, 6:*77*
  traffic jams, 2:64, *64*

Robeson, Paul, 8:204; 1:19; 6:178

Robespierre, Maximilien, 8:204

Robin Hood, 5:14, *14*, 77

robins, 1:*141*

Robinson, Jackie, 1:19, 120; 3:156

Robinson, Smokey, and the Miracles,
  5:25

Robinson Crusoe (Defoe), 2:44; 3:29

robots, 6:78–79, *78, 79*; 4:190; 6:169;
  7:*68*, 69

Roche, Arnaldo, 4:33

rock and roll, 6:81

rock climbing, 5:59, *59*

Rockefeller, John D., 8:204–205;
  1:19; 5:100, 127, 128

rockets, 6:80, *80*; 3:80, *80*; 4:114;
  6:106, 170, 172; 8:31
  missiles, 5:39, *39*
  weapon delivery systems,
  7:150–151

rocking horses, 7:*69*

rock music, 6:81, *81*; 4:113; 5:68, 128; 6:141

rock paintings, 1:175, *175*

rocks, 6:82–84, *82, 83, 84*; 3:33, 154; 7:156

    caves in, 2:29

    cliffs, 2:71, *71*

    and **coal,** 2:81

    and **continents,** 2:113

    crystals, 3:150, *150*

    erosion of, 5:34

    and **geological time,** 3:152, *153*

    metamorphic, 5:34

    and **minerals,** 5:34, *34*

    mining of, 5:35

    in the ocean, 5:122

    and **oil,** 5:128

    and **plate tectonics,** 5:179, *179*

    quarries, 6:41

    and **silicon,** 6:138

rock salt, 6:104–105, *104*

Rockwell, Norman, poster by, 6:12, *12*

Rocky Mountains, 6:85, *85*; 2:92, 113; 5:52, 60, *60*, 93, 109; 7:184

rodents, 6:86, *86*; 6:42

    beavers, 1:125, *125*

    gerbils, 3:157, *157*

    guinea pigs, 3:190, *190*

    hamsters, 4:12, *12*

    lemmings, 4:149

    mice, 5:23, *23*

    nests of, 5:92

    porcupines, 6:7, *7*

    prairie dogs, 3:177, *177*

    rats, 6:53, *53*

    squirrels, 6:182, *182*

    teeth of, 7:*37*

    voles, 7:133, *133*

rodeos, 2:120

Rodgers, Richard, 5:75

Rodin, Auguste, 8:205

    sculpture by, 8:*205*

Rodrigo, Joachín, 2:103

Roe v. *Wade,* 8:182

Roentgen, Wilhelm, 8:205; 6:46; 7:185

Rogers, Ginger, 2:*133*; 5:76

Rogers, Roy, 2:119

Rogers, Will, 5:85, 129

Rojas, Manuel, 4:142

Rolfe, John, 4:108

roller-coasters, 1:49

roller skating, 6:86

Rolling Stones, 4:62; 6:81

Rollins, Sonny, 4:112

Roman Catholicism, *see* **Catholocism, Roman**

Romance languages, 4:138

Romanesque architecture, 5:106, *106*

Romania, 6:87, *87*; 6:168, 184; 7:177–178, 179

Romany people, 4:7, *7*

Rome, Italy, 4:104, 105

    catacombs in, 7:63

    Colosseum in, 6:91, 125

    pilgrimages to, 5:169

    pollution in, 2:64

    Sistine Chapel, 3:133, *133*

Rome and the Roman Empire, 6:87–91, *88, 89, 90, 91*; 4:104–105

    agriculture, 1:22

    alphabet, 1:37

    in **ancient world,** 1:50

    aqueducts, 1:68

    and archaeology, 1:70

    architecture of, 1:73, 74, 75, 76; 2:59

    armor in, 1:85, *85*

    astrology in, 1:92

    and barbarians, 2:135

    bridges, 1:160

    and Britain, 1:53; 3:26, 27

    building materials in, 2:104

    and **Byzantium,** 1:177

    canal systems in, 1:191

    and **Celts,** 2:31

    and **Christianity,** 2:54–55, 58–59

    circuses in, 2:61

    coins of, 2:87, *87*

    cosmetics in, 2:117

    and **Dark Ages,** 2:135

    dictators in, 2:150

    and **dragons,** 2:168

    in **Egypt,** 2:187

    in **Europe,** 3:38

    founding of, 1:13

    Germany in, 3:159–160

    in **Greece,** 3:182

    Hadrian's Wall, 6:111

    horses in, 4:42

    law and legal systems in, 4:143, 144

    legal code of, 1:177

    in **Libya,** 4:153

    literature of, *see* **Greek and Roman literature**

    map of, 8:*17*

    mosaics in, 5:54

    mythology, 3:184–185, *184–185*

    names of, 5:78

    oil lamps in, 4:156

    Pantheon in, 7:43

    papyrus in, 1:151

    as a **republic,** 6:66, 89

    roads built by, 6:77; 7:76

    Saturnalia in, 2:15

    slavery in, 6:146, *146*

    Spain, 6:174

    towns of, 6:87–89, *88*

    weapons used in, 7:150, *150*

Romero, Frank, 4:33

roofs, 1:170, 171

Rooney, Mickey, 5:63, *63*

Roosevelt, Eleanor, 8:206, *206*; 3:82, 83; 5:100; 7:105

Roosevelt, Franklin D., 8:206–207, *206, 207*; 2:*107*, 143; 3:82, 157; 5:100, 160, 185; 7:101, *105*

Roosevelt, Theodore, 8:207, *207*; 2:109; 5:100; 6:167, 175; 7:68, 100

roots, 6:91, *91*; 3:101–102, *101, 102*; 6:122

    holdfast, 6:121

    of **trees,** 7:79–80

    tubers, 7:83, *83*

rope, 6:92, *92*; 3:76

    cables, 1:178

    hoisting (elevator cable), 3:17

    knots, 4:129, *129*

rosemary, 4:25, *25*

Rose, Pete, 1:120

Rosetta Stone, 4:28, *29*

Rosh Hashanah, 3:73

Ross, Betsy, 8:208, *208*; 5:162

Ross, Diana, 5:25

Ross, Nellie Taylor, 7:184

Rossini, Gioacchino, **5**:132
rotational symmetry, **7**:27, *27*
Rotterdam, Netherlands, **5**:92
Roundheads, **6**:39
roundworms, **7**:182, *182*
Rousseau, Jean-Jacques, 8:208; **3**:41
rowing, 6:92
royal colonies, **7**:56
royalties, **2**:115
rubber, 6:93, *93*
rubbish, **5**:186, *186–187*; **7**:77, *77*
Rubens, Peter-Paul, 8:209
    painting by, **8**:*209*
Rudolph, Wilma, **1**:19; **7**:*70*
rugs and carpets, 6:93, *93*
    tapestries, 7:33, *33*
ruminants, **7**:7
rumination, **1**:62; **2**:26
ruminative disorder, **2**:180
rummy, **2**:*11*, 12
runes, **1**:54
running, 6:94, *94*; **4**:184, *184*;
    7:70–72, *70*
Rush, Benjamin, **2**:138
rush hours, **7**:75
Rushmore, Mount, **6**:115, 166, 167,
    167
Russell, George, **4**:112
Russell, William Howard, **2**:124
Russia and the Russian Federation,
    6:95–98, *95, 96, 97, 98*; **1**:88, 89;
    4:111; **6**:148, 168
    and Alaska, **1**:30–31
    in allegory, **1**:35
    ballet in, **1**:111
    circuses in, **2**:61, *61*
    climate in, **2**:73
    Commonwealth of Independent
      States, 2:94
    Communism in, **2**:97
    cosmonauts, **1**:93
    and **Crimean War, 2**:124
    fur hat from, **4**:*15*
    icons from, **4**:62, *62*
    Inuit in, **4**:91, *91*
    Lenin's tomb in, **7**:*63*
    literature of, **3**:41
    poverty in, **6**:*15*
    power stations in, **6**:16–17
    revolution, 6:68, 98, *98*, 168

submarines of, **7**:14
    tanks from, **7**:31
    Trans-Siberian Railway, **6**:49
    in **World War I, 7**:177–178
    see also Soviet Union
Ruth, Babe, **1**:*119*, 120; **4**:186
Rutherford, Ernest, 8:209; **1**:95
Rutledge, John, **6**:165
Ruwenzori, Mount, **5**:61, *61*
Ruwenzori Range, **1**:15
Rwanda, 6:99
Ryan, Nolan, **1**:120
rye, **3**:173, *173*
Ryukyu Islands, **4**:109

Sabah, **4**:176
sabers, **3**:72
Sabin, Albert, **5**:185
Sacajawea, 8:210, *210*; **4**:63; **5**:112
Sacramento, California, **1**:182
sacraments, **2**:55–56
Sacré-Coeur (Sacred Heart) church,
    Paris, **3**:129
Sadat, Anwar, 8:210
sadhus, **6**:102
saffron, **3**:103
sage, **4**:25, *25*
Sahara, 6:99, *99*; **1**:16, 17, 174; **2**:36,
    72, 144, 172; **5**:101, 104; **7**:16
sailing, 6:100, *100*; **1**:147; **6**:*69*, 70;
    7:147, *147*
sailing ships, 6:100–101, *100, 101*;
    6:132–133
St. Augustine, Florida, **3**:99
St. Denis Church, Paris, **1**:76
St. Helena, **2**:95
St. Helens, Mount, **5**:60, *60*; **7**:98, 137
St. Kitts, **7**:157
St. Lawrence Seaway, **1**:192; **5**:100
St. Louis, Missouri, **5**:41, 42, *42*
St. Lucia, 6:102, *102*; **2**:95; **7**:157
St. Mark's Church, Venice, **2**:58
St. Paul, Minnesota, **5**:36, *36*, 37
St. Paul's Cathedral, **8**:*252*
St. Petersburg, Russia, **1**:*76*; **3**:37;
    5:148; **6**:95, 97
St. Peter's Basilica, Rome, **2**:23, *58*;
    8:*191*

saints, 6:102, *102, 103*; 2:23, 56, 59; 3:73
   icons, 4:62, *62*
   in **medieval legends,** 5:15
St. Vincent, 7:157; 2:95
Saladin, 8:210–211; 2:126
salamanders, 6:104, *104*; 1:48
Salem, Massachusetts, 4:189; 7:172
Salem, Oregon, 5:136
Salisbury Cathedral, clock, 2:*74*
saliva, 2:152
Salk, Jonas, 8:211; 5:185
salt, 6:104–105, *104*, 105
   crystals, 2:128, *128*
   in the ocean, 5:125
   removal from water, 7:87
Salt Lake City, Utah, 7:109
Salvation Army, 6:105
Salyut space stations, 6:170
Salzburg, Austria, 1:100
Samaritans, 5:152
Samoa, 1:46; 5:**121, 187**; 7:100
samurai warriors, 4:111, *111*
San, 1:*175*
San Andreas fault, 7:98
San Antonio, Texas, the Alamo in, 7:49, *49*
Sandburg, Carl, 8:211, *211*; 4:65; 5:111
Sandburg, Lilian Steichen, 8:*211*
San Diego, California, 1:182, 183
sandstone, 6:83, 84
Sandwich, Earl of, 1:157
San Francisco, California, 1:182, 183; 2:62, *62*, 87, 179; 6:*29*; 7:*96*, 98
San Juan, Puerto Rico, 6:33, *33*
San Marino, 6:105
San Martín, José de, 8:212, *212*; 1:79
San people (Bushmen), 1:175
San Salvador, El Salvador, 3:16
Sanskrit language, 4:73
Santa Anna, Antonio López de, 8:212; 2:150; 7:49
Santa Claus, 2:57
Santa Fe, New Mexico, 5:97, 98
Santana, Carlos, 4:33
Santiago, Chile, 2:46
São Paulo, Brazil, 11.156, 12.*63*
sapwood, 7:80
Sarajevo, Bosnia, 1:100, 151

Saratoga, Battle of, 1:45
Sarawak, 4:176
Sargent, John Singer, 8:213
Sark, 2:37
Satan (Lucifer), 1:52
satellites, 6:106, *106*; 5:26, 120; 6:172
   communication, 7:38–39, *38*
   and **navigation,** 5:87
   and **planets,** 5:171, 173–174, *173, 174*
   television, 7:42
satin, 7:51
Saturn (planet), 6:159, *159*, 160, 170–171
Saturn rockets, 6:170
Saturn (Roman god), 5:171, *171*, 173–174, *174*
Saudi Arabia, 6:107, *107*; 1:68; 4:126; 5:30
saunas, 3:78
Saurischia, 2:154–155, *155*
Savannah, Georgia, 3:156
savannahs, 1:16
Savery, Thomas, 4:78
Saxons, 1:53–54
saxophones, 5:70, *70*
scales, musical, 5:68–69, *69*
Scalia, Antonin, 4:*145*
scallops, 5:44, *44*
Scandinavia, 6:107; 5:30
   acid rain in, 1:10
   Anglo-Saxons, 1:53
   Denmark, 2:142
   Finland, 3:78, *78*
   literature of, 3:41
   Norse mythology, 5:107
   Norway, 5:114, *114*
   reindeer in, 6:60, *60*
   Sweden, 7:23, *23*
   and **tundra,** 7:84, *84*
   Vikings from, 7:125–126, *125, 126*
scanners, 6:108, *108*; 5:13
scarab beetles, 1:127
Scarlatti, Alessandro, 5:67
scavengers, 1:57; 3:114, 120
scent, in animal communication, 1:56, 64
Scheherazade, 1:68
Schiller, Friedrich von, 3:41

Schoenberg, Arnold, 5:67
Schonberg, Claude-Michel, 5:75
schools, 6:109, *109*; 8:155
   colleges and universities, 2:89
   segregation in, 2:66
   teachers in, 7:35
schooners, 6:*101*
Schubert, Franz, 8:213, *213*; 2:36; 5:67
Schulz, Charles, 2:18; 5:36
Schumann, Robert, 2:103; 5:67
Schurz, Carl, 7:171
Schweitzer, Albert, 8:213
Schwitters, Kurt, collage by, 2:*89*
science fiction, 6:110
scientists, 6:110
Scipio, 8:106
scissors, as levers, 4:151
Scopes, John, trial of, 7:45; 8:66
scorpions, 6:110, *110*
Scotland, 6:111, *111*; 3:25, 27; 6:10; 7:90–94
   Celts in, 2:31–32
   literature of, 3:29
   sheep farming, 1:22
Scott, Dred, 2:67
Scott, Robert F., 1:60–61
Scott, Walter, 8:214; 3:29
screening, in **medicine,** 5:13
screws, 4:170, *170*
scrotum, 6:128
scuba divers, 2:159, *159*
sculpture, 6:112–116, *112, 113, 114, 115, 116*; 3:77; 6:8, *103*
   African, 1:*17*
   Mayan, 5:9, *9*
   in Nineveh, 5:*19*
   Persian, 4:*94*
   purposes for, 6:114–116, *114, 116*
   Renaissance, 6:63
   statue of Zeus at Olympia, 6:124, *125*
scum, 6:153
sea anemones, 6:116, *116*; 1:*56*; 2:115; 6:65, *65*
seacoasts, see **coasts**
Seacole, Mary, 2:124
seals, 6:117, *117*
Sears Tower, Chicago, 4:65, *65*; 6:145
seas, see **oceans and seas**

sea salt, 6:105, *105*
seashore, 6:118–119, *118, 119*; 7:161
  barnacles, 1:117, *117*
  coasts, 2:84–85, *84*
  erosion of, 4:137
  of New Jersey, 5:*96*, 97
  sea anemones, 6:116, *116*
  seaweeds, 6:121, *121*
sea slugs, 5:44, *44*; 6:67
seasons, 6:120, *120*; 2:136
  and climate, 2:72
  and constellations, 2:111, *111*
Seattle, Washington, 7:*137*, 138
seaweeds, 6:121, *121*; 6:118, *119*
  algae, 1:33
  classification of, 2:70
Seawolf (nuclear submarine), 7:*15*
sedges, 6:56
sediment, 6:83–84, *83*
sedimentary rocks, 6:82, 83
seed drills, 1:23; 3:65
seeds, 6:122, *122*
  feeding wild birds with, 1:140
  of flowers, 3:101, 103, *103*
  of fruit, 3:136–137
  of grasses, 3:175
  and nuts, 5:119
  and pollination, 5:185
Seeger, Pete, 3:108
Seeing Eye dogs, 1:145, *145*
Segal, George, sculpture by, 6:*113*
segregation, 1:30; 2:65–66
Seine, River, 3:129
seismologists, 2:179
Sekhmet (Egyptian god), 2:190
selective breeding, 2:165
self-incrimination, 1:136
Selma, Alabama, 1:30; 2:66
semen, 6:128
semiconductors, 3:13; 4:191–192, *192*
Semitic alphabet, 1:37
Senate, U.S., *see* Congress, U.S.
Sendak, Maurice, 2:45
Senegal, 6:122; 3:144; 5:*159*
Senghor, Léopold, 1:18
senses, 6:123, *123*
  and brain, 1:154–155
  ears, 2:175, *175*
  smell, 5:114
Seoul, South Korea, 6:168, *168*

sepals, 3:103, *103*
Sequoyah, 8:214, *214*
seraphim, 1:52
Serbia, 6:124; 1:151; 2:125;
    7:177–178, 188
Serengeti National Park, 1:16
Serra, Father Juniper, 1:182
service academies, 7:106–107
Seton, St. Elizabeth Ann, 8:214–215
Seton, Ernest Thompson, 1:153
sets (badger), 1:107
sets (mathematics), 6:124, *124*
Sevareid, Eric, 5:111
Seven Days, Battle of, 2:68
Seven Wonders of the World,
    6:124–125, *125*; 8:*202*
  Hanging Gardens of Babylon, 5:19
  Zeus at Olympia, 7:43
Seven Years' War, 3:39; 7:136
Seville, Spain, 6:*174*
sewage, 6:126, *126*; 6:56; 7:148, *148*
Seward, William, 1:30–31
sewing, 6:126–127, *127*; 3:66
  embroidery, 3:18, *18*
sewing machines, 2:77; 8:121
sex and sexuality, 6:127–128, *128*
  and mating, 5:7
  and menstruation, 5:17, *17*
  spores and, 6:179
sex discrimination, 6:127
sexually transmitted diseases (STDs),
    6:128
Seychelles, 7:165; 2:95
sgraffito, 6:14, *14*
Shackleton, Ernest, 1:*61*
Shaka the Zulu, 8:215
Shakers, 6:129, *129*
Shakespeare, William, 8:215–216,
    216; 1:136; 2:169; 3:26, 29, 107;
    4:160; 6:111; 7:53–54
Shanghai, China, 2:48, 84–85
shanty towns, 2:64
shapes, 6:129, *129*
  geometry, 3:154–155, *154, 155*
  symmetry of, 7:27, *27*
Shap-ng-tsai, 5:170
Sharjah, 7:90
sharks, 6:130, *130*; 6:123
  teeth of, 7:*36*
Sharp, Cecil, 3:108

Shavuot, 3:113
Shaw, George Bernard, 8:216; 3:29
Sheba, Queen of, 3:34; 4:126
sheep, 6:131, *131*; 2:26, 39, *163*, 166;
    5:*90*; 7:149
  cloning of, 2:76
  farming, 3:62
  ranches, 6:52
  teeth of, 7:36
  wool from, 7:176, *176*
Shelley, Mary, 8:216–217; 3:29; 5:51;
    6:110
Shelley, Percy Bysshe, 8:217, *217*;
    3:29
shellfish, 5:44, *44*, 160
Shepard, Alan, 5:94
Sheraton, Thomas, 3:141
Sheridan, Philip, 2:69, 70
Sheridan, Richard B., 3:29
Sherman, Roger, 2:138
Sherman, William T., 8:217; 2:69,
    70; 3:156; 5:127, 128
Shetland Islands, 6:111
Shiite Muslims, 4:102
Shikibu, Lady Murasaki, 1:90
Shintoism, 6:131; 6:61–62
ships, 6:132–133, *132–133*; 1:147;
    2:*108*; 3:97; 4:78, 175; 7:76
  battleships, 7:178, *178*, 180
  in Civil War, 5:*86*
  clippers, 6:100, *101*
  container, 6:9, *9*
  Liberian registry of, 4:152
  lifeboats of, 4:155, *155*
  Mayflower, 5:*169*
  and merchant marine, 5:18
  Monitor and *Merrimack*, 5:*86*
  of navies, 5:86
  in Pearl Harbor, 5:159–160, *159*
  and pirates, 5:170
  ports and harbors, 6:9–10, *9, 10*
  sailing, 6:100–101, *100, 101*
  slave, 6:147, *147*
  Viking, 7:126, *126*
shock, first aid for, 3:81
Shockley, William, 3:13
shoes, 6:134, *134*
Shoghi Effendi, 1:108
Shona people, legends, 1:21
shooting stars, 5:21

shopping centers, 7:9–10, *10*
Shostakovich, Dimitri, 8:218; 2:103; 5:67
shot put, 7:71, *71*
show-jumping, 6:134, *134*
shrews, 6:135, *135*
shrimp, 6:135, *135*; 2:127, *127*
Shrove Tuesday, 3:73, 113
shrubbery, 6:136, *136*; 7:78–80
Siam, *see* **Thailand**
siamangs, 1:65
Sibelius, Jean, 2:103
Siberia, 1:88; 2:*79*; 3:119, 124
sickle-cell anemia, 1:51, *51*
Sierra Leone, 6:137; 2:95
Sierra Madre, 2:113
Sierra Nevada, 1:183; 5:61, *61*, 93–94, 109
signals:
    electrical, 3:12
    international flag, 3:93, *93*
    radio, 1:94
signals units, army, 1:84
sign language, 6:137, *137*; 2:96, 137
Sikhism, 6:138; 3:73–74, 169; 6:61–62, *62*; 7:*155*
    funerals in, 3:139
    in **India,** 4:73
    pilgrimages of, 5:169
    reincarnation, 6:60, 138
silicates, 6:138
silicon, 6:138; 3:13, *13*, 14
silicones, 6:138
silk, 6:138, *138*; 3:76; 5:57; 7:51, *51*
    painting on, 5:141, *141*
    spiders and, 6:177, *177*
Silko, Leslie Marmon, 5:85
silkscreen printing, 6:28, *28*
Silly Symphonies (Disney), 2:19
silver, 6:139, *139*
    coins, 2:87, *87*
    in Colorado, 2:92
    from South America, 2:90
silverfish, 4:87
silverpoint, drawing, 2:170
Simchat Torah, 3:73
similes, 5:182
Simon, Paul, 3:108
Simpson, Wallis, 7:93
Sinatra, Frank, 5:*75*

Singapore, 6:139; 1:88; 2:64, 95; 4:176
Singer, Isaac, 8:121
Singer, Isaac Bashevis, 1:40, 41; 6:127
Singh, Guru Gobind, 3:74
Singin' in the Rain, 5:76
singing and songs, 6:140–141, *140, 141*; 5:67–69, *68, 69,* 182
    African, 1:21
    anthems, 1:63
    ballads, 1:109
    blues, 1:147
    carols, 2:16, *16*
    choirs, 2:53, *53*
    country and western music, 2:119
    folk music, 3:108, *108*
    hymns, 4:56
    minstrels, 5:37
    musicals, 5:75–76
    operas, 5:132
    rock music, 6:81, *81*
    spirituals, 6:178, *178*
single-parent families, 3:59
Sinhalese alphabet, 1:37
Sinn Féin, 4:97
Sirius, 6:186
sirocco winds, 7:168
Sisters of Charity, 2:114
Sistine Chapel, Rome, 3:133, *133*
Sitting Bull, 8:218, *218*; 6:166–167
Skate, U.S.S., 1:78
skeletons, 6:142, *142*; 3:71; 7:120, *120*
    bones, 1:149
    of buildings, 1:170, *170*
    exoskeletons, 4:86–87, 92, 162, *162*
    human body, 4:48, *48*
skene, 7:53
skiing, 6:143, *143*
skin, 6:143, *143*
    albino, 1:32
    animal fur, 3:140, *140*
    bruises on, 1:164
    eczema, 2:185
    elasticity of, 2:191
    leather, 4:146, *146*
    and **senses,** 6:123
skin grafting, 5:178
Skopje, Macedonia, 4:169

skunks, 6:144, *144*
sky, 6:144, *144*
    astronomers and, 1:93
    constellations in, 2:111, *111*
    Milky Way, 5:32, *32*
    nebulas in, 5:89
    northern lights, 5:113
    observatories and, 5:120
    stars, 6:186–188, *186, 187, 188*
skydiving, 6:145, *145*
Skylab space station, 6:170
    Sun photographed from, 7:*18–19*
skyscrapers, 6:145, *145*; 2:65; 4:65, *65*; 5:100, *100*
    building, 1:169–171, *170*
    elevators in, 3:17, *17*
slag heaps, 4:137
slang, 3:27
slate, 6:84, *84*
Slater, Samuel, 6:70
slavery, 6:146–148, *146, 147, 148*; 4:67, 108; 5:39; 7:32
    Africa and, 1:17–18, 55, 130; 2:14; 4:152, 176
    in Alabama, 1:29, 30
    in American colonies, 1:19
    in American literature, 1:40
    in ancient Greece, 3:181
    Aztec, 1:105
    and Bahamas, 1:108
    and Barbados, 1:116
    and Bermuda, 1:130
    and Brazil, 1:156
    and **Civil War,** 1:19; 2:67, 70
    and Constitution, 1:19; 2:112
    and dancing, 2:132
    and Emancipation Proclamation, 2:67, 68–69, 70
    and **Kansas,** 4:120
    and **pirates,** 5:170
    and Underground Railroad, 1:190; 2:67; 8:234
Slavs, 6:148; 6:124
sleep, 6:149; 2:171
Sleeping Beauty ballet, 1:*110*
"Sleeping Beauty" (fairy tale), 3:107, *107*
sleep-walking, 6:149
sleight-of-hand, 4:173
slide rules, 1:180, *180*

slip trailing, 6:14
Slocum, Joshua, 6:100
sloths, 6:149, *149*
Slovakia (Slovak Republic), 6:149;
    2:130; 6:148
Slovenia, 6:150; 6:124, 148; 7:188
sludge, **sewage,** 6:125, *125*
slugs and snails, 6:150, *150*; 3:19;
    5:44, *44*; 6:*67*
smelting, 5:20; 6:23
Smith, Adam, 2:183
Smith, Arnold, 2:95
Smith, Bessie, 1:147
Smith, John, 1:40; 4:186; 5:94
Smith, Joseph, 8:218; 5:54
Smithsonian Institution, 5:66; 7:140;
    8:121
smog, 1:102; 3:105; 5:187
smoking, 6:151
    as **addiction,** 1:11; 2:172
    and **health,** 4:18, 19
    tobacco, 7:62
smugglers, 6:151, *151*; 3:146; 4:106;
    5:86
snails, *see* **slugs and snails**
snakes, 6:152, *152*; 3:94, *94*, 177;
    6:66
    eggs of, 2:186
    venom of, 7:118, *118*
sneezing, 2:*158*
snooker, 1:135
snow, 6:153, *153*
    and **avalanches,** 1:103
    and **glaciers,** 3:165, *165*
    and **ice,** 4:57, 60
    skiing on, 6:143, *143*
    in **water cycle,** 7:144, *144*, 148
snow leopards, 4:150
Snow White and the Seven Dwarfs, 2:19
snuff, 6:151
soap, 6:153, *153*; 2:148
soccer, 6:154–155, *154*, *155*
socialism, 6:156
Social Contract, The, 8:208
social workers, 6:156
Society of the Cincinnati, 7:121
Society for the Prevention of Cruelty
    to Animals (SPCA), 1:57
sociobiology, 1:64
Socrates, 8:218–219

sodium chloride, 6:104–105
Sofala, Africa, 1:17
Sofia, Bulgaria, 1:172
softball, 6:156; 1:118
softwood, 7:59, 80
soil, 6:157, *157*
    earthworms in, 2:179, *179*
    erosion of, 3:30, 33, *33*
    fertilizers in, 3:72
Sojourner space probe, 6:*170–171*, 171
solar power, 6:158, *158*; 3:20, *21*, 22,
    22
    power stations, 6:16–17
    for **satellites,** 6:106, *106*
Solar System, 6:159–160, *159*;
    6:169–172; 7:108, *108*
    asteroids, 1:91
    comets, 2:94, *94*
    Earth, 2:176–177, *176*, *177*
    meteors and meteorites, 5:21, *21*
    Moon, 5:53, *53*
    planets, 5:171–174, *171*, *172*, *173*,
    174
    space exploration of, 6:169–172
    Sun, 7:18–19, *18–19*
solder, 2:33
solid matter, 5:8
Solomon, 8:219; 3:34; 4:126; 6:32
Solomon, Temple of, 7:44
Solomon Islands, 5:121; 2:95
solstices, 2:136
Solzhenitsyn, Aleksandr, 3:41
Somalia, 6:160, *160*
Somaliland, 1:68
Sondheim, Stephen, 5:75
songs, *see* **singing and songs**
sonic booms, 6:161
sonnets, 5:182
Sons of Daniel Boone, 1:153
Sons of Liberty, 1:43, 44
Sophocles, 3:183
sorcerers and sorceresses, 7:172, *172*
Soto, Gary, 4:33
Soufrière, volcano, 2:13
sound, 6:161, *161*; 3:20; 5:168
    broadcasting, 6:47–48, *47*, *48*
    ears and, 2:175, *175*
    echoes, 2:181, *181*
    insulation of, 4:88–89, *88–89*
    and **microphones,** 5:25, *25*

    in **movies,** 5:64
    and **radiation,** 6:45, *45*, 46
    recording, 6:54, *54*
    speed of, 6:161
    ultrasound, 6:108
    and **vibration,** 7:121
    waves, 7:149
Sousa, John Philip, 8:219, *219*
Souter, David, 4:*145*
South Africa, 6:162, *162*; 1:18; 7:179
    apartheid in, 2:95
    Boer War in, 1:148; 1:18; 2:103;
    7:93
    Bushmen, 1:175; 2:29
    in the Commonwealth, 2:95
    elections in, 2:192, *192*
    flag, 3:93
    gold in, 3:170
    mining in, 3:170, 5:35
    penguins in, 5:161
    racism in, 6:43, 162
South America, 6:163–164; 2:113
    Andes, *see* **Andes**
    bullfighting in, 1:173
    camels in, 1:184
    coffee in, 2:87, *87*
    conquistadores in, 2:109; 1:105;
    6:174
    European colonies in, 3:190; 6:164;
    7:22, 117
    explorers in, 3:50–51
    gauchos in, 2:120
    grasslands in, 3:177, *178*
    Incas in, 4:69, *69*
    literature of, 4:141
    map, 6:*163*
    marsupials in, *185*; 4:185
    mummies in, 5:65
    Native Americans in, 5:82, *82*
    prehistoric people in, 6:20, 21
    roads and highways in, 6:77
    slavery in, 6:146–147, *147*
    Spanish colonies in, 4:69
    wealth sent to Europe from, 2:90
    wildlife in, 7:166, *167*
    see also Latin America; *specific
    countries*
South Carolina, 6:165–166, *165*;
    2:67; 6:148, *148*; 7:56, 100
South Dakota, 6:166–167, *167*; 7:100

Black Hills of, **5**:61, *61*
Mount Rushmore in, **6**:115, 166, 167, *167*
Native Americans in, **5**:*85*
Southern (Antarctic) Ocean, **5**:122, 125, *125*
Southern Christian Leadership Conference (SCLC), **2**:66
southern colonies, **7**:56
South Korea, **6**:168, *168*; **1**:88; **4**:131; **5**:113; **7**:*51*
South Pole, *see* **poles**
Soviet Union, **6**:168; **6**:98, 148
and Afghanistan, **1**:14
in Antarctica, **1**:61
and **Armenia**, **1**:84
and **Belarus**, **1**:128
and **Cold War**, **2**:88; **7**:104–105
collapse of, **3**:40
and **Commonwealth of Independent States**, **2**:94
Communism in, **2**:97
concentration camps in, **2**:103
and **Czech Republic**, **2**:130
and **Estonia**, **3**:34
and **Georgia**, **3**:155
and **Germany**, **3**:159, 160
Kazakhstan, **4**:121
Kyrgyzstan, **4**:132
Latvia, **4**:142
Lithuania, **4**:160
medals of, **5**:12, *12*
Moldova, **5**:42
space exploration by, **6**:169–172, *172*
Turkmenistan, **7**/87, **6**:*93*
Ukraine, **7**:89, *89*
Uzbekistan, **7**:111
and **World War II**, **7**:179–181
see also **Russia and the Russian Federation**
Soyinka, Wole, **1**:18
space, and time, **7**:60
spacecraft, and friction, **3**:134
space exploration, **6**:169–172, *169, 170–171, 172*; **5**:53, 80, 171–174; **6**:80, *80*, 106, *106*
asteroids, **1**:91
astronauts, **1**:93, *93*
and **communication**, **2**:*96*

UFOs, **7**:88
spacelab, **6**:172
space stations, **6**:170, *172*
Spain, **6**:173–174, *173*; **4**:32
American colonies of, **2**:14, 34, 46, 128, 166, 185; **3**:16, 99, 189; **4**:33, 38, 69, 107, 167; **5**:22; **6**:33, *33*, 164; **7**:49, 117
and American Revolution, **1**:45
and **Andorra**, **1**:51
bullfighting in, **1**:173
and California, **1**:182
castles in, **2**:21
cave paintings in, **2**:28; **6**:18
conquistadores from, **2**:109; **1**:105, 148; **5**:22, 77, 82, 164
Crusades in, **5**:28
empire, map, **8**:*51*
explorers from, **3**:50, 51; **7**:103
fascism in, **3**:66
and **Gibraltar**, **3**:163, *163*
literature of, **3**:41
medieval legends of, **5**:14–15
mercury produced in, **5**:18
and **Mexico**, **1**:81, 105, 182
in **Middle Ages**, **5**:28, 29
monarchy in, **4**:126
Pacific colonies of, **5**:113, 165
sombrero from, **4**:*15*
topographic map for, **4**:*181*
Spanish-American War (1898), **6**:175; **6**:33
Spanish Armada, **3**:27; **7**:136; **8**:81, 191
sparrows, **1**:139, 141
Sparta, **3**:181
Spartacus, **6**:146
spawning, **1**:47; **3**:89
special effects, **7**:123
species, **6**:175
classification of, **2**:70
endangered, **3**:19
extinct, **3**:52–53, *52–53*
spectrum, **2**:91, *91*
Speke, J. H., **1**:68
Spencer, Lady Diana, **6**:*14*
Spenser, Edmund, **3**:29
sperm, **6**:*65*, 127, 128
spheres, **6**:129, *129*
spices, **6**:176, *176*; **3**:103, 115

spicules, **6**:179
spiders, **6**:177, *177*; **7**:58, 118
Spielberg, Steven, **5**:63
spikes (flowers), **3**:104, *104*
spinal anesthetic, **1**:52
spine, and chiropractic, **1**:39
spinning, **6**:178; **6**:*93*
spinning wheels, **6**:178
spirits, alcoholic, **1**:33
spirituals, **6**:178, *178*
spoils system, **8**:15, 55
sponges, **6**:179, *179*
spores, **6**:179, *179*
of **ferns**, **3**:72
of **fungi**, **3**:139
of **mosses**, **5**:56
of **mushrooms**, **5**:67, *67*
sports, **6**:180
clothing for, **2**:78
and **games**, **3**:144–146, *145*
Olympic Games, 15.131; *see also* **Olympic Games**
sponsorships of, **1**:*12*
see also specific sports
Spring, Sherwood, **1**:*93*
Springfield, Illinois, **4**:65, 66
springing point, **1**:73, *73*
springs, **6**:181, *181*
springs and wells, **7**:156, *156*
spring tides, **7**:58, *58*
Sputnik spacecraft, **5**:80; **6**:169
Spyri, Joanna, **2**:45
spy satellites, **6**:106
square shapes, **6**:129, *129*
squash (game), **6**:181, *181*
squid, **6**:182, *182*; **5**:44
squirrels, **6**:182, *182*; **6**:86
Sri Lanka, **6**:183, *183*; **1**:88; **2**:95
stagnation, **5**:189
stained glass, **6**:183, *183*; **3**:166
stainless steel, **1**:36; **4**:98
stalactites and stalagmites, **6**:184, *184*; **2**:29
Stalin, Joseph, **8**:220, *220*; **1**:35; **2**:150; **6**:168; **7**:89
Stalingrad, Battle of, **7**:136
stamens, **3**:103, *103*
Stamp Act (1765), **1**:43, 44; **2**:138; **8**:112

stamps, 6:184–185, *184, 185*;
6:11–12, *11*
Standard of Ur, **1**:*50*
Stanton, Elizabeth Cady, 8:220–221;
5:100; 7:173
staple foods, 3:111
starch, 5:168
starfish, 6:185, *185*; 4:92
starlings, 1:139, *139*
stars, 6:186–188, *186, 187, 188*;
6:144, *144*; 7:108, *108*
astrology, 1:92
and **astronomers,** 1:93
and **Big Bang theory,** 1:134
and **black holes,** 1:145
clusters of, 6:187
colors of, 6:*186,* 187
comets, 2:94, *94*
constellations, 2:111, *111*
creation of, 6:186, *187*
double, 6:187
galaxies, 3:143, *143*
and **gravity,** 3:179
meteors, 5:21
Milky Way, 5:32, *32*
names of, 6:188
novas and supernovas, 6:35, 188
and **planets,** 5:171
pulsars, 6:35, *35*
space between, 4:158
and **Sun,** 7:18–19
variable, 6:188
"Star-Spangled Banner, The" (Key),
6:189, *189*; 4:186, *187*; 5:80;
7:135
starvation, 6:189; 3:139
State, U.S. Secretary of, 7:*105*
state and local government, 6:190
law and legal systems, 4:145
state fairs, 3:57, *125*
states, U.S., 7:100; *see also specific*
states
statistics, 6:190, *190*
averages, 1:104
graphs, 3:174, *174*
Statue of Liberty, 3:23; 7:99, *99*
STDs (sexually transmitted diseases),
6:128
stealth aircraft, 1:27
steam, **4**:20

engines, 6:191, *191*; 4:164–165;
6:49–51, 133
power stations, 6:17, *17*
steel, *see* **iron and steel**
Stegosaurus, 2:*155*
Steinbeck, John, 8:221; 1:40, 41,
182; 5:130; 6:34
Stendhal, 3:41
Stenonychosaurus, **2**:*156*
step-families, 3:59
Stephen, St., 6:102
Stephenson, George, 8:221; 7:69
Stevens, John Paul, **4**:*145*
Stevens, Wallace, 1:41
Stevenson, Robert Louis, 8:221;
1:46; 2:45; 3:29
stick insects, 6:192, *192*
Stickley, Gustav, 3:141, 142
stockbrokers, 6:192
Stockhausen, Karlheinz, 3:11
Stockholm, Sweden, 7:23, *23*
stock market, 6:192, *192*; 2:143
stocks, 6:192
Stockton, John, 1:121
Stoker, Bram, 7:115
STOL aircraft, 1:27, 29
stomachs, 7:7, *7*
of **cattle,** 2:26, *26*
and **digestion,** 2:152
human, 4:49, *49*
stone, **sculpture** of, 6:112, 114, *114*
stone circles, 7:7–8, *8*
Stonehenge, 7:7–8, *8*; 5:120; 6:125
stoneware, 6:13
stores and shopping centers, 7:9–10,
9, 10; 5:37
storks, 1:*139, 140*
storytellers, 1:18, 21–22, *22*, 90
stoves and ovens, 7:11, *11*; 5:26
Stowe, Harriet Beecher, 8:222, *222*;
1:40; 2:67, 108
Stowe, Vermont, 7:*119*
Stradivari, Antonio, 8:222, *222*
Strand, Mark, 5:182
Stratford-upon-Avon, England, 7:53,
54
stratosphere, 1:94
Strauss, Johann, Sr. and Jr.,
8:222–223
Strauss, Levi, 2:79

Strauss, Richard, 5:132
Stravinsky, Igor, 8:223, *223*; 2:134;
5:67
stream of consciousness, 8:133
streams, 7:12–13, *12, 13*
Streisand, Barbra, 5:76
streptomycin, 1:63
stress, and nervous breakdowns, 5:18
Strindberg, August, 3:41
stringed instruments, 5:72–73, *72, 73*,
134
string quartets, 5:73, *73*
strip malls, 7:10
stromatolites, 3:*43*
Stuart, Gilbert, 3:82; 6:69
stuntmen, 5:64
Suarez, Xavier, 4:33
subatomic particles, 1:95
submarines, 7:14–15, *14–15*; 2:108;
3:97
submersibles, 7:14
suburbs, 2:65
subways, 7:15–16, *15, 16*
sucrose, 7:17
Sudan, 7:16; 1:84; 5:102
Sudetenland, 7:179
Suetonius, 1:136
Suez Canal, 1:191, 192; 2:189
suffrage, 7:173
suffragettes, 7:16, *16*
Sufism, 4:102
sugar, 7:17, *17*; 3:176; 5:168; 7:37
Suharto, Raden, 4:77
Sukarno, Ahmad, 4:77
Suleiman, 8:223; 5:139
Sullivan, Arthur (Gilbert and
Sullivan), 8:99; 5:132
Sullivan, John L., 1:152
Sullivan, Louis, 8:223–224; 1:74;
4:66
building designed by, 8:*224*
sulphur dioxide, in acid rain, 1:9
sulphuric acid, 1:11; 2:40
Sumer, 1:50
Sumerians, 7:17, *17*; 2:65; 5:19;
7:183, *183*
Sumo wrestlers, 7:182, *182*
Sun, 7:18–19, *18–19*; 1:93; 2:72;
7:108, *108*
and aurora, 5:113

and **calendars**, 1:181, *181*
and **cosmic rays**, 2:117
eclipses of, 2:181, *181*
energy from, 3:20, *21*
at **Equator**, 3:32
and food chains, 3:114
and **gravity**, 3:179
heat from, 4:20, *20*, 21
light of, 4:156–157, 158
Midnight, 5:31, *31*
orbit of, 5:32
and **photosynthesis**, 1:24, 33, 107;
   5:168
and **planets**, 5:171–174
protection from, 4:15, *15*
and **radiation**, 1:94; 6:*45*, 46
and **rainbows**, 6:51
and **seasons**, 6:120, *120*
solar power of, 6:158, *158*
solar system of, 6:159–160, *159*
as **star**, 6:186–188
and **sundials**, 2:74, *75*
and **tides**, 7:58, *58*
and **weather**, 7:153
and white light, 2:91
Sunbelt, 7:101
sunblock, 6:46
Sunday, Billy, 4:93
sundials, 7:61
Sundiata Keita, 1:22
sunflowers, 4:*120*, 121
Sunnis, 4:102
sunspots, 7:19
Sun Yat-sen, 8:224
Super Bowl, 1:12; 3:116, 156
superconductivity, 7:19, *19*
Superior, Lake, 4:135; 5:108; 7:171
supermarkets, 7:9
supernovas, 6:35, 188
supersonic speed, 6:161
superstitions, 7:20; 1:41–42
Supreme Court, U.S., 4:144, *145*
   and **Civil Rights Movement**, 2:65,
      66
   and **Constitution**, 2:112
   and separation of powers, 2:112
   and slavery, 2:67
surfing, 7:20, *20*
surgeons, 7:21, *21*, 75
surgery:

anesthetics for, 1:52
   plastic, 5:178
Suriname, 7:22; 6:164
surveying, 7:22
suspension bridges, 1:160, *160*, 161,
   161; 2:50
Sutton Hoo, England, 1:*54*, 174
swallows, 1:139, 140
Swan Lake (Tchaikovsky), 1:*110*, 111
swans:
   courtship dance of, 1:*55*
   migration of, 1:138
   see also **birds**
Swaziland, 7:22, *22*; 2:95; 3:93;
   4:126
Sweden, 7:23, *23*; 3:41; 6:107; 7:125
Swift, Jonathan, 8:224–225; 2:44;
   3:29
swifts, 1:139
swimming, 7:24, *24*; 7:146
swing (jazz), 4:112
switching (electronic), 3:12
Switzerland, 7:25, *25*; 6:125
Sydney, Australia, 1:98, *98*, 99;
   2:84–85
syllogisms, 5:165
Sylvester (Warner Bros.), 2:19
symbols, 7:26, *26*; 4:115, *115*
   dragons, 2:167–168
   flags, 3:93, *93*
   hieroglyphics, 4:28, *28*, 29
   icons, 4:62, *62*
   logos, 2:146, *146*, 147; 7:*74*
   on **maps**, 4:182, *182*
   trademarks, 7:74, *74*, 176
symmetry, 7:27, *27*; 6:129, *129*
symphonies, 7:28
synagogues, 7:28, *28*; 4:118
synapses, 5:91, *91*
synoptic charts, 7:153
synthetic fibers, 7:29
Syria, 7:29, *29*; 1:50; 4:148; 5:30, 148

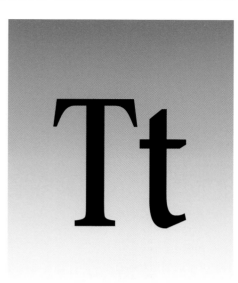

table tennis, 7:30, *30*

tadpoles, 1:47, *48*
tae kwon do, 4:186
Taft, William Howard, 8:225, *225*;
   2:33; 4:145; 5:127, 128; 7:101
Tagore, Rabindranath, 1:90
Tahiti, 5:187, *187*
tai-chi, 4:186
Taillefer, Christian, 1:*133*
tails, prehensile, 1:62
Taiwan, 7:30, *30*; 2:52; 4:111
Tajikistan, 7:31; 6:168
Taj Mahal, 4:*71*, 73
Takamine, Jokichi, 4:40
Talbot, William Henry Fox, 5:167
Tale of Peter Rabbit, The (Potter), 2:45,
   45
talk shows, 7:42
Tallahassee, Florida, 3:99
Tallchief, Maria, 5:85
tambourines, 5:75, *75*
Taney, Roger, 4:145
Tanganyika, 7:32
Tanganyika, Lake, 1:16; 7:32
tankers, 6:100, *100*, 132, *132–133*
tanks, 7:31, *31*; 7:180
tank trucks, 7:*82*
tank units, army, 1:84
tanning, **leather**, 4:146, *146*
Tantalus (Greek god), 3:184
Tanzania, 7:32, *32*; 2:95
Taoism, 7:32; 6:61–62
tapestries, 7:33, *33*

tapeworms, 7:33, 182, *182*

tap roots, 6:91, *91*

tariffs, 7:73

Tarkington, Booth, 4:74

Tasman, Abel, 5:101; 7:33

Tasmania, 7:33; 1:99; 2:*84*

Tasmanian devil, 4:*185*; 7:33

Tasmanian wolf, 4:*185*

tattoos, 2:117

Tatum, Art, 4:112

taxes, 7:34

   customs duties, 6:151

   excise, 6:151

   as percentages, 5:164

   tariffs, 7:73

Taylor, Edward, 1:40

Taylor, Elizabeth, 5:*63*, 64

Taylor, Mildred D., 2:45

Taylor, Zachary, 8:226, *226*; 7:101, 128

TB (**tuberculosis**), 7:83

Tchaikovsky, Pyotr Ilyich, 8:226; 1:110, 111; 2:103; 5:67; 6:98

tea, 7:34, *34*; 3:*63*

Tea Act (1773), 1:43–44; 2:138

Teach, Edward (Blackbeard), 5:170

teachers, 7:35

Teapot Dome scandal, 8:107

Technicolor movies, 5:62, *62*

technology, 7:35; 3:23

tectonic processes, *see* **plate tectonics**

Tecumseh, 8:227; 4:74; 5:127, 128

teddy bears, 7:68, *69*

teenagers, 1:11; 6:33

teeth, 7:36–37, *36, 37*

   of cats, 2:*25*

   elephant tusks, 3:15, *15*, 16

   and **fluorine**, 3:105

   ivory, 4:106

   of rodents, 6:86

   of sharks, 6:130, *130*

Teflon, 5:177

Tegucigalpa, Honduras, 4:38

telegraph, 7:37, *37*; 1:178; 6:*47*, 48

Telemann, Georg Philipp, 5:67

telephones, 7:38–39, *38, 39*; 1:79; 4:166

   communication, 2:96

   and **fax machines**, 3:68, *68*

and **information technology**, 4:82–83, *83*, 90

and **lasers**, 4:141

telescopes, 7:40, *40*; 4:150; 5:38, 133

   in **observatories**, 5:120, *120*

   orbiting, 6:106, 169, 172

telethons, 2:38

television, 7:41–42, *41, 42*; 5:13

   advertising, 1:12–13

   broadcasting, 6:48

   cartoons, 2:18–19

   cathedral for, 2:*22*, 23

   censorship of, 2:33

   and **compact discs**, 2:97

   and **electronics**, 3:12–13

   loudspeakers, 4:166, *166*

   MTV, 5:65

   video, 7:123

Telford, Thomas, 1:160

telharmonium, 3:11

tempera, 5:140

temperature, 7:43, *43*; 7:55, *55*, 168

   absolute zero, 2:88; 7:19

   body, 7:134

   and **climate**, 2:72–73

   and **cold**, 2:88

   for **cooking**, 2:114

   freezing, 4:57

   global warming, 3:168, *168*

   heat, 4:20, *20*, 21, *21*

   hypothermia, 4:56

   and **superconductivity**, 7:19, *19*

   and **weather**, 7:152–153

Temple, Shirley, 5:64

temples, 7:43–44, *43, 44*; 7:52

   Buddhist, 1:*130, 167*

   Hindu, 4:30, *30–31*

   Jewish **synagogues** and, 7:28, *28*

tempo, musical, 5:69

Tennessee, 7:44–45, *44*; 2:68; 7:100

Tennessee Valley Authority (TVA), 7:45

tennis, 7:46–47, *46, 47*; 6:70

Tennyson, Alfred, Lord, 3:29

Tenochtitlán, Mexico, 1:104, *104–105*, 105; 2:65

tension, 3:117

tents, 1:187, *187*; 2:61, 3:177, *178*; 5:48, *48*

Teotihuacán, Mexico, 1:104

Teresa of Avila, St., 8:227; 3:41; 6:102

Teresa of Calcutta, Mother, 8:227, *227*; 4:26

Tereshkova, Valentina, 8:228

terminal velocity (skydiving), 6:145

termites, 7:48, *48*; 1:62; 4:87

terns, 1:138, *138*, 140

terrapins, 3:19; 7:66–67

terrestrial television, 7:42

territories, of animals, 4:8

terrorists, 7:48

testes, 6:127, *128*

testosterone, 4:40

Texas, 7:49–50, *49*; 2:67; 4:99, *99*; 7:103

Texas Rangers, 7:49–50

text, 7:176

textiles, 7:50–51, *51*; 4:78, 189

   cotton, 2:118–119, *118*

   designers, 2:146

   kente cloth, 3:*162*

   knitting, 4:128

   lace, 4:134, *134*

   sewing, 6:126–127, *127*

   tapestries, 7:33

   see also **silk**

Thailand, 7:52, *52*; 6:*93*

   Buddhist monks in, 5:*45*

   factory in, 3:*115*

   monarchy of, 4:126

   royal palace of, 5:*147*

   and **World War II**, 7:179

Thales, 8:228

Thanksgiving, 3:73, 113; 4:14

Thatcher, Margaret, 8:228, *228*; 6:25; 7:94

theaters, 7:53–54, *53–54*; 2:169; 5:134

theme parks, 1:49

theodolites, 7:22

Theodosius, 5:131

theremin (instrument), 3:11

Theremin, Leon, 3:11

thermionic valves, 7:115

thermodynamics, 4:20

thermometers, 7:55, *55*; 5:18; 7:43, *43, 152*

thermonuclear bombs, 1:96

thermoplastics, 5:178

thermos bottles, 1:24
thermostats, 7:55, *55*
Theseus, 4:26
Third World, 7:55; 2:148–149
    famine in, 3:60
    Peace Corps in, 5:158–159, *159*
    poverty in, 6:15, *15*
    starvation in, 6:189
Thirteen Colonies, 7:56, *56*; 2:90;
    7:102
    and American Revolution, 11.43,
        map, 1:*43*, 44
    Connecticut, 2:107
    and Declaration of
        Independence, 2:138–139
    Delaware, 2:140
    Georgia, 3:156
    Jamestown, 4:108, *108*
    Maryland, 4:186
    Massachusetts, 4:189
    New Hampshire, 5:94
    New Jersey, 5:96
    New York, 5:99
    North Carolina, 5:109
    Pennsylvania, 5:162
    Rhode Island, 6:69
    slavery in, 1:19
    South Carolina, 6:165
    Virginia, 7:128
Thirty Years' War, 7:136
Thomas, Clarence, 4:*145*
Thomas, Dylan, 3:29; 5:181
Thomas, Seth, 2:75
Thomas Aquinas, St., 8:228–229
Thomism, 8:228
Thomson, Charles, 2:138
Thomson, Joseph, 1:95
Thor (Norse god), 5:107
thorax, 4:168
Thoreau, Henry David, 8:229–230;
    1:40; 4:189
Thorpe, Jim, 3:116; 5:85, 129
Thousand and One Nights, A: see
    Arabian Nights
Three Mile Island, 5:163
threshing machine, 1:*23*
Thucydides, 3:181, 183
Thumb, Tom, 8:*21*
thunderstorms, 7:57, *57*; 2:80; 4:8
Thutmose III, king of Egypt, 5:147

thyme, 4:25, *25*
Tiananmen Square uprising, 2:52
Tianjin, China, 2:48
Tiber River, 1:160
Tibet, 7:57, *57*; 4:*18*, 29, *29*
ticks, 7:58; 1:85
tidal power, 7:58; 3:22; 6:16–17
tides, 7:58, *58*
    floods and, 3:98
    seashore, 6:118–119, *119*
    and seaweeds, 6:121
Tien Shan mountains, 4:132
tigers, 7:59, *59*; 2:24–25; 5:*190*; 7:26
Tigris River, 1:50; 5:30
timber, 7:59; 3:*78*, 121, *121*; 7:80,
    174, *174*, 175, *175*
time, 7:60–61, *60–61*
    and Big Bang theory, 1:134
    calendars, 1:181, *181*
    candles, 2:7
    carbon dating, 1:71; 2:10
    clocks and watches, 2:74–75, *74*,
        75
    day and night, 2:136
    geological, 3:152–153
    measurement of, 5:10, 11
timelines:
    Civil Rights Movement, 1:66
    English history, 3:24–25
    European history, 3:38–40
    evolution, 3:*44–45*
    prehistoric people, 6:*20–21*
    Rome and the Roman Empire,
        6:88–89
    U.S. history, 7:105
    world history, 9:12–17
time zones, 7:60–61, *60–61*
tin, 7:62; 4:173; 5:20; 6:23, *23*
"Tintin" (Hergé), 2:18, *18*
tires, 7:62, *62*; 1:24, 133, 134
tissue culture, 2:76
tissues (cell), 2:30
Titan (Greek god), 3:184
Titanic, 4:59, *59*
Titian, 8:230
    painting by, 8:*230*
Titicaca, Lake, 1:51, 148; 4:134
Tito (Josip Broz), 8:230–231; 7:188
Tivoli Gardens, Copenhagen, 1:49

TNT, 3:52
toads, 7:62; 1:47–48; 4:140; 7:118,
    166
tobacco, 7:62, *62*; 2:172; 4:18; 5:110;
    6:151
Togo, 7:63, *63*
Tokyo, Japan, 4:109, *110*; 6:192
Toledo, Ohio, 5:127, 128
Tolkien, J. R. R., 8:231; 2:45; 3:29
Tolstoy, Leo, 8:231, *231*; 3:41; 6:98
Toltec people, 1:41, 104; 6:21
    pyramids of, 6:40, *40*
Tom and Jerry (Hanna-Barbera), 2:19
tomatoes, 3:136, *136*
tombs, 7:63, *63*; 2:33, 188, *189*
    Mausoleum of Halicarnassus,
        6:125, *125*
    paintings in, 2:*189*; 3:*35*
    pyramids, 6:40, *40*
    tombstones, 2:59
Tombstone, Arizona, 1:81
Tompion, Thomas, 2:75
Tonga, 2:95; 4:126; 5:121, 187
tongue, 7:131
Tonle Sap River, 1:183
tonsils, 7:63; 4:68
tools, 7:64–65, *64–65*; 7:35
    carpentry, 2:16–17
    of chimpanzees, 2:46
    of Native Americans, 5:85
    of prehistoric people, 6:22, *23*
Topeka, Kansas, 4:120
topographic maps, 4:181, *181*
Torah, 7:28
tornadoes, 7:66, *66*
Toronto, Canada, 1:189
tortoises and turtles, 7:66–67, *66*,
    67; 3:45; 5:31; 6:66, *66*
Torvill and Dean, 4:62
Toscanini, Arturo, 8:232
totem poles, 5:85, *85*
Tour de France, 1:12; 2:129, *129*;
    3:128
tourism, 7:67, *67*
Tours, Battle of, 7:136
Toussaint L'Ouverture, François-
    Dominique, 8:232; 4:10
towns, *see* cities and towns
Townshend Acts (1767), 1:43, 44;
    2:138

toxicology, 5:182
toys, 7:68–69, *68, 69*
 dolls, 2:164, *164*
 Lego, 2:*142*
 springs in, 6:181
Toy Story (Disney), 2:18–19
track and field, 7:70–72, *70, 71, 72*
traction elevators, 3:17, *17*
tractors, 3:65
tractor-trailers, 7:82–83, *82, 83*
trade, 7:73, *73*; 7:101
trade deficits, 7:73
trade fairs, 3:57
trademarks, 7:74, *74*; 7:*176*
 logos, 2:146, *146, 147*
 patents, 5:158
trade winds, 2:73; 7:168
Trafalgar, Battle of, 7:136
tragedies, 2:169
trains, *see* railroads
trampolines, 3:192
Transcendentalism, 8:229
transcendental meditation (TM), 5:15
transcontinental railroad, 6:51
transformers, 7:74, *74*; 3:9
transistors, 3:12, *13*
transmigration, 6:60
transmission:
 radio, 6:47–48, *47, 48*
 television, 3:12
transpiration, 3:101; 4:147; 7:80
transplants, 7:75
transportation, 7:75–76, *75*
 aircraft, 1:25–27, *25, 26, 27*
 automobiles, 1:101–102, *101, 102*
 bicycles, 1:133, *134*
 bullet trains, 4:*111*
 railroads, 6:49–51, *49, 50–51*
 rivers, 6:71, *71*
 roads and highways, 6:77, *77*
 segregation in, 2:65, *66*
 ships, 6:132–133, *132–133*
 subways, 7:15–16, *15, 16*
 trucks, 7:82–83, *82, 83*
 in tunnels, 7:78.85; 7:85
 see also boats
transport planes, 1:27
Trans-Siberian Railway, 6:49
trash, 7:77, *77*; 2:64; 5:186, *186–187*
 and recycling, 6:55, *55*

used in art, 6:116
Travers, P. L., 2:45
Travis, William B., 7:49
Treasure Island (Stevenson), 2:45
treeline, 5:60
trees, 7:78–80, *78–79, 80*; 5:175, *176*
 autumn foliage, 4:190
 bark of, 7:*78, 79*, 80
 conifers, 3:101, 119, *119*
 diseased, 2:*158*
 destruction of, 3:19, 30, 121, *121*, 186
 forests, 3:118–121, *118, 119, 120, 121*
 leaves, 4:147, *147*
 palm, 5:149, *149*
 and paper, 5:151
 roots of, 6:91, *91*
 seeds, 6:122
 shrubbery, 6:136, *136*
 timber from, 7:59, 174
 wood from, 7:174, *174*
 in woodlands, 7:175, *175*
Trenton, New Jersey, 5:96
Trevino, Lee, 4:33
Trevithick, Richard, 4:78, 165; 6:191
trials, 4:143
triangles, 6:129, *129*
tricycles, 1:133
trigonometry, 7:81, *81*
Trinidad and Tobago, 7:81, *81*; 2:14, 15, 95; 7:157
triode valves, 3:13
Tripoli, Libya, 4:153, *153*; 6:*105*
Trojan War, 7:82; 1:*13*; 3:182, 183; 4:26, 64; 5:126
tropical fish, 1:67
tropics, 7:82
 rain forest, 1:16
 see also Equator
troposphere, 1:94
trotting, 6:94
trucks, 7:82–83, *82–83*
Trudeau, Garry, 2:18
truffles, 5:67
Truman, Bess, 3:82
Truman, Harry S., 8:232–233, *233*; 3:82; 4:131; 5:41, 42; 7:101
Trumbull, John, painting by, 2:*139*
trumpets, 5:71, *71*

trumps, 2:11
truss-girder bridges, 1:161, *161*
trust-busting, 8:107
Truth, Sojourner, 8:233; 1:19
Ts'ao Hsueh-chin, 1:90
Tuareg people, 6:99, *99*
tuataras, 6:66, *66*
tuberculosis, 7:83
tubers, 7:83, *83*
Tubman, Harriet, 8:234, *234*; 1:19
Tucson, Arizona, 1:81, 82
Tudor, Larry, 4:13
Tull, Jethro, 1:23
tumors, cancer, 2:7
tundra, 7:84, *84*
tungsten, 5:20
tuning, television, 7:42
Tunisia, 7:85; 5:16; 6:*91*
tunnels, 7:85, *85*
 Channel, 2:38; 6:50, *50–51*; 7:*94*
turbines, 7:86, *86*; 3:7, 23; 4:55; 7:65, 146, 169, *169*
 jet engines, 4:114, *114*
 power stations, 6:16–17, *16, 17*; 6:191
 on ships, 6:133
Turgenev, Ivan, 3:41
Turin, Italy, 4:105
Turkey, 7:86, *86*; 1:88; 2:64; 4:34; 5:30; 7:178
 in ancient world, 1:50
 and Crimean War, 2:124
 and Cyprus, 2:130
 Kurds in, 4:131
 mosque of Hagia Sophia, 1:73, 177, *177*; 6:125; 7:86
 prehistoric people in, 6:23
 see also Ottoman Empire
turkeys, 7:87, *87*; 1:142
Turkmenistan, 7:87; 6:93, 168
Turner, J.M.W., painting by, 5:*143*, 145
Turner, Nat, 1:19; 6:147
turtles, *see* tortoises and turtles
Tuskegee Institute, 1:19; 8:241
Tutankhamen, 8:234; 2:188; 5:65, *65*; 6:40
Tutu, Desmond, 8:234–235, *234*
Tuvalu, 5:121; 2:95

TVA (Tennessee Valley Authority), 7:45
Twain, Mark, 8:235, *235*; 1:40; 2:45, 108; 4:160; 5:41, 42, 93
tweed, 7:51
Tweety Pie, 2:19
twigs, 7:79, *80*
twisters, 7:66, *66*
"Tyger, The" (Blake), illustration, 8:*26*
Tyler, John, 8:235–236, *235*; 7:101, 128
Tyndale, William, 1:131
type, 7:88, *88*; 6:26–27, *26, 27*
typesetting, 6:26–27, *26, 27*
typewriters, 7:88, *88*; 7:176
typhoons, 4:54
Tyrannosaurus, 2:156, *156–157*
tyrothricin, 1:63

Uccello, Paolo, 2:168
UFOs, 7:88; 5:38
Uganda, 7:89; 2:*78*, 95
U.K.: *see* **United Kingdom**
Ukraine, 7:89, *89*; 6:168
Ulm Cathedral, Germany, 2:22
ultrasound, 5:13
ultrasound scanners, 6:108
ultraviolet rays, 7:18
Ulysses, 4:26
umbels, 3:104, *104*
Umm al-Qaiwain, 7:90
Uncle Sam, 7:104, *104*
Underground Railroad, 1:190; 2:67; 8:234
Undset, Sigrid, 3:41
unemployment, 3:18
Unicorn tapestries, 7:*33*
unidentified flying objects (**UFOs**), 7:88
Union Jack, 7:91, *91*
United Arab Emirates, 7:90, *90*; 5:30
United Kingdom, 7:90–94, *90–94*
    African colonies of, 1:18, 151, 186; 2:90, 189; 4:123, 151, 176; 5:8, 102; 6:137, 160; 7:22, 32, 63, 89, 189
    American colonies of, 1:29, 116, 129; 2:34, 90; 4:65, 174, 189; 5:94, 95, 110; 6:164; 7:137
    in Antarctica, 1:61
    Asian colonies of, 1:164; 2:90; 4:39, 176; 5:76; 6:139, 183
    and Australia, 1:99; 2:90
    and **Boer War,** 1:148; 2:103
    and Canada, 1:190
    Caribbean colonies of, 2:14, 90; 6:102
    Chinese trade with, 2:50–51
    Church of England in, 2:60
    colonies of, 3:40, 76, 162, 163, 190
    Commonwealth of Nations, 2:95
    and **Crimean War,** 2:27, 124
    and **Cyprus,** 2:130
    England, 3:24–27
    in EU, 3:41
    and Falklands, 1:79
    flag of, 7:91, *91*
    French and Indian War, 3:132
    and **Gibraltar,** 3:163, *163*
    and **India,** 4:73
    and **Irish Republic,** 4:95–97
    kings and queens of, 4:125–126, *126*
    knights in, 4:128, *128*
    laws and legal systems, 4:144, 145
    measurement in, 5:10–11, *11*
    medals in, 5:12, *12*
    Middle Eastern colonies of, 5:131
    Northern Ireland, 4:97
    parliament of, 5:156
    prime ministers of, 6:25
    reservoirs in, 1:68
    Scotland, 6:111, *111*
    Wales, 7:134
    and War of 1812, 3:82, 99; 7:135
    welfare state in, 7:94
    in **World War I,** 7:177–178, *178*
    in **World War II,** 7:179–181, *179, 181*
    see also **British Isles;** *specific countries*
United Nations, 7:95, *95*
    and **Africa,** 1:18
    and **developing countries,** 2:149
    flag, 3:93
    and GPS, 5:87
    and **human rights,** 4:52
    and **Israel,** 4:118
    and **Korean War,** 4:131
    and **Kuwait,** 4:132

New York headquarters of, **5**:99
and **refugees**, **6**:59
UNICEF, **4**:11
United States of America, **7**: 96–105, *96–105*; **2**:*62*; **5**:*108*, 109
NOTE: Most of the articles in this encyclopedia have at least one reference to the U.S., but all of them cannot be listed because of space limitations. The following are some of the major U.S. articles and references:
and **African Americans**, **1**:19–20, *20*
American literature, **1**:40–41
American myths and legends, **1**:41–42, *42*
American Revolution, **1**:43–45, *43–45*
Amish in, **1**:46
in **Antarctica**, **1**:61
army in, **1**:84; **7**:101, 107, *107*
Articles of Confederation, **2**:107, 112
Asians in, **4**:67–68
Bill of Rights, **1**:135–136
Civil Rights Movement in, **2**:65–66; **8**:*140*
Civil War, **2**:67–70
and **Cold War**, **2**:88
Congress of, **2**:106–107, *106, 107*; **5**:156
Constitution, see **Constitution, U.S.**
courts of law, **4**:143-145, *143*
Declaration of Independence, **2**:138–139, *139*; **1**:44, 45
Depression, Great, in, **2**:143, *143*
design in, **2**:46–47
exploration of, **7**:103; **8**:*147*
FBI, **3**:69, *69*
first ladies, **3**:82–83, *82–83*; **7**:101
flag of, **3**:93, *93*; **4**:*187*
Gettysburg Address, **3**:161, *161*
in **Gulf War**, **1**:27; **4**:95
Hispanics in, **4**:32–34, *33*
history of, **7**:102–105
Hollywood, **4**:36, *36*
immigration in, **4**:67–68, *67*
Jamestown colony, **4**:108, *108*

in **Korean War**, **4**:131
law and legal systems in, **4**:143–145, *145*
Liberty Bell, **4**:152; **7**:*104*
maps of, **1**:*43*; **5**:*83, 108*; **7**:*97, 102*; **8**:*147*; *see also maps in all state entries*
Mason-Dixon Line in, **7**:103
medals of, **5**:12, *12*
movies in, **5**:62–64, *62, 63*
and **NAFTA**, **5**:22; **7**:73
and **NASA**, **5**:80
national anthem of, **4**:186; **6**:189
national parks in, **5**:81, *81*; *see also names of specific parks*
Native Americans, **5**:82–85, *82–85*
patents in, **5**:158
and **Pearl Harbor**, **5**:159–160, *159*
Pilgrims, **5**:169–170, *169, 170*
political parties in, **5**:185
population of, **7**:*102*
presidents, **6**:24; **7**:101
Prohibition in, **6**:30
proverbs and sayings in, **6**:32
and **Puerto Rico**, **6**:33, *33*
Pulitzer Prize in, **6**:34
Puritans, **6**:39
railroads in, **6**:49–51, *49*; **7**:*103*
and **refugees**, **6**:59
as a **republic**, **6**:66
Rocky Mountains, **6**:85, *85*
Shakers, **6**:129, *129*
slavery in, **6**:147, 148, *148*
Spanish-American War, **6**:175
state and local government in, **6**:190
states of, list, **7**:100; *see also entries for each state*
stores and shopping centers, **7**:9–10, *9, 10*
Supreme Court, **4**:144, *145*
territories of, **3**:189; **5**:121, 165; **6**:175; **7**:100
Thirteen Colonies of, **7**:56, *56*, 102
timeline, **7**:105
time zones, **7**:*61*
Uncle Sam, **7**:*104*
in **Vietnam War**, **7**:124
War of 1812, **7**:135, 139

wars and warfare, **7**:136
Washington, D.C., **7**:138–141, *138–141*
women's movement in, **7**:173
in **World War I**, **7**:177–178, *178*; **8**:*190*
in **World War II**, **5**:159–160, *159*; **7**:*104*, 105, 179–181, *179–181*
ZIP codes in, **7**:191
U.S. Air Force Academy, **7**:106, *106*
U.S. Marine Corps, **7**:106, *106*
U.S. Military Academy, **7**:107, *107*; **2**:87
U.S. Naval Academy, **7**:107, *107*; **4**:186
universal joint, **7**:147
Universe, **7**:108, *108*
Big Bang theory, **1**:134; **2**:177
galaxies in, **3**:143, *143*
see also **Solar System**
Unknown Soldiers, **tombs** of, **7**:63
Ur, **1**:50; **2**:65; **4**:95
Ural Mountains, **2**:113; **3**:38; **6**:96
uranium, **1**:96; **5**:20, 115; **6**:45
Uranus, **5**:171, 173, 174; **6**:159, *159*, 160, 171
Urban II, Pope, **2**:126
Ure, Andrew, **7**:55
Uriel, archangel, **1**:52
urine, **1**:146; **4**:50, 124
Uruguay, **7**:109; **6**:164
U.S.S.R., *see* **Soviet Union**
Utah, **7**:109–110, *109*; **2**:67; **5**:54, 98; **6**:85, *85*; **7**:100
uterus, **6**:128
U Thant, **7**:95
Uther Pendragon, King, **1**:86
Uthman the Turk, **5**:139
Utigard Falls, Norway, **7**:145
utopias, **7**:110; **4**:74
Uzbekistan, **7**:111; **6**:168

vacations, camping, 1:187

vaccinations, 7:111; 3:31, 161; 4:68, 81

vacuum cleaners, 7:111, *111*

vacuums, 7:111, *111*; 4:88–89

Vaduz, Liechtenstein, 4:154

Valadez, John, 4:33

Valdez, Luis, 4:33

Valdivia, Pedro de, 2:46

Valens, Ritchie, 4:33

Valenzuela, Fernando, 4:33

Valera, Eamon de, 4:97

Valley Forge, Pennsylvania, 1:45

valleys, 7:112–114, *112–113, 114*; 7:145, *145*

Vallire, Jean, 4:47

Valmiki, 1:90

valves, 7:115, *115*; 3:13

vampires, 7:115, *115*; 1:122

Van Buren, Martin, 8:236, *236*; 5:100; 7:101

Vancouver, British Columbia, 1:189

Van Duyn, Mona, 5:182

Van Gogh, Vincent, 8:236–237; 5:*140*, 144

vanilla, 5:136

Vanuatu, 5:121; 2:95

Vargas Llosa, Mario, 4:142

Vasari, Georgio, 1:136

vascular cambium, 7:80

Vatican City, 7:116, *116*; 2:56; 4:105

vaudeville, 5:75

Vaughan, Sarah, 4:112

Vaughan Williams, Ralph, 1:63; 3:108

vaults (architecture), 1:73, 76

Vaux, Calvert, 8:183

Vega, Garcilaso de la, 4:141

Vega spacecraft, 6:171

vegetables, 7:116, *116*; 3:103

    beans, 1:123

    corn, 2:116

vegetarians, 7:117

veins, blood, 4:19, *19*

Velásquez, Diego, 8:237

    painting by, 8:*237*

Velasquez, Jorge, 4:33

veneers, 7:174

Venera space probes, 6:*170*, 171

Venezuela, 7:117, *117*; 6:164

Venice, Italy, 4:104, 105

venom, 7:118, *118*

Venus (planet), 5:171, *172*, 174; 6:159, *159*, 160, 170, 171

Verdi, Giuseppe, 8:237, *237*; 5:67, 132

Vermeer, Jan, 8:238

    paintings by, 5:*142–143*; 8:*238*

Vermont, 7:118–119, *119*; 7:100

Verne, Jules, 8:238; 3:41; 6:110

Verrazano, Giovanni de, 5:99; 7:103

vertebrates, 7:120, *120*; 1:58; 3:44, 71, *71*

    heads of, 4:17

    senses of, 6:123, *123*

    skeletons of, 6:142, *142*

Vesalius, Andreas, 5:*13*; 7:21

Vespucci, Amerigo, 8:238; 7:117

Vesuvius, Mount, 5:60, *60*; 6:88; 7:133

veterans, 7:121

Veterans Affairs, Department of (VA), 7:121

veterinarians, 7:121

vibration, 7:121, *121*; 6:161

Vicksburg, Battle of, 2:68, 69

Victor Emmanuel II, king of Italy, 4:105

Victoria, queen of England, 8:238–239, *239*; 2:124; 4:125; 5:148; 7:92, 93, 122

Victoria, Lake, 5:102; 7:32

Victoria Falls, 6:125; 7:145, *190*

Victorian Age, 7:122, *122*; 7:92

vicuñas, 4:161

video, 7:123, *123*

    cameras, 1:185; 7:41, 123, *123*

    recording, 6:54, *54*

Vienna, Austria, 1:100

Vientiane, Laos, 4:139

Vietnam, 7:124; 1:88; 2:*64*; 3:132

    and **Cambodia,** 1:183

    Communism in, 2:97

    monsoons in, 5:50

    refugees ("Boat People") from, 6:59

Vietnam War, 7:124; 2:88; 4:139; 7:136

    and **peace movement,** 2:66; 5:159

Vijayakumar, Kalamandalam, 5:*33*

Viking orbiter, 6:170, *170*, 171

Vikings, 7:125–126, *125, 126*; 1:53, 192; 2:142, 168; 3:26, 187; 4:97, 174; 5:114

    burial mounds of, 1:174

    names of, 5:78

villages, 7:127, *127*

Villa-Lobos, Heitor, 8:239

villas, Roman, 6:89

villeins, 3:75

Vinson Massif, Antarctica, 1:60

violins, 5:73, *73*, 134

Virgil, 8:239; 1:13; 3:183; 6:92; 7:82

Virginia, 7:128–129, *128*; 2:68, 70; 7:56, *56*, 100

    General History, 1:40

    Jamestown colony in, 4:108, *108*

    and **Kentucky,** 4:122

Virgin Islands, 7:129; 7:100, 157

virtual reality (VR), 7:130, *130*; 6:110

viruses, 7:131, *131*; 1:107; 2:70, 158; 4:81

    colds and coughs, 2:88

    epidemics of, 3:31

    HIV, 1:23

visas and passports, 5:158

vitamins, 7:131; 2:158; 3:111; 5:12, 32; 7:116, 117

Vitruvius, 1:74, 76

Vivaldi, Antonio, 8:240, *240*; 2:103; 5:67

Vlad the Impaler, 7:115

vocal cords, 7:131, *131*

vodka, 1:33
voice, 7:131, *131*
  choirs, 2:53, *53*
  singing and songs, 6:140–141,
    140, 141
volcanic rocks, 6:83
volcanoes, 7:132–133, *132*; 1:15;
    2:13; 4:103; 5:60, *60*; 7:98, 137
  and crater lakes, 4:134, *135*
  in Hawaii, 4:16–17, *17*
  and lava, 6:82, *82*
  in Mexico, 5:22
  in New Zealand, 5:101
  on ocean floor, 5:122
  in Oceania, 5:121
  and plate tectonics, 5:179, *179*
  in Russia, 6:96
  in St. Lucia, 6:*102*
  on Venus, 5:171, *172*
voles, 7:133, *133*; 6:86
Volga River, 3:37
volleyball, 7:133; 7:187
Volta, Alessandro, 8:240
voltage, 3:7, 9; 7:74
Voltaire, 8:240; 3:41
Volta River, 1:174
voodoo, 7:134
Vostok, Antarctica, 1:60
Vostok spacecraft, 6:169
voting:
  and Constitution, 2:112
  in democracy, 2:141
  in elections, 2:192, *192*
voting rights, 2:66; 7:16, *16*, 139, 173
Voting Rights Act (1965), 2:66
voussoirs, 1:72, *73*
Voyager spacecraft, 5:171–174; 6:171
VR (virtual reality), 7:130, *130*
VTOL aircraft, 1:27
vultures, 1:139–140, 142; 4:*106*
vulvas, 6:128

wadis, 6:75
Wagner, Richard, 8:241, *241*; 2:36;
    5:67, 132
Walden Pond, 8:*229*
Waldheim, Kurt, 7:95
Wales, 7:134; 3:25, 26, 27; 7:90–94
  Celts in, 2:31–32
  dragons in, 2:167, 168
  literature of, 3:29
Walesa, Lech, 8:241; 5:183
Walker, Madame C. J., 1:19
walking, 7:72
Wallace, Alfred Russel, 3:42; 7:167
Wallace's Line, 7:167
walnuts, 5:119
Walpole, Robert, 6:25
walruses, 6:117, *117*; 7:36
Walton, Izaak, 3:89
warehouses (air cargo), 1:28
warlocks, 7:172
warm- and cold-bloodedness, 7:134;
    4:27; 6:66
Warner Brothers, 2:19
warning coloration, 7:118
War of 1812, 7:135; 4:167, 186, 187;
    6:189, *189*; 7:139
War on Poverty, 8:131
warp threads, 7:154, *154*
Warren, Earl, 1:182; 4:145
Warren, Robert Penn, 5:182
wars and warfare, 7:135–136
  appeasement in, 7:179
  armor for, 1:85, *85*

  bombs, 1:149
  castles under siege, 2:21, *21*
  cavalry in, 2:27, *27*
  impressment in, 7:135
  major battles, 7:136
  Napoleonic, 5:79–80, *79, 80*
  navies in, 5:86, *86*
  and peace movement, 5:159
  U.S. Congress and, 5:160
  veterans of, 7:121
  weapons for, 7:150–151, *150, 151*
  see also armies; *specific wars*
Warsaw, Poland, 5:183
Warsaw Pact, 5:86
Wars of the Roses, 3:26
Wasatch Range, 7:110
washing machines, 7:136, *136*;
    7:*189*
Washington, Booker T., 8:241, *241*;
    1:19, 29, 40, 41; 7:128
Washington, D.C., 7:138–141,
    138–141; 4:186–187; 7:10, 16, 96,
    100, 135
  Civil Rights march on, 2:66
  Library of Congress in, 2:115;
    4:152
  Mint in, 2:87
  slavery abolished in, 2:70
Washington, George, 8:242, *242*;
    1:42; 3:82; 5:82; 6:167; 7:100,
    101, 102, 121, 128, 138–139, 141
  and American Revolution, 1:44,
    45, *45*; 2:138
  and Constitution, 2:112
  portraits of, 5:*144*
Washington, Martha, 3:82
Washington, Mount, 5:95, *95*
Washington (state), 7:137–138, *137*;
    7:100
Washington Crossing the Delaware
    (Leutze), 1:*45*
Washington Monument, 7:140
wasps, 7:142, *142*; 4:87; 5:92; 7:118
watches (timepieces), 2:74–75, *75*
water, 7:143, *143*; 2:40; 3:14, 111;
    4:160
  algae in, 1:33
  baptism in, 1:116
  bubbles, 1:164, *164*
  cooking in, 2:114

and **deserts**, 2:144
and **drought**, 2:172
and **erosion**, 3:33, *33*
evaporation of, 1:178
and **fish**, 3:84–87, *86–87*
floating on, 3:97, *97*
floods of, 3:98–99, *99*
and **forests**, 3:121
frozen (ice), 4:57, *57*
and **gardens**, 3:147, *147*
"hard," 6:153
hydrotherapy, 1:39
for **irrigation**, 4:99, *99*
in oases, 5:119
in **oceans** and **seas**, 5:122–125, *125*
in **ponds**, 5:188–189, *188–189*
in **rivers**, 6:71–75, *74*
soap and, 6:153
as steam, 5:8
in **wetlands**, 7:159–161, *160–161*
water buffalo, *see* **buffalo**
water clocks, 2:74
watercolors, 5:140–141, *141*
water cycle, 7:144, *144*; 6:51, *51*; 7:*143*
waterfalls, 7:145, *145*; 7:*190*
Waterloo, Battle of, 7:136
water parks, 1:49
water power, 7:146, *146*; 3:7, 9, 22; 4:99; 6:75
  hydroelectric, 4:55
  power stations, 6:16–17, *17*
  tidal, 7:58
  waterfalls, 7:145
water-skiers, 7:*147*
Waters, Muddy, 1:147; 5:39
water sports, 7:146–147, *146*, *147*; 5:187; 7:24, *24*
water supplies, 7:148, *148*
  aqueducts, 1:68, *68*
  and **dams**, 2:131
  irrigation, 4:99, *99*
  and **sewage**, 6:126
water table, 7:156, *156*
water vapor, 3:105
water wheels, 4:99; 6:17; 7:146, *146*
Watson, James (Crick and Watson), 8:61
Watson-Watt, Robert, 4:92; 6:44

Watt, James, 8:242; 4:78; 6:191
watts, 3:8, 20
wavelength, 2:91; 6:45–46, *45*, 47; 7:149
waves, 7:149, *149*; 2:84, *84*, 85
  formation of, 5:125, *125*
  light, 2:91
  and **radiation**, 6:45–46, *45*
  radio, 6:47–48, *47*, *48*
  sound, 6:161
  tidal, 7:58
  tsunamis, 2:179
  vibration of, 7:121
wax, 7:149
  candles, 2:7
  honeycombs and, 4:38
Wayne, Anthony, 4:74
Wayne, John, 5:*63*
weapon delivery systems, 7:150–151, *151*
weapons, 7:150–151, *150*, *151*; 2:27; 5:20, *20*
  armor and, 1:85, *85*
  bombs, 1:149
  boomerangs, 1:9
  cannons, 2:8, *8*
  for **fencing**, 3:72, *72*
  germs, 3:161
  gunpowder, 3:52
  guns, 3:190
  in **Middle Ages**, 5:*28*
  missiles, 5:39, *39*
  nuclear, 1:96, *96*, 149
  tanks, 7:31, *31*, 180
weapons systems, 7:151
weasels, 7:152, *152*; 6:144
weather, 7:152–153, *152–153*
  and **atmosphere**, 1:94
  balloons, 1:94, 112
  and **barometers**, 1:117
  and **climate**, 2:72–73
  clouds, 2:80, *80*
  drought, 2:172
  hailstones, 4:8
  hurricanes, 4:54, *54*
  monsoons, 5:50, *50*
  NOAA forecasts of, 6:106
  northeasters, 4:190
  radar, 6:44
  rain, 6:51, *51*

  satellites, 6:106
  thunderstorms, 7:57, *57*
  tornadoes, 7:66, *66*
  wind and, 7:168, *168*
weathering, 3:33, *33*
weather vanes, 1:*52*; 7:*153*
Weavers, the, 3:108
weaving, 7:154, *154*; 7:51
  baskets, 5:84
  rugs and carpets, 6:93
  tapestries, 7:33
Web: *see* World Wide Web
webs, spider, 6:177, *177*
Webster, Daniel, 8:242–243; 5:94, 95
Webster, Noah, 8:243; 2:151
weddings, 7:155, *155*; 4:184
wedges, *170*; 4:170
weft threads, 7:154, *154*
weight, 7:156
  of atmosphere, 1:94
  and **gravity**, 3:179
  and **mass**, 4:188
Weil's disease, 6:53
Welk, Lawrence, 5:111
Welles, Orson, 5:63
Wellington, Duke of, 8:243–244; 6:25
Wellington, New Zealand, 5:101
Wells, H. G., 6:110
wells and springs, 7:156, *156*, *157*
Welty, Eudora, 5:39
Wesak, 3:74
Wesley, John and Charles, 8:244, *244*; 6:31
Western Union, 7:37
West Indies, 7:157, *157*; 2:95, 115; 5:109
  literature of, 4:141–142
  see also **Caribbean**
Westinghouse, George, 8:244–245; 1:155
Westminster Abbey, London, coronations in, 4:126, *126*
West Point, USMA, 2:87; 7:107, *107*
West Virginia, 7:158–159, *158*; 1:161; 2:81; 7:100
West Side Story (Bernstein), 5:75; 8:25
wetlands, 7:159–161, *160–161*
whales, 7:162–163, *162*; 3:94; 5:123, *124*; 6:7, 123; 7:149

blowholes of, 5:114

as **endangered species,** 3:19, *19*

migration of, 5:31

Wharton, Edith, 1:40, 41

wheat, 7:163, *163*; 3:63, 64, *64*, 173, *173*, 176, 178, *178*; 4:120, 121

wheatears, Greenland, 1:138, *138*

Wheatley, Phillis, 8:245; 1:19, 20, 40

wheels, 7:164, *164*; 4:169, *169*, 170, *170*; 7:76

railroad, 6:49, *49*

roller skate, 6:86

symbolism of, 7:26

tires for, 7:62, *62*

whiskers, of cats, 2:24

whiskey, 1:33

whist, 2:11, *11*

Whistler, James McNeill, 8:245; 4:189

painting by, 8:*245*

White, E. B., 8:246, *246*; 1:40, 41

White, Walter, 8:246; 1:19

white dwarfs, 6:187

White House, 3:82–83; 7:139, *140*, 141

white light, 2:91

White Mountains, New Hampshire, 5:95, *95*

white witches, 7:172

Whitman, Marcus and Narcissa, 8:246–247; 7:137, 138

Whitman, Walt, 8:247, *247*; 1:40; 5:100

Whitney, Eli, 8:247–248; 2:107, 108; 3:156

Whit Sunday, 3:74

Whittier, John Greenleaf, 1:40; 4:189

Whittle, Frank, 3:96; 4:114

Who, the (performers), 6:81

Wiesel, Elie, 8:248

Wigglesworth, Michael, 1:40

Wigman, Mary, 2:133

wigs, 4:10, *10*, 15

Wilbur, Richard, 5:182

wild cards, 2:11

wildebeest, 5:31; 7:*32*

Wilde, Oscar, 8:248, *248*; 3:29

Wilder, Laura Ingalls, 2:135; 7:171

Wilder, Thornton, 1:41; 2:169

Wilderness, Battle of, 2:68, 70

wildlife, 7:165–167, *165, 167*

conservation of, 2:109–110

feeding, 1:140

gardens for, 3:147

habitats of, 4:8, *8*

migration of, 5:31

protection of, 1:57

of **tundra,** 7:84

in **wetlands,** 7:159–161, *160–161*

Wile E. Coyote, 2:19

William I (the Conqueror), 8:248–249; 3:26, 27; 4:125; 5:105; 7:136

William and Mary, 8:249, *249*; 4:125

William IV, king of England, 7:92

William of Sens, 1:74

Williams, Daniel Hale, 8:249; 1:20

Williams, George, 7:187

Williams, Hank, 1:29

Williams, Roger, 8:250; 6:69

Williams, Tennessee, 1:41; 2:169; 5:39

Williams, William Carlos, 1:41

Williamsburg, Virginia, 7:56, 129

Wills, William, 3:51

Wilmut, Ian, 2:76

Wilson, Edith Bolling Galt, 3:82, *83*

Wilson, Edward O., 1:64

Wilson, Woodrow, 8:250, *250*; 3:82, 83; 5:96, 97; 7:101, 128

wind, 7:168, *168*; 7:152–153

and **atmosphere,** 1:94

and balloons, 1:112

and **climate,** 2:72–73

in deserts, 2:144

and **erosion,** 3:33, *33*

hurricanes, 4:54, *54*

measurement of, 7:153, *153*

monsoons, 5:50, *50*

as pollinator, 3:104, *104*

and sailboats, 1:147

tornadoes, 7:66, *66*

Wind in the Willows, The (Grahame), 2:45

windmills, 7:86, 169, *169*

wind power, 7:169, *169*; 3:9, 22

power stations, 6:16–17

sailing ships, 6:100–101, *100, 101*

Windsor, Duke and Duchess of, 7:93

windsurfing, 7:147, *147*

Windward Islands, 7:157

wine, 7:170, *170*; 1:32; 3:128, *128*; 7:187

Winfrey, Oprah, 1:20; 5:39

Winnie-the-Pooh (Milne), 2:45; 8:*167*

winter sports, 7:170

Winthrop, John, 8:250–251; 4:190

wire, 7:170

cables, 1:178

copper, 2:114

filament, 3:7

insulation of, 4:88–89

Wisconsin, 7:171–172, *171*; 7:100

wishing wells, 7:156

witches, 7:172, *172*; 1:42; 4:11, 189

Wizard of Oz, The (book), 2:45; 4:121

Wizard of Oz, The (movie), 5:62, *62*

wizards, 7:172

Wolfe, James, 7:91

Wolfe, Thomas, 1:40, 41

Wollstonecraft, Mary, 8:251, *251*; 7:173

wolves, 7:173, *173*

Tasmanian, 4:*185*

wombats, 4:*185*

wombs, 6:128

women, in **track and field,** 7:70–72, *70*

women's movement, 7:173; 7:16, *16*

and **Civil Rights Movement,** 2:66

and Nineteenth Amendment, 2:112

wood, 7:174, *174*; 7:59, 80

and **carpentry,** 2:16–17, *16, 17*

from **forests,** 3:120, 121, *121*

as **fuel,** 3:138

lignin of, 6:136

and **paper,** 5:151, *151*

sculpture of, 6:112, *112*

shrubbery, 6:136, *136*

toys of, 7:68, 69

Wood, Grant, 4:93

Wood, Natalie, 5:64

Woodcraft Indians, 1:153

woodcuts, 6:28, *28*

woodlands, 7:175, *175*; *see also* **forests**

woodpeckers, 1:139, *139*, 141

Woods, Granville T., 1:19

Woodstock Music and Art Fair, 6:81

woodwind instruments, 5:70, *70*, 134
wool, 7:176, *176*; 3:76, *76*
   knitting, 4:128
   spinning, 6:178
Woolf, Virginia, 3:29; 8:133
Woolley, Leonard, 7:17
wooly mammoths, 6:19, *19*
word processors, 7:88, *88*; 7:176
Wordsworth, William, 8:251; 3:29
work, and **heat,** 4:20, *20*
World Bank, 2:149
World Cup:
   soccer, 6:154–155, *155*, 180
   track and field, 7:72
World Health Organization (WHO),
   2:149
World Series, baseball, 1:*119*, 120
World Trade Organization, 7:73
World War I, 7:177–178, *178*; 7:95,
   136
   France and, 3:132
   Germany and, 3:160
   Italy and, 4:105
   start of, 1:100
   tanks in, 7:31
   United Kingdom in, 7:93
   United States in, 7:104
World War II, 7:179–181, *179–181*;
   3:40, 7:95, 136
   atomic bombs in, 1:96; 4:32, 111
   in Austria, 1:100
   and Belarus, 1:128
   concentration camps in, 2:103,
     103
   declaration of, 2:*107*
   defense industries, 1:81, 182–183;
     2:108, 143
   in **Florida,** 3:100
   France in, 3:132
   Germany in, 2:*37*; 3:160
   gliders in, 3:167
   Italy in, 4:105
   Japan in, 1:96; 2:52, 107; 4:16, 32,
     111; 5:113
   Nazis in, 4:37, 118
   in the Pacific, 5:113, 121
   Pearl Harbor and, 4:16, 111;
     5:159–160, *159*
   in Russia, 6:168

United States and, 7:104, *105*,
   179–181
victory bonds sold in, 6:12
   Yugoslavia and, 7:188
World Wide Web, 4:90
worms, 7:182, *182*; 2:179, *179*; 4:92
   earthworms, 6:157
   silkworms, 6:138, *138*
   tapeworms, 7:33
worsteds, 7:176
Wounded Knee massacre, 6:167
Wren, Christopher, 8:252
   church designed by, 8:*252*
wrestling, 7:182, *182*
Wright brothers, 8:252–253; 1:25;
   3:96, 167; 5:111, 127, 128
   aircraft of, 1:*25*; 3:96; 5:*111*; 8:*252*
Wright, Frank Lloyd, 8:253; 1:74,
   81; 4:65, 66; 7:171, 172
   buildings designed by, 1:*75*
   house designed by, 8:*253*
Wright, Richard, 1:20, 41; 5:39
writing systems, 7:183, *183*
   alphabets, 1:37, *37*
   Anglo-Saxon, 1:54
   braille, 1:154
   Chinese, 2:50, *50*
   in **communication,** 2:96
   cuneiform, 5:19; 7:17
   and **drawing,** 2:170
   hieroglyphics, 1:105; 2:187; 4:28,
     28
   languages, 4:138–139
Wyclif, John, 8:253; 1:131; 6:31
Wyoming, 7:184–185, *184*; 2:81;
   7:100

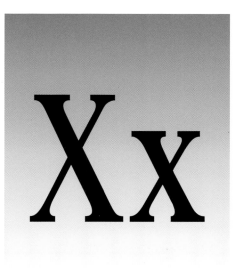

xerography, 5:166, *166*
Xerxes, 8:254; 4:94
X-rays, 7:185, *185*; 3:*127*; 6:45, 46,
   108; 7:18; 8:205
xylem tubes, 7:80
xylophones, 5:74, *75*

yachts, 7:186, *186*; 1:147; 6:70, 100;
   7:147
yaks, 2:26, 39, 166
Yale, Linus, Jr., 4:164
Yangtze River, China, 6:74
yarn, 3:*189*; 7:51
Yasunari, Kawabata, 1:90
Yeager, Chuck, 3:96; 7:158
yeasts, 7:187; 1:125, 137

Yeats, William Butler, 8:254; 3:29

Yellowstone National Park, 3:162, *162*; 5:52, 81; 6:85; 7:*114*, 184, 185

Yeltsin, Boris, 8:254–255, *255*; 6:98

Yemen, 7:187; 5:30

Yenisey River, Russia, 6:74

Yerkes Observatory, 7:*40*; 8:122

Yetis (abominable snowmen), 5:51

Yevtushenko, Yevgeny, 3:41

Yggdrasil, 2:168

Yiddish language, 1:41

yin and yang, 7:26, *26*, 32

Yirawala, bark painting by, 1:9

YMCA and YWCA, 7:187

yoga, 7:188; 4:121

Yogi Bear, 2:19

yogurt, 7:188; 1:107

yogurt cheese, how to make, 2:39

yolk, egg, 2:186, *186*

Yom Kippur, 3:73; 4:118

Yordonidis, Dimitrion, 4:184

Yorktown, Battle of, 1:44; 7:136

Yoruba people, 1:16, 21

Yosemite National Park, 1:183; 5:81, *81*

Young, Brigham, 8:255; 5:54; 7:109

Young, Cy, 1:120

Young, Lester, 4:112

Yuan Dan, 3:73

Yugoslavia, 7:188; 1:151; 2:125; 4:169; 6:59, *59*, 124, 148, 150

Yukon River, 1:31

Yukon Territory, Canada, 1:*189*

yurts, 3:177, *178*; 5:48, *48*

Zz

Zaïre (**Congo**), 2:105, *105*

Zaïre (Congo) River, 2:105, *105*; 6:74

Zambia, 7:189, *189*; 2:95

Zangla bridge, India, 1:*160*

Zanzibar, 7:32

Zapata, Emiliano, 8:255–256, *255*

zebras, 7:189–190, *190*; 3:*178*; 4:42–43

Zen Buddhism, 1:167

Zenger, John Peter, 8:256, *256*

Zeppelins, 7:178

   Hindenburg, 1:112, 113, *113*

zero, 7:143

   absolute, 7:19, 43

Zeus (Greek god), 3:184–185

   statue of, 6:124, *125*

Zhou Enlai, 8:256, *256*

Ziegfeld, Florenz, 5:75

Ziegfeld Follies, 5:75

ziggurats, 5:120; 7:17

Zimbabwe, 7:190, *190*; 1:17; 2:55, 95; 6:24

zinc, 7:191

ZIP codes, 7:191; 6:11–12

zippers, 7:191, *191*

zodiac, signs of, 1:92, *92*, 181

Zola, Emile, 3:41

zoologists, 7:191

zooplankton, 5:175, *175*

zoos, 7:192, *192*; 2:109

Zoroastrianism, 4:85, *85*

Zworykin, Vladimir K., 7:42

Acknowledgments

OXFORD AMERICAN CHILDREN'S ENCYCLOPEDIA

Editor, U.S.:

Ann T. Keene

Designers:

Cheryl Rodemeyer
  The Design Shop
  Torrington, CT

Gecko Ltd.

Oxprint Ltd.

Jo Bowers

Jack Donner (Volume 9)

Contributors:

Ann T. Keene

Philip Koslow

Charles Patterson

Adriane Ruggiero

Sean Dolan

Charles T. Bartunek

Thomas J. Bartunek

Picture research:

Patricia Burns and Ann T. Keene

Indexer:

Nancy Wolff

Consultants, U.S.:

Ann Bay
  Director, Office of Education
  National Museum of American History
  Smithsonian Institution
  Washington, D.C.

Dr. Frank De Varona
  Visiting Associate Professor of Education
  Florida International University/
  Superintendent (retired), Region I
  Dade County Public Schools
  Miami, Florida

Dr. Nellie Graham
  Coordinator of Social Studies
  Atlanta Public Schools
  Atlanta, Georgia

Dr. Henry G. Kiernan
  Director of Curriculum
  West Morris Regional High School District
  Chester, New Jersey

Sue Struthers
  Director of Youth Services
  Riverside Public Library
  Riverside, California

Leonard Tallevi
  Chairman
  Department of Social Studies
  Scarsdale Middle School
  Scarsdale, New York

Dr. Raymond Wicks
  Director of Curriculum
  Catholic Education Office
  Archdiocese of St. Louis
  St. Louis, Missouri

U.K. editor:

Ben Dupré

U.K. contributors:

Dr. R. E. Allen
Bridget Ardley
Neil Ardley
Tom Arkell
Dr. Stephen Ashton
Peter Aykroyd
Jill Bailey
Professor Chris Baines
Dr. Christopher Baldick
Peter Ball
Norman Barrett
Penny Bateman
Brian S. Beckett
Dr. John Becklake
Sue Becklake
H. C. Bennet-Clark
Dr. Michael J. Benton
Jane Bingham
Johnny Black
Alan Bloomfield
Dr. Brian Bowers
Professor Adrian Brockett
John R. Brown
Eric Buckley
Ben Burt
Gerald Butt
Arthur Swift Butterfield
Richard C. Carter
Kate Castle
Professor Joan M. Chandler
Mary Cherry
Ian Chilvers
Jean Cooke
Jeremy Coote
Mike Corbishley
Judith Court
Hilary Devonshire
Tony Dr.ake
Professor Michael Dummett
Professor T. H. Elkins
Mark Espiner
David Fickling
Elizabeth Foster
John L. Foster
Dr. Bernard J. Freedman
David Glover
Gib Goodfellow
Susan Goodman
Dr. Alastair McIntosh Gray
J. M. Gullick
Gerald Haigh
Michael Harrison
Margaret Hebblethwaite
Peter Hebblethwaite
Sonya Hinton
John Hodgson
Peter Holden
Janet E. Hunter
Michael Hurd
Paul James
David Jay
Rob Jeffcoate
Richard Jeffery
Dr. Terry Jennings
Astley Jones

Stephen Keeler
Rosemary Kelly
Margaret Killingray
Sheila Kitzinger
Ann Kramer
Clive A. Lawton
Diyan Leake
Vivienne M. Little
Ann Low-Beer
Keith Lye
Vicki Mackenzie
Dr. Nicholas Mann
Bridget Martyn
Kenneth and Valerie McLeish
Peter Mellett
Haydn Middleton
Dr. N. J. Middleton
Dr. Jacqueline Mitton
Peggy Morgan
National Epilepsy Association
Dr. Roger Neich
Iain Nicolson
Paul C. Noble
John O'Connor
Catherine O'Keefe
Dr. Stuart Owen-Jones
Chris Oxlade
David Parkinson
Tony Pawson
Dr. David Pimm
Henry Pluckrose
Joyce Pope
Stephen Pople
Philip Pullman
Jeremy Purseglove
Judy Ridgway
Professor James Riordan
R. J. Ritchie
John Robottom
Lois Rock
Dr. Alisdair Rogers
Stewart Ross
Theodore Rowland-Entwistle
Ann Schlee
Michael Scott
Daljit Sehbai
Louise Spilsbury
Imogen Stewart
Derek Strange
John N. Stringer
Jeffery Tabberner
Liz Tagert
Professor Charles Taylor
Peter Teed
Dr. Nicholas Tucker
Pauline Vincent
John N. Walker
Roger Watson
Dr. Philip Whitfield
Patrick Wiegand
Elizabeth Williamson
Mark Wilson
Gillian A. Wolfe
Jenyth Worsley
Jill A. Wright

Principal U.K. consultants:

John Brown
  Flexible Learning Adviser
  Southwest Region
  England

Dr. Henry Bennet-Clark
  Lecturer in Invertebrate Zoology
  Oxford University
  Oxford, England

Ian Chilvers
  Editor, Oxford Dictionary
  of Art
  Oxford University Press
  Oxford, England

Tony Drake
  Head of Economics and Head of
  Upper School
  Oxford School
  Oxford, England

Joyce Pope
  Formerly Senior Lecturer
  Natural History Museum
  London, England

Stephen Pople
  Formerly Head of Physics
  Withywood School
  Bristol, England
  Author of Science to 14 and
  other books

Charles Taylor
  Emeritus Professor,
  University of Wales;
  Formerly Professor of
  Experimental Physics
  Royal Institution
  London, England

Peter Teed
  Formerly Headmaster
  Goole Grammar School
  Goole, Humberside, England

Patrick Wiegand
  Lecturer in Geographical
  Education
  University of Leeds
  Leeds, England

and the children and staff of
Blunsdon St. Andrew School
  Blunsdown, Wiltshire, England
Henry Bellairs Middle School
  Bedworth, Warwickshire,
  England
St. Edward's School
  Paddington, London, England
Stonesfield County Primary School
  Stonesfield, Oxfordshire, England
Woodstock Primary School
  Woodstock, Oxfordshire,
  England

Other U.K. consultants:

Dr. Terry Allsop
Dr. Stephen Ashton
Dr. Christopher Baldick
Rev John Barton
Dr. G. T. Bath
Marigold Best
Dr. John Blair
Jean Bolam
Professor Keith Branigan
Professor Adrian Brockett
Dr. Peter Carey
Professor William Chafe
Ian Chilvers
Mike Farr
Dr. Honor Gay
Dr. David Gellner
Dr. Andy Gosler
Dr. Daniel Greenstein
Dr. Narayani Gupta
Gerald Haigh
Michael Harrison
Peggy Heeks
Michael Hurd
M. Mashuq ibn Ally
Dr. Brian Keeble
Dr. Margaret Kinnel
Dr. Katherine Krebs
Clive A. Lawton
Helen Lewins
Henrietta Leyser
Bryan Loughrey
Professor James Lydon

Keith Lye
Shirley Matthews
Dr. George McGavin
Vivien McKay
Dr. Euan McKendrick
Professor W. H. McLeod
Dr. Stuart Milligan
Professor Clyde A. Milner II
Professor Kenneth O. Morgan
Peggy Morgan
Dr. Chandra Muzatfar
Dr. Christopher A. Norris
Dr. Beth Okamura
Dr. Judith Okely
Quentin Oliver
Padraig O'Loingsigh
Professor J. H. Paterson
Chris Powling
Jan Powling
David A. Preston
Judith Salmon
Dr. Ian Scargill
Dr. Andrew Sherratt
Dr. Harry Shukman
Professor Harvard Sitkoff
Margaret Spencer
Louise Spilsbury
Janet Stevenson
John Stringer
Dr. Nicholas Tucker
Anita Tull
Ben Watson
Dr. Robert Youngson

Credits

Diagrams and Illustrations

Gary Tong **1** 24b, 59r, 95, 101, 104tl, 117br, 118, 121, 134, 147, 155tl, 170; **2** 91, 92, 106, 111, 116, 121, 161l; **3** 17, 79, 134; **4** 21tr, 36, 41, 45, 143; **5** 129l, 192br; **6** 11, 44, 45; **7** 14, 15, 38.

Other diagrams and illustrations **1–8** by Graham Allen, Sophie Allington, Victor Ambrus, Norman Arlott, John Barber, Julian Baum, Brian Beckett, Richard Berridge, Jenny Brackley, Stefan Chabluk, Jim Channell, Priscilla Coleman, Peter Connolly, Michael Courtney, Paul Doherty, Simon Driver, Gecko Ltd., Tony Gibbons,

David Hardy, Nick Harris, Nick Hawken, Gary Hincks, Richard Hook, Ray Hutchins, Information Design Unit/Russel Birkett, Christopher Jarman, Harold Jones, Jones Sewell Associates, Peter Joyce, Frank Kennard, Gillian Kenny, Elizabeth Kerr, Joan Kiddell-Monroe, Linden Artists, Mick Loates, Vanessa Luff, Kevin Madison, David Moore, Richard Morris, David Murray, OUP, Denys Ovenden, Oxford Illustrators Ltd., Raynor Design, Paul Richardson, Terry Riley, Jim Robbins, Andrew Robinson, Chris Rothero, Martin Sanders, Mike

Saunders, Steve Seymour/Bernard Thornton Artists, Howard Twiner, Peter Visscher, Brian Watson, Steve Weston, Michael Woods, Mel Wright.

Maps

Gary Tong—**3–7** all U.S. state maps; **5** 83, 108 (inset); **7** 102, 139; **8** 147; Cheryl Rodemeyer—**1–2** all U.S. state maps *except* **1** 31 (Susan Fearey), and all state locater maps; other maps **1–8** by European Map Graphics, Oxford Illustrators Ltd. and OUP.

Abbreviations

The following abbreviations have been used:
t = top, b = bottom, c = center, l = left, r = right

Archive	Archive Photos, New York City
Art Resource	Art Resource, New York City
Bridgeman	The Bridgeman Art Library
Coleman	Bruce Coleman
Corbis-Bettmann	Corbis-Bettmann, New York City
Harding	Robert Harding Picture Library
Hulton	Hulton Deutsch Picture Company/Hulton Getty Collection
Hutchison	The Hutchison Library
Lane	Frank Lane Picture Agency
Kobal	The Kobal Collection
Mary Evans	Mary Evans Picture Library
NHPA	Natural History Photographic Agency
OSF	Oxford Scientific Films
Peter Newark	Peter Newark's American Pictures/Western Americana
Planet	Planet Earth Pictures
SPL	The Science Photo Library
Spooner	Frank Spooner Pictures

Volume 1

9bl Pitt Rivers Museum; 9tr Harding; 12l Vandystadt/Allsport; 12–13 Hershey Community Archives, Hershey, PA; 13 Scala/Art Resource; 14 Hutchison; 17bl Hutchison; 17tr Liverpool Museum; 20 Digging It Up Archives; 22 New York Public Library; 23l Hulton; 25br Boeing Commercial Airplane Group/Peter Middleton Associates; 25bl Science Museum, London; 25t Flight/Quadrant Picture Library; 25r Quadrant Picture Library; 25c, b British Aerospace; 27l Boeing Commercial Airplane Group/Peter Middleton Associates; 27r U.S. Air Force; 28bl Peter J. Schulz/Chicago Department of Aviation; 28br Paul Van Riel/Harding; 28–29 DRS Productions/Zefa; 30 Dan Brothers/Alabama Bureau of Tourism and Travel; 31 Alaska Division of Tourism; 33 Jan Hinsch/SPL; 34 Gunter Heil/Zefa; 35 OUP/British Film Institute; 36 Bob & Clara Calhoun/Coleman; 38 J. Allan Cash Ltd; 42 Palmer Hayden Collection, Museum of

Photographs

African American Art, Los Angeles; 44 The American Antiquarian Society; 45 AKG London; 46 Archive; 47 Michael Fogden/OSF; 48 Michael Fogden/Coleman; 49 Archive; 50 Courtesy of the Trustees of the British Museum, London/AKG London; 51t Patricio Goycolea/Hutchison; 51b Jackie Lewin, Royal Free Hospital, London/SPL; 52 Museum of American Folk Art, New York City; 53t Courtesy of the Trustees of the British Museum, London/OUP; 53b OUP; 54tl, bl, r Courtesy of the Trustees of the British Museum, London/OUP; 55 Jeff Lapore/Photo Researchers Inc/OSF; 56 Roger Jackman/OSF; 57 Lynx; 61l Scott Polar Reserach Institute, Cambridge/Harding; 61r Geoff Renner/Harding; 62t Breck P. Kent/Animals Animals/OSF; 62b Peter Davey/Coleman; 64t Kim Taylor/OSF; 64b P.J. Devries/Partridge Productions Ltd./Coleman; 65 R.I.M.Campbell/Gorilla Research/Coleman; 66 D. DeMello/Wildlife Conservation Society, New York City; 67 George Grall/National Aquarium, Baltimore; 68l Ronald Sheridan Ancient Art & Architecture Collection; 68r Mary Evans; 69 James Green/Harding; 70 African Burial Project, New York City; 71t, c, b Courtesy of the Trustees of the British Museum, London; 72 Colorsport; 73 Zefa; 74 Short Ford and Associates/School of Engineering and Manufacture, De Montfort University, Leicester; 75t Archive; 75b OUP; 76tl OUP; 76b Harding; 76–77 T.E. Clark/Hutchison; 77t Richard Bryant/Arcaid; 77b Paul Rafferty/Arcaid; 78 Jorg Torbitzsch/Zefa; 81 Archive; 83t A. C. Haralson/Arkansas Department of Parks and Tourism; 83b Carol Farneti; Partridge Films Ltd/OSF; 90 Bridgeman/Art Resource; 91 S.A. & J. Mitton/NASA; 92 Giraudon/Art Resource; 93 NASA/SPL; 96 US Navy/SPL; Norbert 98t Julia Thorne/Harding; 98c B Croxford/Zefa; 98b Andrew Mola/Zefa; 99 E.T. Archive; 100 V. Phillips/Zefa; 102t and b N.

Wright/National Motor Museum, Beaulieu; 102c National Motor Museum, Beaulieu; 103 Walt Kuhn/Indianapolis Motor Speedway; 104–105 E.T. Archive; 105r American Museum of Natural History; 106tl Camilla Jessel; 106br Bubbles; 106 all other pictures S. & R. Greenhill; 107 Alastair Shay/OSF; 110bl Archive; 110bl Harding; 110–111 Harding; 111 Edgeworth Productions/Stockmarket/Zefa; 112 Herbert Schwind Okapia/OSF; 113t Goodyear Tire and Rubber Company; 113b AKG London; 108l Hulton; 114l Ed and Karen Crockett/Ohio State University Marching Band; 114–115 Hulton; 115t J. Allan Cash Ltd.; 115b Barry Hicks/Britain on View; 117 Mike Price/Coleman; 119tl Otto Greule/Allsport; 119bl Little League Baseball, Inc.; 119r National Baseball Hall of Fame Library, Cooperstown, NY; 120 Archive; 121 Libby Howells; 122 Stephen Dalton/NHPA; 123 American Soybean Association; 124l Leonard Lee Rue III/Coleman; 124r Dan Guravich/OSF; 126 Kim Taylor/Coleman; 127 Thomas Eisner, Cornell University; 128 Zefa; 129 Archive; 130l Hummel/Zefa; 130r Paul McCullagh/OSF; 131 Courtesy of the Trustees of the British Museum, London/Phaidon; 132 Philadelphia Museum of Art; 133l Cycleurope; 133r Neatwork; 137 APV Crepaco, Inc.; 140 G. K. Brown/Ardea London; 141l D. Robert Franz/Cornell Laboratory of Ornithology; 141rt Art Biale/Cornell Laboratory of Ornithology; 141rb J. R. Woodward/Cornell Laboratory of Ornithology; 142l Giljsbert Van Frankenhuyzen/Cornell Laboratory of Ornithology; 142rt and rb Isidor Jeklin/Cornell Laboratory of Ornithology; 143t Mary Tremaine/Cornell Laboratory of Ornithology; 143bl Zig Leszcynski/Animals Animals/OSF; 143br Gordon Langsbury/Coleman; 144l S. & R. Greenhill; 144r OUP; 145 The Seeing Eye

of Morristown, NJ; 146 Prof. Aaron Polliak/SPL; 148 Robert Frerck/Harding; 150 OUP; 153 Boy Scouts of America; 156 Hutchison; 157 OUP; 160tl Seque/Hutchison; 160l Harding; 160r Dave Brinicombe/Hutchison; 163l Richard Packwood/OSF; 163tr John Murray/Coleman; 163b Roy Rainford/Harding; 164 Paolo Koch/Harding; 165 Harding; 166t Ann & Bury Peerless; 166b OUP; 167 Zefa; 168t Bernard Regent/Hutchison; 168b Kathie Atkinson/OSF; 169 John Miller/Harding; 170 National Westminster Bank; 171 copyright 1960 Allegra Fuller Snyder/Buckminster Fuller Institute, Santa Barbara, CA; 172l Brian Beckett; 172r Richard Packwood/OSF; 173t Caterpillar; 173b E. Jauregui/Zefa; 174 Ian Griffiths/Harding; 175l Simon Trevor/Coleman; 175r Carol Jopp/Harding; 176l Silvestris/Mueller/Lane; 176r Thomas Eisner, Cornell University; 177 J.H.C. Wilson/Harding; 178 Travel Photo International; 179 OUP; 180t Sarah Errington/Hutchison; 180b Sheila Terry/Rutherford Appleton Laboratory/SPL; 181 Giraudon/Bridgeman; 182 Michele and Tom Grimm/Los Angeles Convention and Visitors Bureau; 184 Mickey Gibson/Animals Animals/OSF; 186 Michael Fogden/Coleman; 187 Jenny Woodcock/Bubbles; 189tl, tr G. Hunter/Zefa; 189br Harding; 191t Walter Rawlings/Harding; 191b K. Kerth/Zefa; 192 Harding.

Volume 2

8t David Hughes/Coleman; 8b Jost Amman, *Fronsberger's Book of War*/Mary Evans; 9 Martyn F. Chillmaid/Harding; 11–12 Martin Sookias/OUP; 15 Christian Zuber/Coleman; 16l Mary Evans; 16r Adam Woolfitt/Harding; 18t Reproduced by permission of United Feature Syndicate Inc./Knight Features; 18b Herge/Moulinsart 1966; 20l G. Heller/Harding; 20–21, 21tr Harding; 22tl Peter Parks/OSF; 22tr Harding; 22br Bernard Regent/Hutchison; 23 Eckhard Gollnow/Zefa; 24 Norbert Rosing/OSF; 25t Terry Whittaker/Lane; 25b Alan and Sandy Carey/OSF; 26 K. Wothe/Coleman; 27 Philadelphia Museum of Art; 28b James Wellard/Sonia Halliday Photos; 28–29 Allschwil-Basel/Colorphoto Hinz ; 29b James Wellard/Sonia Halliday Photos; 31r, 32t OUP; 34 Ian Griffiths/Harding; 35 Kevin Schafer; 36 The Image Bank; 37t Kim Taylor/Coleman; 37b Janos Jurka/Coleman; 39 Atlantide SDF/Coleman; 40t Stan Osolinski/OSF; 40b British Petroleum; 42 Linda Spigelmeyer, Pleasant View Egg Farms, Winfield, PA; 43t Caroline Penn/Impact; 45 Penguin Books Ltd.; 46 Helmut Albrecht/Coleman; 47t Dallas & John Heaton/Colorific; 47b Sarah Errington/Hutchison; 49t J. Allan Cash Ltd;

49b Paolo Koch/Zefa; 50 OUP; 51 Harding; 52 Heidelberg University; 53 Carlos Reyes/Andes Press Agency; 54tl Harding; 54tr F. Jackson/Harding; 55bl Colorific; 55tr Hutchison; 55br A. Krause/Rex Features; 56tl Zefa; 56bl E. Simamor/Harding; 56tr Jorg Trobitzsch/Zefa; 57 Carlos Reyes/Andes Press Agency; 58tl Gascoigne/Harding; 58tr Peter Brown/Arcaid; 58–59 Zefa; 60 Archive; 61l Damm Fr/Zefa; 61r A. Roberts/Zefa; 62tl National Snow and Ice Data Centre/SPL; 62b Earth Satellite Corporation/SPL; 63 Harding; 64bl Zefa; 64tr Harding; 69 Archive; 70 National Archives; 74t Hutchison; 74b, 75t Michael Holford; 75bl National Maritime Museum, Greenwich/Michael Holford; 75bc, br Swatch; 76l Hulton; 76r Zefa; 78bl Geoff Tompkinson/SPL; 78br Zefa; 79t Tim Sharman; 79bl Levi's/Schilland & Co.; 79br Christina Dodwell/Hutchison; 83 United States Coast Guard; 84t R. Smith/Zefa; 84b Nick Holt/Zefa; 85 R. Halin/Zefa; 87t J. Allan Cash Ltd; 87b Ashmolean Museum, Oxford; 88 A. B. Dowsett/SPL; 89l *Opened by Customs*, by Kurt Schwitters, DACS 1996 Tate Gallery; 89r Tate Gallery; 90 Brian Moser/Hutchison; 93 Pikes Peak County Attractions Association; 95 Al Bello/Allsport; 96t Clive Bromhall/OSF; 96b NASA/SPL; 98t Ontario Science Centre; 98b Silva (UK) Ltd.; 99t AKG London; 99b Maxis Ltd; 100 University of Pennsylvania Archives; 101bl Intel; 102 Dr. Jeremy Burgess/SPL; 103 AKG London; 104 Tarmac Construction/F.R. Logan Ltd.; 105t Frieder Sauer/Coleman; 105b Zefa; 107 Franklin D. Roosevelt Library; 108 Mystic Seaport; 110l Colin Milkins/OSF; 110r Harding; 115 Allan Power/Coleman; 117 Rex Features; 119l Leidmann/Zefa; 119r Dave Hogan/Rex Features; 120 Peter Newark; 122 G. Ziesler/Coleman; 123b David Parker/SPL; 124l Christie's Colour Library; 124br Hulton; 125bl Herbert Kranawetter/Coleman; 125tr Jen & Des Bartless/Coleman; 126 Sonia Halliday Photos; 127r Peter Parks/OSF; 128tl Sinclair Stammers/SPL; 128tr Dr. Jeremy Burgess/SPL; 128br Archive; 129bl Pascal Rondeau/Allsport; 129tr Mike Powell/Allsport; 130 Hutchison; 131r Harding; 132tr Nick Sidle/The Dance Library; 132lc Tim Jarvis; 132br Darryl Williams/The Dance Library; 133t Kobal; 133b Hulton; 134b Rex Features; 136 Harding; 137 Starkey Laboratories Ltd.; 139 United States Capitol Art Collection; 140 R. Wilmshurst/Coleman; 141 Delaware Tourism; 142 Legoland, Denmark; 143 Copyright Dorothea Lange Collection, Oakland Museum; 144bl Sunak/Zefa; 144–145 Colin Monteath/OSF; 145t Coleman; 145cr Hutchison; 146l, top to bottom—Nike Corporation, Apple MacIntosh Computers, Inc., Shell Oil Co.,

VAG, McDonald's Corporation; 146br London Transport Museum; 147 Coca-Cola, Inc.; 150bl Diamond International Magazine; 150tr Louise Spilsbury; 153t John Mitchell/OSF; 153b American Museum of Natural History; 157 Archive; 158l Jonathan Watts/SPL; 158r Leonard Lee Rue III/Coleman; 159l Richard Folwell/SPL; 159r Dr. George Gornacz/SPL; 162tl Gerard Lacz/NHPA; 163tl G.A. Maclean/OSF; 163c V. Shone/Gamma/Spooner; 164l, tr Trustees of the Victoria & Albert Museum, London; 164b Norton & Company; 165tl R Pitman/Earthviews/Lane; 167l J. Carmichael/NHPA; 167br Harding; 168 National Gallery, London; 169bl Ian Griffiths/Harding; 169 Donald Cooper/Photostage; 170 Magyar Szepm Veszeti Muzeum, Budapest/AKG London; 171 Bonhams, London/Bridgeman; 172 Robert Frerck/Harding; 173bl J. Allan Cash Ltd.; 173tr Premier Percussion Ltd; 174tl Peter Newark; 174br Hutchison; 175t John Cancalosi/Coleman; 175cl Jane Burton/Coleman; 175cr Leonard Lee Rue III/Animals Animals/OSF; 176 NASA; 177 Worldsat International/NRSC/SPL; 178 V. Shone/Gamma/Spooner; 180 Terence Le Goubin/Colorific; 182 Sue Wells/ICCE; 185r Travel Photo International; 187 J. Allan Cash Ltd.; 188 Damm/Zefa; 189t, b, 190 Trustees of the British Museum, London/Michael Holford; 191 Dunlop Slazenger International Ltd; 192 AP/Worldwide Photos.

Volume 3

7 Gordon Garradd/SPL; 11 Mick Hutson/Redferns; 12 Quadrant Picture Library; 13t John Howard/SPL; 13b Don Thomson/SPL; 15 Mickey Gibson/Animals Animals/OSF; 16 Jonathan Scott/Planet; 19tr WWF; 19c Norman Myers/Coleman; 19b Charles Bishop/Planet; 20 Mike Powell/Allsport; 22 Francois Duhamel/Mega/Rex Features; 30bl Richard Packwood/OSF; 30tr Henneghein/Coleman; 33 Hutchison; 35 Scala; 42 Equinox; 43t Jan Taylor/Coleman; 43b Dept. of Geology, College of Cardiff, University of Wales; 47, 48tl John Reader/SPL; 50 British Library, London; 51t Hulton; 51b British Library, London; 52l Sturrock/Network; 54 Patti Murray/Animals Animals/OSF; 54b Stephen Dalton/OSF; 56b Richard Doyle, *Fairyland*/Mary Evans; 57 Harding; 58t Arthur Rackham/Mary Evans; 58b Goebel/Zefa; 60l Arnaud Borrel/Gamma/Spooner; 60r Mark Boulton/Coleman; 61t Zefa; 62t Steenmanns/Zefa; 62b Heilman/Zefa; 63t Orion Press/Zefa; 63b A.J. Deane/Coleman; 64 Dennis Orchard/Coleman; 66tr Trustees of the Victoria & Albert Museum, London; 66bl Defile Lanvin/Stills/Rex Features; 69 FBI; 70b M. R. Phicton/Coleman; 72t David Cannon/Allsport; 72b John Shaw/Coleman;

73, 74 (all photos) Chris Honeywell/OUP; 75 Zefa; 76l SPL; 76br Harding; 77 Metropolitan Police; 78 Bernard Regent/Hutchison; 80tr John Shaw/Coleman; 80br H. Armstrong/Zefa; 82bl Smithsonian Institution; 82tr Library of Congress; 83tl UPI/Corbis-Bettmann; 83bl Franklin Delano Roosevelt Library; 83br John F. Kennedy Library; 86t David Thompson/OSF; 86–87 Dick Clarke/Planet; 87r Carl Roessler/Coleman; 90–91 Kim Westerskov/OSF; 92 Kim Westerskov/OSF; 94 Gunter Ziesler/Coleman; 95t Geoff Dore/Coleman; 95b Mik Dakin/Coleman; 98 John Fennell/Coleman; 99 Chip Hires/Gamma/Spooner; 100 U.S. National Park Service; 102 (all) Brian Beckett; 103t Alain Compost/Coleman; 105 J. Pfaff/Zefa; 106t Granada TV/Hutchison; 106b John Egan/Hutchison; 107t AKG London; 107b Corbis-Bettmann; 108t Harding; 108b Rex Features; 110–111 Keller/Zefa; 115 Harding; 116tr Stephen Dunn/Allsport; 118t Harding; 118b Travel Photo International; 120t Peter Ward/Coleman; 120b Fritz Prenzel/Coleman; 121tl Harding; 121br Luiz Claudio Marigo/Coleman; 122 Fort Ticonderoga Museum; 123l J Fennell/Coleman; 123r Sinclair Stammers/SPL; 124bl Frieder Sauer/Coleman; 124tr Gunter Ziesler/Coleman; 125 4-H Youth Development, University of Nebraska, Lincoln; 126t Tom Ulrich/OSF; 126b Gregory Sams/Photo Researchers; 127t, b Kim Taylor/Coleman; 128l Adam Woolfitt/Harding; 128r Pictchal, Sibapress/Rex Features; 129 Streichan/Zefa; 130 Trustees of the Victoria & Albert Museum, London/Bridgeman; 131l Chateau de Versailles, France/Bridgeman; 131tr Hulton; 133 Vatican Museums & Galleries, Rome/Bridgeman; 134–135 Michael Fogden/OSF; 135tl Stephen Dalton/OSF; 135tr John Gerlach/OSF; 136l (all) Brian Beckett; 136r, top to bottom— Hackenberg/Zefa, Hans Reinhard/Zefa, Harding, Robert Francis/Harding, Hans Reinhard/Coleman, Hans Reinhard/Zefa; 137tr Kim Taylor/Coleman; 137b State of Florida, Department of Citrus; 139 Frans Lanting/Coleman; 140 Tony Martin/OSF; 141 American Museum, Bath, England; 142tr City Art Gallery, Bristol; 142br St. Louis Art Museum; 143t NOAO/SPL; 143b Royal Observatory, Edinburgh/SPL; 145t Arthur Leipzig copyright 1950; 145b Metropolitan Museum of Art; 147bl Ken Gillham/Harding; 147tr C. Jopp/Harding; 148bl Dr. Jeremy Burgess/SPL; 148tr Kim Westerskov/OSF; 150 ICA/Bart Curren, courtesy of the Gem Bureau; 152 Harding; 157t Georgia-Pacific Corporation; 157b Jane Burton/Coleman; 158 Streichan/Zefa; 159tr Tim Sharman; 159br N. Schaefer/Zefa; 160 Associated Press/Topham Picture Source; 161 Library of Congress; 162l U.S. National Park Service; 162r Juliet Highet Brimah/Hutchison; 163 Archive; 164bl Jeff Foott/Coleman; 164tr Girl Scouts of the U.S.A.; 166 Wienke/Zefa; 167 T. Souter/Hutchison; 169 Eyal Bartov/OSF; 170tl Paul Brierley; 170c Peter Newark; 170br David Cannon/Allsport; 171br Mark Newman/Lane; 176tl Heilmann/Zefa; 176br H. Rivarola/Coleman; 177 John Shaw/Coleman; 178tl Hunter/Zefa; 178tr Sunak/Zefa; 178bl Harding; 178br Leonard Lee Rue III/Coleman; 179 C. Bowman/Harding; 180 Travel Photo International; 181 Harding; 187bl W. Schmidt/Zefa; 187r Rex Features; 189 J. G. Fuller/Hutchison; 190 Francisco Jerize/Coleman; 191 Colorsport; 192 Dimitri Lundt/Colorsport (TempSport).

Volume 4

7t Tim Sharman; 7b Galt Toys; 8 Gordon Langsbury/Coleman; 9tr P. M. Andrews/SPL; 10t British Library, London/Bridgeman; 10b Mark Wilson; 11t S. & R. Greenhill; 11b Mexico Ministry of tourism; 12 Jane Burton/Coleman; 13tr PH/Zefa; 13bl Didier Klein/Vandystadt/Allsport; 14 Stephen J. Krasemann/Coleman; 15tl Meyer/Liaison/Gamma/Spooner; 15tc William & Humbert Bodega/Harding; 15tr Gina Corrigan/Harding; 17 Hawaii Visitors and Convention Bureau; 18 Felix Greene/Hutchison; 22 Rod Williams/Coleman; 23b Westland Group plc; 24b Trustees of the British Museum, London/OUP; 27l Kim Taylor/Coleman; 29tl Art Resource; 29b Dieter & Mary Plage/Coleman; 30tl Trustees of the British Museum, London; 30bl Brian Warriner Ltd/Harding; 30–31 Ann & Bury Peerless; 31r R. Halin/Zefa; 32 Eric & David Hosking; 33 F. Carter Smith for the *New York Times*; 35br Richard Martin/Vandystadt; 36 Archive; 37cr Philippe Plailly/SPL; 38 David Parker/SPL; 39 Cameraman/Zefa; 41l Hans Reinhard/Coleman; 42–43 Lane; 46b Richard Bryant/Arcaid; 48tl London Scientific Films/OSF; 48cl J.C.Revy/SPL; 48bl London Scientific Films/OSF; 52tl Amnesty International; 53t Damm/Zefa; 53b John Mackinnon/Coleman; 54bl Harding; 54tr J.G. Fuller/Hutchison; 55b WWF/G. W. Frame/Coleman; 57tl Jeff Foott/Coleman; 58br C. M. Dixon Photo Resources; 59bl Hunter/Zefa; 59br Mary Evans; 60 Planet; 61t John Jennings; 61b Dave Kelly/Reuters/Archive; 62l Vandystadt/Allsport; 62r Werner H. Mueller/Zefa; Idaho Department of Commerce; 65 Illinois Bureau of Tourism; 67 Aldus Archive; 69r American Museum of Natural History; 69l Brian Boyd/Colorific; 70bl Michael Freeman/Coleman; 71tr Hutchison; 71br Sassoon/Harding; 72 Starfoto/Zefa; Indiana Department of Commerce; 76 Liba Taylor/Hutchison; 77b J. Fields/Zefa; 78 Hulton; 79tr Conran Design Group; 79br Lyn Gambles/Hutchison; 80tr Cathy Blackie; 81r Chris Honeywell/OUP; 82 TRH Pictures; 83t Hank Morgan/SPL; 83br Paul Shambroom/SPL; 84bl Alon Reininger/Colorific; 84tr Hutchison; 85bl Luca Invernizzi Tettoni/Photobank/Harding; 85tr Ann & Bury Peerless; 86bl G.I. Bernard/OSF; 86–87 Anthony Bannister/NHPA; 91tr Steennans/Zefa; 91br Derek Fordham; 92tl Ken Lucas/Planet; 93 National Corn Growers Association; 94br Sassoon/Harding; 96tl Carlos Guarita/Impact Photos; 96b Zefa; 98b British Steel; 99t Walter Rawlings/Harding; 99b Heilman CW2 290A3/Zefa; 100l Liba Taylor/Hutchison; 100–101 NAAS; 100tr V. Wentzel/Zefa; 102br, 103 Zefa; 104 Prato/Coleman; 106 M. P. Kahl/Coleman; 107 Claudia Wright/Partridge Productions Ltd/OSF; 108 Jamestown-Yorktown Foundation, Williamsburg, VA; 110cl Nigel Blythe/Harding; 110tr Japanese National Tourist Organization; 110br Hunter/Zefa; 114 Trustees of the Victoria & Albert Museum, London/Michael Holford; 111b Japan Information Center; 112bl Nick Elgar/Rex Features; 112–113 Corbis-Bettmann; 113bl Hulton; 113tr Rodger Jackman/OSF; 114tr Rolls-Royce; 115tr Sotheby's; 115br Compix; 116bl Jackson/Harding; 117tl Neville Kenton/Zefa; 117br Liba Taylor/Hutchison; 118t H. J. Kreuger/Zefa; 118b Jackson/Zefa; 119bl Patrick Fagot/NHPA; 119tr Frithfoto/Coleman; 120 Kansas State University Cooperative Extension Service; 122 Kentucky Department of Travel; 123br John Jennings; 126tr Sipa Press/Rex Features; 126br Michael Freeman/Coleman; 127bl Royal Aerospace Establishment, Farnborough; 128l Scala/OUP; 130 Erwin & Peggy Bauer/Coleman; 131 Library of Congress; 132 Meryl Levin/Impact Visuals; 133 David Leahy/SPL; 134tl Trustees of the Victoria & Albert Museum, London; 135tr Walter Rawlings/Harding; 138 M. Macintyre/Hutchison; 139 Coleman; 140tl Peter Parks/OSF; 141 Jerry Mason/SPL; 145 Mike Theiler/Reuters/Archive; 146 J. Allan Cash Ltd.; 148t Harding; 149 Michael Leach/OSF; 150 Mary Grant/Coleman; 153l O. Langrand/Coleman; 153r Alastair MacEwen/OSF; 154 G. I. Bernard/OSF; 155 RNLI; 156t Zefa; 159t Peter Davey/Coleman; 159b G. Ziesler/Coleman; 161t C. B. & D. W. Frith/Coleman; 161bl Harding; 162bl Northeast Fisheries Science Center, Woods Hole, Massachusetts; 162tr Maine Office of Tourism; 162br Colin Milkins/OSF; 165tr Ron Ziel/Millbrook House Ltd.; 166bl Kim Taylor/Coleman; 167 New Orleans Metropolitan Convention and Visitors Bureau, Inc.; 171tl Konrad

Patretti/Coleman; 179t Harding; 179b Rex Features; 180tr Morgan Library/Archive; 182t London Zoo; 183 U.S. Geological Survey; 184 Darrell Ingham/Allsport; 185 Carolina Biological Supply Co./OSF; 186 Gerard Planchenault/Allsport; 187 U.S. National Park Service/Ft. McHenry National Monument and National Shrine; 188tl No Theatre of the Kongo School, Kyoto/Werner Forman Archive; 188bl Ursula Didoni/Linden Museum, Stuttgart; 188tr OUP; 188br Werner Forman Archive; Sarah Hood/Massachusetts Office of Travel and Tourism; 192 Open Road.

Volume 5

7bl Andy Purcell/Coleman; 7tr Ray Richardson/Animals Animals/OSF; 9 Christopher Rennie/Harding; 10r Alexander Tsiaras/SPL; 13 E. T. Archive; 15 Wallace Collection, London/Bridgeman; 18 Suzanne Williams/OUP; 19 Courtesy of the Trustees of the British Museum, London/Michael Holford; 20 Trustees of the British Museum, London/Werner Forman Archive; 21l (all) Rudie H. Kuiter/OSF; 21c Dr. J. Mitton/OUP; 21r American Meteorite Laboratory; 22 Mexican Government Tourism Office; 23t Bridgeman; 23b G. Kinns/Joyce Pope; 24 Tulip Time Festival, Holland, MI; 26tr David Scharf/SPL; 26b IBM; 28t British Library, London/AKG London; 28b The Pierpont Morgan Library; 31 Eugen/Zefa; 32t Ronald Royer/SPL; 33t Brian E. Rybolt/Impact Photos; 33b (all) OUP; 34l Trustees of the British Museum (Natural History), London; 34r Harding; 35 Tony Craddock/SPL; 36 Minnesota Tourism Division; 38c Hutchison; 38b OUP; 39 Boeing Aerospace/TRH Pictures; 40 Peter Newark; 42 Missouri Division of Tourism; 43b Hans Reinhard/Coleman; 44tl Ken Lucas/Planet; 45t Douglas Dickens; 45b Guenet/Figaro Magazine/Gamma/Spooner; 46–47 Museum of Mankind; 47tr Rex Features; 47b Ashmolean Museum, Oxford; 48tl Harding; 48br Anthony Bannister/OSF; 49t Leonard Lee Rue III/Coleman; 59bl Horus/Zefa; 52bl Glacier National Park/U.S. National Park Service; 53r S. Nielsen/Coleman; 54 Harding; 55r Hutchison; 56l Stephen Dalton/NHPA; 56r Richard Packwood/OSF; 57t Mary Plage/Coleman; 57b Nexus/Suzuki; 58tl OUP; 58tr Mike Hewitt/Allsport; 59tr Nathan Bilow/Allsport; 59bl Spayway/John Cleare/Mountain Camera Picture Library; 60–61b Jen & Des Bartlett/Coleman; 62, 63 (all) Kobal; 65bl Trustees of the British Museum, London/Michael Holford; 65br Harding; 66 Collections of Henry Ford Museum and Greenfield Village; 67tl Scott Camazine/OSF; 70t OUP; 70bl Harding; 71t, bl, 72t OUP; 72br Paul Van Riel/Harding; 73t, bl, 74bl OUP; 75tr MGM/Samuel Goldwyn/Kobal; 76 T. H. C.

Wilson/Harding; 77bl Jim Clare/Partridge Films Ltd./OSF; 77br Joe Van Worner/Coleman; 79 Erich Lessing/Musée du Louvre, Paris/AKG London; 80 Musée de l'Armée, Paris; 81 Mike Floyd/Yosemite Museum/U.S. National Park Service; 82 Hanbury-Tenison/Harding; 84tl Art Gallery of Ontario; 84tr Library of Congress; 84bl Dept. of Library Services, American Museum of National History; 84br National Museum of American Art/Art Resource; 85l Harding; 85tr Smithsonian Institutution/National Anthropological Archives/Aldus Archives; 85br Department of Library Services, American Museum of National History; 86 Library of the Union League Club of Philadelphia; 87 Suzanne Williams/Bibliothèque Nationale Paris MSFR150f21/E. T. Archive; 88 Nebraska Department of Economic Development; 89b Anglo-Australian Telescope Board; 90t Robert Francis/Harding; 90b David Gellner; 92 Steenmanns/Zefa; 93 Las Vegas News Bureau; 95 Bob Grant/New Hampshire Office of Travel and Tourism Development; 96 New Jersey Travel and Tourism; 98 Archive; 100 Photodisc; 102t Hutchison; 102b Zefa; 104 V. Englebert/Zefa; 105bl, 106 OUP; 111 Clay Nolen/North Carolina Travel and Tourism; 112t Dawn Charging/North Dakota Tourism Department; 112b J. Allan Cash Ltd.; 113 Norbert Rosing/OSF; 114 Kotoh/Zefa; 115 Martin Bond/SPL; 119b Andy Price/Coleman; 120t Lovell Telescope, Jodrell Bank Science Centre; 120b Roger Ressmeyer, Starlight/SPL; 121 Nicholas Devore/Coleman; 123 Norbert Wu/OSF; 126 Zig Leszczynski/Animals Animals/OSF; 127 Columbus Convention and Visitors Bureau; 130 Fred Marvel/Oklahoma Tourism; 131t Sporting Pictures (U.K.) Ltd.; 131b Mark Boulton/ICCE; 132t Archive; 132b Haroldo Palo/NHPA; 133tr M. P. Price/Coleman; 134b Harding; 134–135 Baltimore Symphony Orchestra; 136 Terry Heathcote/OSF; 137 Larry Geddis/Oregon Tourism; 138tr Len Rue, Jr./Animals Animals/OSF; 139 NASA/SPL; 140 OUP; 140l Bibliothèque Nationale, Paris/Bridgeman; 142bl Galleria degli Uffizi/Erich Lessing/AKG London; 142–143 Rijksmuseum, Amsterdam/AKG London; 143tr National Gallery, London; 143b AKG London; 144 National Gallery of Art, Washington, D.C.; 145b Musée d'Orsay, Paris/VG-Bild/Kunst, Bonn/AKG London; 145t Metropolitan Museum of Art; 146t Metropolitan Museum of Art; 146b Bridgeman; 147t Prato/Coleman; 147b Harding; 148 Archive; 150t Lacz Lemoine/NHPA; 150b WWF/Timm Rautert/Coleman; 152 Colorsport; 153bl Dieter Grathwohl/Zefa; 153tr M. P. L. Fogden/Coleman; 154tr J. L. G. Grande/Coleman; 154bl Hulton; 155 Sara Cedar Miller/Central Park Conservancy; 156 K. Wothe/Coleman; 157 Cern Photo; 159tr

Peace Corps; 159bl Hawaii Visitors and Convention Bureau; 160 Luca Invernizzi Tettoni/Harding; 161t John Boyd/OSF; 163 Independence National Historical Park; 164 J. Allan Cash Ltd.; 167bl Peter Parks/Jonathan Watts/OSF; 167tr Sutcliffe Gallery c/o Whitby Literary & Philosophical Society/Frank Meadow Sutcliffe; 168 Roger Wilmshurst/Coleman; 169 Archive; 170 Kevin Galvin/Plymouth County Development Council; 171 Armstrong Roberts/Zefa; 172t NASA; 172c SPL/NASA; 172b NASA/J. Mitton; 173, 174bl NASA/SPL; 175 Peter Parks/OSF; 180 D. Parer & F. Parer-Cook/Ardea; 181 "Snake," by Keith Bosley, reproduced by permission of the publishers Angus Robertson (U.K.); 183 Tim Sharman; 184t S. & R. Greenhill; 184b Lambert/Archive; 186l P. Schwartz/Sipa-Press/Rex Features; 186tr R.P. Lawrence/Lane; 186–187b Andrew McClenaghan/SPL; 187 Tahiti Tourisme; 189 Robert Maier/Silvestris/Lane; 190tr Adam Woolfitt/Harding; 190b M.P. Price/Coleman; 191t R. Wilmshurst/Coleman.

Volume 6

7t Anthony Bannister/NHPA; 8bl San Lorenzo in Lucina, Rome/Bridgeman; 8tr Giraudon; 9 Benelux/Zefa; 10t Harding; 10b G. R. Richardson/Harding; 11l Harding; 12 National Archives, Washington, D.C.; 13br Harold Rose/Harding; 14tl Steve Benbow/Impact Photos; 14tr S. & O. Matthews; 14cr OUP; 14br City Museum & Art Gallery, Stoke-on-Trent, England; 18bl Neil Bromhall/OSF; 18tr Allschwil-Basel/Colorphoto Hinz; 19tr Novosti (London); 19br Trustees of the British Museum (Natural History), London; 25 Alain Compost/Coleman; 26l (all) Archivi Alinari; 26b OUP; 27r Ontario Science Centre; 27b Butler & Tanner (Printers) Ltd.; 28bl, br Courtesy Talbot Christie, Oxford Printmakers Co-operative Ltd./Photo: Martin Sookias/OUP; 28tr AKG London; 29 Archive; 33bl Bob Krist/Puerto Rico Tourism/courtesy Hill & Knowlton; 35l Smithsonian Institution/SPL; 36tl Erwin & Peggy Bauer/Coleman; 37tl Stephen Dalton/NHPA; 37br Alain Compost/Coleman; 38t Henson Associates Inc.; 39 Hutchison; 40bl Mexican Ministry of Tourism; 40tr Michael Holford; 42 G. I. Bernard/OSF; 43 C. C. Lockwood/Animals Animals/OSF; 46 Mary Plage/Coleman; 49br Ian Robinson/Harding; 50tl AKG London; 50br Amtrak; 50–51 Paul van Riel/Harding; 52l Bill Reaves/Texas Department of Transportation; 52r OUP; 53tl Rod Williams/Coleman; 53br Stephen Dalton/NHPA; 55bl Norman Tomalin/Coleman; 55tr Gupta/Network Photographers; 57 George McCarthy/Coleman; 59 Jobard/Rex

Features; 60tl Ian Dickson/Rex Features; 60br Wally Herbert/Harding; 61 Kaluzny-Liaison/Gamma/Spooner; 62tl J. H. C. Wilson/Harding; 62tc, r Hutchison; 63bl Biblioteca Central Nationale; 63bc, br Phaidon Archive; 64tl Scala; 64tr Trustees of the National Gallery, London; 64bl Scala; 65l Barrie E. Watts/OSF; 65r Don Fawcett/SPL; 66l H. Rivarola/Coleman; 67br OSF; 68 Nigel Dennis/NHPA; 69bl C. A. Browning/Rhode Island Tourism Division; 70 Maurice Harvey/Hutchison; 71 Hutchison; 72 Stephen Dalton/NHPA; 74t Jack Wilburn/OSF; 74c G. A. Maclean/OSF; 74b John & Gillian Lythgoe/Planet; 75 copyright Alex S. MacLean/Landslides, Cambridge, MA; 76l Zefa; 76–77 H. Armstrong/Zefa; 77tr Streichan/Zefa; 78b Rover; 78tr Photofest; 79tl Harding; 79br Siemens; 81l Rex Features; 81r J. Mel/Rex Features; 82tr Martyn F. Chillmaid/OSF; 82l Trustees of the British Museum (Natural History), London; 83r Dept. of Geology, College of Cardiff, University of Wales; 84bl Breck P. Kent/Earth Scenes; 84tr Cathy Blackie; 85t Stan Osolinski/OSF; 85b Bernard Regent/Hutchison; 86 Partridge Films Ltd./OSF; 87 Merillon/Vioujard Rou/Gamma/Spooner; 88 J Schoerrken/Zefa; 89bl Trustees of the British Museum, London/Michael Holford; 89br Antiquities Museum, Newcastle; 91bl Michael Holford; 91tr Brian Beckett; 92 Bridon International Ltd.; 93t Damm/Zefa; 93b Zefa; 94t Globus Brothers/Zefa; 94b Gunter Ziesler/Bridgeman; 95t Goebel/Zefa; 95b Ann T. Keene; 98 Erich Lessing/Lenin Library, Moscow/AKG London; 99b Val & Alan Wilkinson/Hutchison; 100br Japan Ship Center; 102 K. Gillham/Harding; 103tl Bridgeman; 103bl Borromeo/Art Resource; 103br Ann T. Keene; 104tl Jack Dermid/Bridgeman; 104br ICI Chemicals & Polymers; 105 C. Gascoigne/Harding; 106tr NASA/SPL; 107tr Bernard Gerard/Hutchison; 108t Phillips; 108b Dr. M. Phelps & Dr. J. Mazziotta *et al.*/*Neurology*/SPL; 110 Carol Hughes/Bridgeman; 111 Harding; 112bl Museo dell'Opera del Duomo, Florenz/AKG London; 111tr Foto Leidmann/Zefa; 113tl Sotheby's; 113r Collection of Whitney Museum of American Art/photograph by Jerry Thompson/copyright George Segal/licensed by VAGA, New York, NY; 114tl Harding; 119br Naturhistorisches Museum, Vienna/Erich Lessing/AKG London; 115tl Frederick Remington Art Museum, Ogdensburg, NY; 116t Tate Gallery; 115b YSP; 116c Carl Roessler/Planet; 117t Kim Taylor/Coleman; 117b N. Schwirtz/Coleman; 120t John Walmsley; 121 Charles & Sandra Hood/Coleman; 123t Wendy Shattil & Bob Rozinski/OSF; 123c Jane Burton/Coleman; 123b Alastair Shay/OSF; 127 Maryland Historical Society; 129t Metropolitan Museum of Art; 130cr Norbert Wu/Planet; 131tl Hans Dieter Brandl/GDT/Lane; 131br J. Watkins/Lane; 132tr Paul Amos Photography; 134r Holly Stein/Allsport; 135tl Eric & David Hosking; 135br Jane Burton/Coleman; 137 OUP; 138 Jane Burton/Coleman; 139 Museum of Fine Arts, Boston, MA; 140tl Reg Wilson; 140br David Redfern/Redferns; 141tr Homer Sykes/Impact Photos; 141b Harding; 143tl David Cannon/Allsport; 144bl Anglo-Australian Telescope Board; 144tr Jeff Foott Productions/Coleman; 145t Didier Klein/Allsport; 145b Harding; 146 Hulton; 147bl Trustees of the British Museum, London; 147t Wilberforce Museum, Hull, England; 148tl Mansell Collection; 148tr Peter Newark; 149 Michael Fogden/OSF; 150 Jane Burton/Bridgeman; 151 Mary Evans; 152tl C. B. & D. W. Frith/Bridgeman; 153tl Dr. F. Sauer/Zefa; 153tr Freytag/Zefa; 153b Procter & Gamble; 155bl Chris Cole/Allsport; 155tr Ben Radford/Allsport; 158bl J. Pfaff/Zefa; 160 Hutchison; 162tr Goebel/Zefa; 165 Charleston Area Convention and Visitors Bureau; 167b Tim Schoon/South Dakota Tourism; 168t Archive; 169 NASA/SPL; 170–171 NASA; 172 Novosti (London); 173 Michael Collins/Zefa; 174tl Patrimonio Nacional Biblioteca del Monasterio de El Escorial; 174br Hulton; 177r Gordon Langsbury/Coleman; 178 Fisk University Library; 179t Joe Dorsey/OSF; 179b John Shaw/Coleman; 180l, top to bottom—Chris Cole/Allsport; Hulton; Clive Mason/Allsport; Gerard Planchenault/Allsport; 180c, top to bottom—Martin Sookias/OUP; Pascal Rondeau/Allsport; Chris Cole/Allsport; 180r, top to bottom—Guido Benetton/Vandystadt/Allsport; David Cannon/Allsport; Holly Stein/Allsport; Didier Klein/Vandystadt/Allsport; 182r Larry West/Lane; 183bl Damm/Zefa; 183tr S. Halliday & L. Lushington/Sonia Halliday Photos; 184tl M. Serban/Zefa; 184br Archive; 185 bl Archive, all others OUP; 185tr C. Carvalho/Lane; 186 D. F. Malin/Royal Observatory, Edinburgh & A-ATB; 188 Anglo-Australian Telescope Board; 189 National Museum of American History, Smithsonian Institution; 192tl H. Rivarola/Bridgeman; 192br Stefano Amantini/Coleman.

Volume 7

8 National Trust Photographic Library/Art Resource; 9 Library of Congress; 10 Minnesota Office of Tourism; 11t Salter Clark Associates (Philips); 11b Ianthe Ruthven/Michael Holford; 15 U.S. Navy; 16t French Government Tourist Office; 16b Mansell Collection; 17b Trustees of the British Museum, London; 18–19 NASA; 19r David Parker, University of Birmingham High TC Consortium/SPL; 20 James Don/Zefa; 21 Blaine Harrington III/Zefa; 22 G. Ricatto/Zefa; 23b Damm/Zefa; 24 Stockmarket/Zefa; 25b J.A.L. Cooke/OSF; 27t Alastair Shay/OSF; 27b Adrian Neville/Harding; 29 Nigel Blythe/Harding; 30br Alain Evrard/Harding; 32bl Sarah Errington/Hutchison; 32tr Leidmann/Zefa; 33 Musée Cluny, Paris/Lauros-Giraudon/Bridgeman; 34 M. Rock/Hutchison; 37br Archive; 38t J. J. Firefighting Appliances/Bodleian Library, Oxford; 40t Yerkes Observatory; 42 LWT London Studios/Neil Osborne; 43tr Roy Rainford/Harding; 44bl OUP; 44br Tennessee Tourist Development; 46tl Ann & Bury Peerless; 46bc Archive; 46tr Allsport; 46br Colorsport; 47br Hulton; 48 Bob Goodale/OSF; 49 Corbis-Bettmann; 51tl, tr Harding; 51bl Coleman; 52 Zefa; 53bl, tr F. Jackson/Harding; 54 Ann T. Keene; 55l Philips/Brooks Plews Associates; 56 Colonial Williamsburg Foundation; 57b Melanie Friend/Hutchison; 59 Gunter Ziesler/Coleman; 62l Goodyear (Great Britain) Ltd.; 62br Christine Pemberton/Hutchison; 63l J. Brun/Harding; 63tr Jon Bradshaw/Colorific; 65tr Harding; 66t Archive; 66br Frans Lanting/Coleman; 67tl Gerald Cubitt/Coleman; 68t Museum of London; 68cl Trustees of the Victoria & Albert Museum, London; 68cr Atlascraft Ltd.; 68bl Tomy UK Ltd./Cascolor; 68br Hornby Hobbies; 69bl Michael Kahn/Hutchison; 69tr, br Trustees of the Victoria & Albert Museum, London; 70tl Harding; 70bl Archive; 72 Mike Hewitt/Allsport; 74t copyright McDonald's Corporation; 74b Peebles Power Transformers; 75 Mark Cator/Impact Photos; 77l Harding; 81 Harding; 82t Caterpillar; 82–83 Pickfords Removals/Mike Blenkinsop Studios; 83tl Wolfgang Neeb/Zefa; 83r Prato/Coleman; 84 Konrad Wothe/OSF; 85 Eurotunnel/OA Photos Ltd; 86l GEC Turbine Generators Ltd/OUP; 86r Adam Woolfitt/Harding; 87 Archive; 89 Zefa; 90 Neil McAllister/Coleman; 91tr Yale Center for British Art; 92tl *Illustrated London News* Picture Library; 92b Trustees of the Victoria & Albert Museum, London; 94tl Camera Press; 94br Eurotunnel; 95 Zefa; 96 Zefa; 98 Grand Canyon National Park; 99 New York City Convention and Visitors Bureau; 103 Oakland Museum/Aldus Archive; 104t Archive; 104b Corbis-Bettmann; 105t Franklin D. Roosevelt Library; 105b Archive; 106t United States Air Force; 106b United States Marine Corps; 107t United States Army; 107b United States Naval Academy; 109 Church of Jesus Christ of Latter-day Saints; 112–113 Hans-Peter Merten/Coleman; 114t Yellowstone National Park; 114b William McPherson/Coleman; 115r Kobal; 116l Rex Features; 117 H. Strass/Zefa; 118 A. J. Stevens/Coleman; 119 copyright David Brownell; 121 Zefa; 122 Bodleian Library,

Oxford; 123t Panasonic; 125bl Martyn F. Chillmaid; 125br York Archaeological Trust; 127bl Gavin Hellier/Harding; 127tr S. Pern/Hutchison; 128 Ann T. Keene; 130 Peter Menzel/SPL; 131tr Prof. Luc Montagnier, Institut Pasteur/SPL; 132tl F. Salmoiraghi/Stockmarket/Zefa; 133 Press-Tige Pictures/OSF; 137 Washington Tourism Division; 140t Bill Clark/copyright Parks and History Association; 140b Carol Highsmith/copyright Parks and History Association; 141 (all) copyright Parks and History Association; 142bl J. A. L. Cooke/OSF; 142tr Joyce Pope; 145tr H. Steenmans/Zefa; 146bl Denis Boulanger/Allsport; 146tr Gerry Clyde/Michael Holford; 147l Norman Barrett; 147tr Pascal Rondeau/Allsport; 147br A. Morgan/Harding; 151 Westland Group; 152l Hans Reinhard/Coleman; 153tr Peter Menzel/SPL; 154tr J. G. Fuller/Hutchison; 155tl W. H. Mueller/Zefa; 155br Hutchison; 157 Ann T. Keene; 158 David Fattaleh/West Virginia Division of Tourism; 160bl Gerald Cubitt/Coleman; 160–161 Walter Rawlings/Harding; 161br Geoff Dore/Coleman; 162tl James D. Watt/Planet; 163 Chad Coppess/South Dakota Tourism; 164t Alexandre/Zefa; 165 Stan Osolinski/OSF; 169t Harding; 169b T. Braise/Stockmarket/Zefa; 170 Hutchison; 171 Wisconsin Division of Tourism; 172 AKG London; 173 Yellowstone National Park; 174tl Harding; 178bl Topham Picture Library; 178tr Musée des Deux Guerres Mondiales/E. T. Archive; 179bl Hulton; 180 (all) OUP; 181tl AKG London; 181br Imperial War Museum/Macdonald/Aldus Archive; 182br Vandystadt/Allsport; 183 Trustees of the British Museum, London/Michael Holford; 184 Wyoming Tourism; 185br Harding; 186 Reuters/Archive; 189 Hugh Stockhill/Oxfam; 190t Jonathan Scott/Planet; 190br David Cayless/OSF; 192t Randa Bishop/Colorific; 192b Frank Fournier/Contact Press Images/Colorific.

Volume 8

Any photos in Vol. 8 not credited here are from the collections of the Library of Congress.

9tl Swarthmore College Peace Collection; 9b Library of Congress; 11bl UPI/Corbis Bettmann; 10 Colorsport; 11tl Mary Evans; 12l Library of Congress; 12r Chicago Historical Society; 14bl Gert Scutz/AKG London; 14tr Photri-Zefa; 16 Free Library of Philadelphia/Art Resource; 18 Rex Features; 19t Private Collection/Bridgeman; 19tr Mary Evans; 21tl Archive; 21b Bridgeman; 22 Library of Congress; 23bl Hulton; 23tr Hulton; 24 Scala/Art Resource; 25tl Archive; 25br Peter Newark; 26 Pierpont Morgan Library/Art Resource; 27t J. L. Charmet; 27b Peter Newark; 28 Erich Lessing/AKG London; 30tr Mary Evans; 31 Hulton; 32

National Portrait Gallery, London; 33 Corbis-Bettmann; 34 Kunsthistorisches Museum, Vienna; 35l Library of Congress; 37l Archive; 37r, 38l Mary Evans; 39 Office of Presidential Correspondence; 40 Paluan/Art Resource; 42 Peter Newark; 45tl Corbis-Bettmann; 45br Giraudon/Art Resource; 46 Carl Van Vechten Collection, Library of Congress/Ann T. Keene; 47 Bridgeman; 48l AKG London; 48tr Erich LEssing/Art Resource; 49 Art Resource; 50 Royal Collection; 51b Popperfoto; 52 Private Collection/Bridgeman; 53 OUP; 55br courtesy of The White House; 56 Peter Newark; 58tl Scala; 62 Hulton; 63 Mathew Brady/Peter Newark; 64 Francis Lochon/Spooner; 65 Mary Evans; 66 Mary Evans; 69 Metropolitan Museum of Art, New York City; 71 J. Sommer Collection/Archive; 72 courtesy Ann T. Keene; 74 National Portrait Gallery, Smithsonian Institution; 75 Corbis-Bettmann; 77t Metropolitan Museum of Art, New York City; 77b Hulton; 78b Michael Holford; 79 Hulton; 82tr Prado, Madrid/Bridgeman; 81 Bedford Estates, Woburn Abbey; 82 OUP; 85 UPI/Corbis-Bettmann; 86tr Archive; 89 Popperfoto; 90 Corbis-Bettmann; 91tl AKG London; 94 Rex Features; 95 Popperfoto; 97 Hermitage, St. Petersburg/Bridgeman; 99 San Francesco, Upper Church, Assisi/Bridgeman; 101 The Jane Goodall Institute; 102tl Photofest; 105 Library of Congress; 106 U.S. Senate Historical Office; 108 U.S. Senate Historical Office; 109 Bryn Colton/Rex Features; 110 Library of Congress; 112 Palazzo Barberini, Galleria Nazionale, Rome/AKG London; 115tl OUP; 115br, 116bl, 116tr Hulton; 117 Art Resource; 118bl National Museum of American Art, Washington, D.C./Art Resource; 118tr Mary Evans; 120 Collection of Whitney Museum of American Art, New York City; 122 Mary Evans; 123 AKG London; 125 Mary Evans; 127 Peter Newark; 130 U.S. Senate Historical Office; 132tl Library of Congress; 132br Pierpont Morgan Library/Art Resource; 133 National Portrait Gallery, Washington, D.C./Art Resource; 134 San Francisco Museum of Modern Art; 135 Tate Gallery, London; 136bl Hulton; 136–137 Rex Features; 137t Smithsonian Institute; 137br Popperfoto; 138 Archive; 140tl Hulton; 140br Mary Evans; 141t Mary Evans; 141b Hulton; 143 Bond/Zefa; 144 Nastional Archives, Washington, D.C.; 146 Royal Library, Windsor; 149 AKG London; 150AKG London; 151 IDAF; 153t Archive; 154 IDAF; 156 Drennan/New York Times Co./Archive; 157 Corbis-Bettmann; 158 AKG London; 163t Bythnier/Rex Features; 163b R. R. Donnelley & Sons Company Archives; 164 AKG London; 165 Photofest; 166 Galleria dell'Accademia, Florence/Bridgeman; 167 Howard Coster/Popperfoto; 169tl Erich

Lessing/Art Resource; 170 Popperfoto/Archive; 171 The Henry Moore Foundation; 172 Reuters/Pressens Bild/Archive; 173 courtesy Ann T. Keene; 174 Edward Owen/Art Resource; 175 Musée Condé, Chantilly/Erich Lessing/AKG London; 176 Harding; 177tl Yosemite National Park; 177br Hulton; 178 Schloss Charlottenburg, Berlin/Bridgeman; 179 Popperfoto; 181tl Florence Nightingale Museum Trust; 182tl Nobel Foundation; 182c Hulton; 183bl Art Resource; 183tr J. Allan Cash Ltd.; 184 Schalkwijk/Art Resource; 185 AKG London; 186 Chateau de Versailles/Giraudon/Bridgeman; 188 Library of Congress; 189 Peter Newark; 190t Library of Congress; 190b Hulton; 191t Vatican Library/Ann T. Keene; 191b Patrimonio Nacionale, Madrid; 193b Art Resource; 194 detail from *The School of Athens*, Vatican Museums and Galleries, Rome/Bridgeman; 195l Peter Newark; 195tr J. Paul Getty Museum, Malibu, CA; 197 Reuters/Archive; 198 AKG London; 200 Villa Farnesina, Rome/Bridgeman; 201t courtesy Ronald Reagan Library; 201b Bridgeman; 202t Mary Evans; 202br Trustees of the British Museum, London; 203 San Francisco Museum of Modern Art; 205b Art Resource; 205t J. L. Charmet/SPI; 206bl United Nations/Franklin D. Roosevelt Library; 206tr FPG/Harding; 208 Archive/Lambert; 209 Erich Lessing/AKG London; 210 Frederick Remington Art Museum; 211 Carl Sandburg Collection, University of Illinois Library; 212 Corbis-Bettmann; 213 Bridgeman; 214 National Portrait Gallery, Smithsonian Institution/Art Resource; 215 OUP; 216l Library of Congress; 216b OUP; 217 OUP; 218 Trustees of the Victoria & Albert Museum, London/AKG London; 219 Corbis-Bettmann; 220t AKG London; 220br Photofest; 222bl Hulton; 222tr Library of Congress; 223 Ann Ronan/Image Select; 224 Chicago Architecture Foundation; 225 Hulton; 227 Kobal; 228 Harding; 229 copyright Bonnie McGrath; 230 National Gallery, London; 231bl Douglas Dickens; 231tr Zihnioglu/Witt/Rex Features; 234tl Corbis-Bettmann; 234br Hulton; 235tl Library of Congress; 237bl Metropolitan Museum of Art; 237tr Rex Features; 238 Rijksmuseum, Amsterdam; 239 AKG London; 240 Hulton; 241bl OUP; 241t AKG London; 244 OUP; 245 Erich Lessing/Art Resource; 246 New York Times Co./Archive; 247 Library of Congress; 248tl Archive; 248r Kobal; 249 Hulton; 251 AKG London; 252bl Impact Photos/John Sims; 252tr Mary Evans; 253 Archive; 254 Walter Rawlings/Harding; 255tl Hulton; 255r Harding; 256bl Corbis-Bettmann; 256tr School of Oriental and African Studies, London.